AND GOD KNOWS THE SOLDIERS

AND GOD KNOWS THE SOLDIERS

The Authoritative and Authoritarian in Islamic Discourses

Khaled M. Abou El Fadl

University Press of America,® Inc.
LANHAM • NEW YORK • OXFORD

4720 Boston Way
Lanham, Maryland 20706

12 Hid's Copse Rd.
Cumnor Hill, Oxford OX2 9JJ

Printed in the United States of America
British Library Cataloging in Publication Information Available

Library of Congress Cataloging-in-Publication Data

Abou El Fadl, Khaled, 1963-
And God knows the soldiers : the authoritative and authoritarian in Islamic discourses / by Khaled Abou El Fadl.
p. cm
Rev. ed. of: The authoritative and authoritarian in Islamic discourses. 1997.
Includes bibliographical references and index.
1. Authority—Religious aspects—Islam. 2. Hadith—Evidences, authority, etc. 3. Islamic law. 4. Wahhåbåyah. 5. Islam—Doctrines. I. Abou El Fadl, Khaled, 1963-. Authoritative and authoritarian in Islamic discourses. II. Title.
BP165.7 .A26 2001 297.6—dc21 2001037567 CIP

ISBN 0-7618-2084-1 (pbk. : alk. paper)
ISBN 0-7618-2083-3 (cloth : alk. paper)

™ The paper used in this publication meets the minimum requirements of American National Standard for Information Sciences—Permanence of Paper for Printed Library Materials, ANSI Z39.48—1984

Dedication

This work is dedicated to my very first teacher in Islamic law, my mother Afaf.

Contents

I

The Short Legacy of a Short Book

بسم الله الرحمن الرحيم

Justification and Confession

My wife Grace deserves all the credit, or blame, for the re-publication of this book. While I very much hoped that it would remain in print, I could not overcome the sense of relentless exhaustion that the very thought of this book induced in me. It seems that this work had consumed a good chunk of my life for the past four years. A book that started out as a statement of protest and longing turned out to be a taxing intellectual voyage. For these past years, I have been coping with suspicions, censorship, and a healthy dose of marginalization. So when Grace suggested that this work should stay in print, I shrugged my shoulders and resigned to the comforts of lethargy. But Grace wrote the book proposal to University Press of America, and presented me with reviews, comments, and, eventually, the book contract. In many ways, considering my lack of initiative, she should be writing this preface, but she declined to do so and instead asked me to explain the reasons for my indolence.

This book has had a long and arduous history. In 1996, a Muslim basketball player refused to stand up for the American national anthem and the ensuing controversy inspired the writing of this book. But this book is rooted in a much longer and more complicated dynamic. Growing up in the Middle East, I had the opportunity to witness first-hand some of the most remarkable transformations in the intellectual history of contemporary Islam. I grew up surrounded by what in retrospect seem to have been adolescent dreams of the re-birth of the Islamic Civilization—a Civilization that was going to be the beacon of freedom, justice, and dignity. This Civilization was going to recreate the dignity and beauty of the Prophet's experience in Medina. None of the ideas were concrete, but there was a sense that the pioneers of the early twentieth century, such as Rashīd Riḍā (d. 1354/1935) and Muḥammad ʿAbduh (d. 1323/1905), had paved the road for the coming of an Islamic renaissance. I was well aware of the impact of the shameful 1967 defeat upon Arab Muslims, but my family and teachers often asserted that the 1967 defeat proved the futility of Pan-Arab nationalism, and that the only plausible recourse was to return to Islamic authenticity.[1] One was weaned on the ideas of Jalāl Kishk who argued that the significance of the 1967 military defeat paled in comparison to the spiritual or intellectual defeat. The most dangerous threat was not foreign military dominance, but the external cultural invasion that persuaded Muslims to distrust the coherence or validity of their Islamic heritage. The real struggle was not territorial or military but cultural and civilizational. Whether it be Marxism, communism, secularism, capitalism or liberalism—these are alien cultural categories designed to undermine and dissipate Islamic intellectual autonomy and worth.[2] It is important to note, however, that this intellectual orientation was not introspective—it was far more interested in asserting independence from the "other" than in exploring the reality of this independence. There were rather interesting assumptions that informed the idea of the Islamic Civilization, but the source of these assumptions were rarely explored. For instance, one grew up with the conviction that Islam liberated women and afforded them full and equal rights, that Islam is fundamentally egalitarian and

---

[1] Fouad Ajami, *The Arab Predicament: Arab Political Thought and Practice Since 1967* (Cambridge: Cambridge University Press, 1981).

[2] Muḥammad Jalāl Kishk, *Akhṭar min al-Naksah* (Kuwait: Dār al-Bayān, 1967); *idem, al-Ghazw al-Fikrī,* 4th ed. (Cairo: al-Mukhtār al-Islāmī, 1975); idem, *al-Naksah wa al-Ghazw al-Fikrī* (Beirut: Dār al-Kitāb al-ʿArabī, 1969).

democratic in orientation, and that social justice is a basic Islamic value.[3] Adhering to these assumptions was an act of resistance to the onslaught of cultural invasions coming from the East and West. Cultural invaders sought to persuade Muslims that the Islamic cultural heritage is inferior and defective, and that it is incapable of fulfilling the higher values of humanity.

This period of relative intellectual delusional repose was short-lived. Arab Muslims were approaching an age when the relative liberalism of Muḥammad ʿAbduh and Rashīd Riḍā would be considered heretical. The paradigms of the cultural autonomists were being turned against them—an age where caring about values such as gender equality, social justice, or democracy would be considered proof of "selling out" and of adopting the categories of the colonizer. I, like many other Muslims, experienced the euphoria of the 1973 war and the unrelenting "let-down" in its aftermath. It was not a clear victory, and perhaps not a victory at all, over Israel, and in retrospect, it increasingly looked like a mass sacrifice of life primarily to facilitate a shift from the Soviet to the American camp. The 1973 war turned out to be a financial windfall to the oil-rich countries of the Arabian Gulf, and to the corrupt elites of Egypt. Events after the 1973 war followed with dazzling, and demoralizing, speed. Oil prices spiraled upwards in 1973, the Lebanese Civil War started in 1975, the Egyptian President Anwar Sadat started implementing his Open Door policy in 1975 and eventually signed the Camp David accords in 1978, Afghanistan was invaded in 1979, the Iranian Revolution was ignited in the same year, Iraq invaded Iran in 1980, the Islamists were massacred in Syria in 1982, Israel invaded Lebanon in the same year, and the short-lived democratic experiment in Egypt came to an end at the hands of Sadat, the supposed pioneer of democracy, shortly before his assassination in 1981. All of these events disabused even the most dauntless person of any sense of security or assuredness about the future. The highs and lows were too many and too frequent. Especially after the sharp rise in oil prices, the puritan ideology of Wahhābism, one suspects, funded by Saudi money, started spreading in

[3] Muḥammad Quṭb, *Shubuhāt Ḥawl al-Islām* (Cairo: Dār al-Shurūq, 1974); ʿAlī Sharīʿatī, *On the Sociology of Islam*, trans. Hamid Algar (Berkeley: Mizan Press, 1979), 119-120.

the Muslim world.[4] The same period of the late seventies and early eighties witnessed the proliferation of what became known as *al-taṭarruf al-dīnī* (religious extremism), especially in the Arabic speaking world.[5]

Colonialism has played a major role in displacing the traditional institutions of authority and legitimacy in the Muslim world. But the above series of events systematically demolished whatever institutions had emerged in the post-Colonial period. In retrospect, it seems that every institution or thought that one had once believed in or trusted had crumbled. In this intellectual vacuum, puritanism and religious extremism found ample space for growth. The puritanism of the late

---

4 Wahhābism is a puritan theology whose foundations were set in place by the eighteenth-century advocate Muḥammad b. ʿAbd al-Wahhāb (d. 1787). The tenets of this theology are developed in his book, *Kitāb al-Tawḥīd alladhī huwa Ḥaqq Allāh ʿalā al-ʿAbīd* (Cairo: Dār al-Maʿārif, 1974). In the late eighteenth-century, the Wahhābī doctrine was merged with the political and military might of the Āl Saʿūd in the Arabian Peninsula in an effort to challenge Ottoman hegemony in the region. This challenge to Ottoman power was quashed by Egyptian forces under the direction of Muḥammad ʿAlī (r. 1805-1848). Nevertheless, the Wahhābī ideology would be resuscitated in the early twentieth-century under the leadership of ʿAbd al-ʿAzīz b. Saʿūd, who succeeded in merging the Wahhābī puritanical theology with the political and military might of his neighboring tribes, thereby establishing the nascent beginnings of what would become Saudi Arabia. Michael Cook, "On the Origins of Wahhabism," *Journal of the Royal Asiatic Society,* Series 3, 2.2 (1992): 191-202; William L. Cleveland, *A History of the Modern Middle East* (Boulder: Westview Press, 1994), 116-117, 215-216; Hüseyin Hilmi Iṣik, *The Religion Reformers in Islam.* 3rd ed. (Istanbul: Waqf Ikhlas Publications, 1978), 112-121, Muḥammad Khalīl Harrās, *al-Ḥarakah al-Wahhābiyyah: Radd ʿalā Maqāl li al-Duktūr Muḥammad al-Bahī fī Naqd al-Wahhābiyyah* (Beirut: Dār al-Kitāb al-ʿArabī, n.d.); LansinÈ Kaba, *The Wahhabiyya: Islamic Reform and Politics in French West Africa* (Evanston: Northwestern University Press, 1974), 5; Lawrence Paul Goldrup, "Saudi Arabia: 1902-1932: The Development of a Wahhābī Society," (Ph.D. diss., University of California Los Angeles, 1971). More than just a nationalist ideology, Wahhābī theology has permeated the thought of Muslim communities worldwide. See Khaled Abou El Fadl, *The Conference of the Books: The Search for Beauty in Islam* (Lanham, Md.: University Press of America, 2001), which documents the spread of Wahhābī thought among Muslims in the West. The nineteenth-century Wahhābī movement in India associated with Syed Aḥmad (d. 1832) shares the same name as the Arabian ideological movement, but is distinct in its origins. See Fasihuddin Balkhi, *Wahabi Movement* (New Delhi: Classical Publishing Company, 1983); Qeyamuddin Ahmad, *The Wahabi Movement in India* (Calcutta: Firma K.L. Mukhopadhyay, 1966). For a critique of the Wahhābī doctrine, see the work by Muḥammad b. ʿAbd al-Wahhāb's brother, Sulaymān b. ʿAbd al-Wahhāb, *al-Ṣawāʿiq al-Ilāhiyyah fī al-Radd ʿalā al-Wahhābiyyah,* ed. Bassām ʿAmqiyyah (Damascus:

1970s and 1980s reflected a rabid hostility to all forms of academic social knowledge or critical intellectualism. However, this hostility was not directed only at Western or Eastern social and political theories, but at the Islamic intellectual tradition as well. Classical intellectual orientations such as Muʿtazilism, Ashʿarism, Maturīdism, the whole juristic tradition of disputation and deductive reasoning, and the theology of Sufism were considered an aberration and corruption. The only true and real Islam was the Islam of *Ahl al-Sunnah wa al-Jamāʿah*—a hopelessly vague label referring to those who follow the true *Sunnah* of the Prophet and the true practice of the real Muslims. For example, one of the often-quoted Prophetic traditions in this period was one that asserted that close to the end of time, Islam will split into 73 sects and that all of them will end in Hellfire except for one—the one that embodies the true Islam.[6] Presumably, the *Ahl al-Sunnah wa al-Jamāʿah* is this one group. A fundamental component of this puritan trend was the belief that the real Islam was practiced at the time of the Prophet, the four Rightly Guided Caliphs, and the fifth Rightly Guided Caliphate of

---

Maktabat Ḥarrā', 1997). See also ʿAbd al-Qādir Ibn al-Sayyid Muḥammad al-Kīlānī, *al-Nafḥah al-Zakiyyah fī al-Radd ʿalā al-Firqah al-Wahhābiyyah* (Damascus: Maṭbaʿat al-Fayḥā', 1340 A.H.); Ḥüseyn Hilmi Iṣik, *Advice for the Wahhābī*, 2nd ed. (Istanbul: Özal Matbaasi, 1978), and Muḥammad al-Ḥusayn Āl Kāshif al-Ghiṭā', *Naqḍ Fatāwā al-Wahhābiyyah* (Beirut: Markaz al-Ghadīr, 1999).

[5] Not all puritanical groups are Wahhābī. Wahhābism, at different points of its development, relied on an ideology known as Salafism. Salafism advocates the return to the pristine origins of the rightly guided predecessors—usually, this refers to the Prophet and his Companions. Salafism also calls for the abandonment of the accumulations of the past, superstition, and the outdated legal tradition. Consequently, Salafism calls for the re-kindling of the use of *ijtihād* (independent legal thinking) by a resort to the original sources of the Qur'ān and *Sunnah*. Salafism is also opposed to blind adherence to legal precedent or the traditional legal schools of thought. Wahhābism, in its present form, is a particular orientation within Salafism. Wahhābism exhibits a greater hostility than Salafism to Sufism, the juristic heritage, and all forms of rationalistic orientations in the Islamic tradition. It is fair to say that all puritanical groups in the Muslim world are Salafī in orientation but not necessarily Wahhābī.

[6] Muḥammad b. ʿAbd al-Karīm Abī Bakr Aḥmad al-Shahrastānī, *al-Milal wa al-Niḥal*, eds. Amīr ʿAlī Mihannā and ʿAlī Ḥasan Fāʿūr, 5th ed. (Beirut: Dār al-Maʿrifah, 1996), 1:20; Abū Muḥammad al-Yamanī, *ʿAqā'id al-Thalāthah wa al-Sabʿīn Firqah*, ed. Muḥammad b. ʿAbd Allāh Zarabān al-Ghāmidī (Medina: Maktabat al-ʿUlūm wa al-Ḥikam, 1414 AH), 1:3.

ʿUmar b. ʿAbd al-ʿAzīz (r. 99/717–102/720). The balance of Islamic history was a corruption because pre-modern Muslims got into the habit of engaging in intellectual sophistry, divided into schools of thought, and split into competing points of view. In many ways, the puritanical thinking of organizations such as *Jamāʿat Anṣār al-Sunnah*, *al-Jamāʿāt al-Islāmiyyah*, and *Jamʿiyyat al-Iṣlāḥ* was far more devastating to the legitimacy and authority of the Islamic intellectual heritage than the vulgar ravishings of Colonialism. Colonialism exemplified the oppression and hostility of the outsider, but post-colonial puritanism posed a far more subtle and difficult challenge to the legitimacy of the Islamic intellectual heritage.

The Wahhābī school of thought, empowered by its newfound wealth, was easily accommodated by the anti-intellectual and ahistorical trends of the late 1970s and 1980s. In fact, I believe it is fair to say that by the 1990s Wahhābism had become the dominant system of thought in the Muslim world.[7]

The Wahhābism of the post-1975 period, although puritan, does not advocate austerity or asceticism. In many ways, Wahhābism is the ultimate form of religiously sanctioned consumerism. There is very little in Wahhābī theological works about the evils of materialism or the condemnation of wealth. In effect, Wahhābism proved well suited for an era that had witnessed the steady retreat of Marxist and Socialist ideologies and the proliferation of consumer and service-based economies in the Muslim World. Conducting trade and commerce is regarded as a high moral value in Wahhābī thought partly because the Prophet himself was a merchant.[8] In Wahhābī thought, material luxury and the consumption

[7] Ahmad Dallal has convincingly argued that puritanical ideas of Wahhābism in the 18th Century were not representative of the intellectual movements of the age. In fact, Wahhābism seems to have been perceived as a fanatical fringe system of thought, and Muḥammad b. ʿAbd al-Wahhāb, himself, came under severe criticism by his contemporaries. See Ahmad Dallal, "The Origins and Objectives of Islamic Revivalist Thought, 1750-1850," *Journal of the American Oriental Society* 113.3 (1993): 341-359. I would argue that Wahhābism remained a fringe theology until the economic fortunes of its oil rich supporters improved dramatically.

[8] Perhaps contemporary Wahhābism is an aggravated form of what Marshall G.S. Hodgson described as the mercantile values of Islam. Marshall G.S. Hodgson, *The Expansion of Islam in the Middle Periods,* vol. 2 of *The Venture of Islam: Conscience*

of the commercial products of non-Muslims is not reproachable in any sense. However, importing any of the social or political institutions of non-Muslims is considered immoral. Furthermore, buying and using the commercial products of non-Muslims is not considered a form of emulating the West, yet importing ideas related to such issues as gender relations, social justice, political power, or even critical methods of analysis are strongly condemned as following in the footsteps of the infidel. As far as religion is concerned, Wahhābism advocates simplicity of belief and correctness of practice. Hence, most issues related to religion can and should be reduced to a simple and single answer. Wahhābī thought also exhibits an extreme form of distrust of all forms of social theory, and considers intellectualism a form of devilish sophistry. Importantly, unlike other Islamic ideologies, Wahhābism is an ideology of political pacifism—there is very little emphasis on the ideal of the Caliphate or correct government. Rebellion against a government that implements the positive law of Islam is forbidden even if this government perpetuates social or economic injustice.[9]

One of the most traumatic aspects of the spread of this form of puritanism was its attitude and treatment of women. As if Muslim men were projecting their feelings of disempowerment and defeat upon women, one witnessed a concerted attempt to exclude women from all facets of public life. Puritan movements appropriated women's dignity into a symbol of honor for men. Men were empowered—or felt empowered—if they could guard "their" honor. Furthermore, the social and cultural defeat of Muslims was displaced upon women, so that the

---

and History in a World Civilization (1974; reprint, Chicago, Ill.: University of Chicago Press, 1977), 62-151. On Max Weber and the commercial ethic in Islam see Patricia Crone, "Weber, Islamic Law, and the Rise of Capitalism," in eds. Toby E. Huff and Wolfgang Schluchter, *Max Weber and Islam* (New Brunswick, New Jersey: Transaction Publishers, 1999), 247-272; Wolfgang Schluchter, "Hindrances to Modernity: Max Weber on Islam," 53-138 in Ibid.; Maxime Rodinson, *Islam and Capitalism*, trans. Brian Peace (Austin, Tex.: University of Texas, 1978); Bryan S. Turner, *Weber and Islam* (London: Routledge and Kegan Paul, 1974).

9 Ṣāliḥ b. Fawzān b. ʿAbd Allāh Ibn Fawzān, *al-Muntaqā min Fatāwā Faḍīlat al-Shaykh Ṣāliḥ b. Fawzān b. ʿAbd Allāh al-Fawzān*, ed. ʿĀdil b. ʿAlī b. Aḥmad al-Farīdān (2nd ed. Madīnah: Maktabat al-Ghurbān al-Athariyyah, 1997), 1:386-388; *Fatāwā al-Lajnah al-Dāʾimah li al-Buḥūth al-ʿIlmiyyah wa al-Iftāʾ*, ed. Aḥmad b. ʿAbd al-Razzāq al-Dawīsh (Riyadh: Dār ʿĀlam al-Kutub, 1991), 4:332.

visible role of women in society became a symbol for the dominance of Western cultural paradigms.[10] Ironically, the television set, the VCR, the satellite dish, and the mobile telephone were manifestations of modernity and progress, but a woman revealing her hair or shaking hands with men was a symbol of cultural defeat.[11] In some of its more vulgar forms, the puritan trend blamed women for God's abandonment of Muslims and the ensuing Muslim predicaments in the modern world. It is because of the promiscuity of women and their flouting of their sexual charms, so the argument went, that corruption spread in society, and this angered God to the point of allowing Muslims to be at the mercy of their enemies. Part of this dynamic was the associating of any position that restricts the movement or visibility of women with the "true" Islam. Any argument that reached contrary conclusions became associated with the Westernizing and corrupting of Islam. Most importantly, any attempt to read or interpret Islamic sources in a way that granted greater freedom to women, by definition, became illegitimate

[10] Part of this dynamic was the political symbolism that accompanied the discarding of the veil by Muslim women in the Colonial age. In some countries, women renounced the veil in a public act of protest against the restrictions imposed upon women in Muslim societies. However, this was also a symbol of adopting the culture and mannerisms of the Colonizer. Importantly, the discarding of the veil was often argued on Islamic grounds—i.e., it was justified on the grounds that Islam liberated and empowered women. Of course, this contributed to the notion that the failure to wear the veil is a symptom of the cultural invasion of Muslim societies. See the diaries of Hudā Sha'rāwī, who led women in a movement to discard the veil. Huda Shaarawi, *Harem Years: The Memoirs of an Egyptian Feminist*, trans. Margot Badran (New York: The Feminist Press, 1987). On the dynamics of unveiling during the Colonial period see Leila Ahmed, *Women and Gender in Islam* (New Haven: Yale University Press, 1992), 125-188. My point, however, is that whether one is speaking of discarding the veil or imposing the veil both discourses remain locked into the paradigms of Colonialism and Westernization—one position is a move Westward and the other position is an anti-Westward. Being anti-Westward, however, does not mean that an Islamic authenticity is being preserved or protected. Whether a person defines himself or herself by following the example of the one, or defines himself or herself by being the antithesis of the other, in both cases, the result is that self-integrity and self-determination are ultimately denied. As I demonstrate later on in this book, the pro-veiling positions are not necessarily mandated by an Islamic authenticity either.

[11] Many of these contradictions are noted in Olivier Roy, *The Failure of Political Islam*, trans. Carol Volk (Cambridge, Mass.: Harvard University Press, 1994), 82-83.

and was dismissed as the product of idolizing the West.[12] On the other hand, any position that restricted or excluded women even if unsupported by text or legal precedent was considered, by definition, Islamic.

I am not claiming that many of these prejudices were not already embedded in Arab Muslim culture. Even puritanism does not emerge from a cultural vacuum. Nevertheless, the discourses of puritanism were discourses of privilege and alienation. Puritanism stood in a self-proclaimed privileged position judging the living history and culture of Arab Muslims. Armed with its construct of the true Islam, it stood in a position of privilege judging the authenticity and validity of the historical legacy and the experienced culture of other Muslims. The effect of this dynamic was a profound sense of alienation from everything collectively remembered or experienced. Both the remembered and the experienced represented paradigms of corruption and deviation that could not be endorsed without a degree of defensiveness. As such, puritanism constructed both history and society as the externalized other, but this other was not to be studied or analyzed. Rather, this "other" had to be cleansed and transformed—the other had to be persuaded, forcefully if need be, to understand the extent of his deviation.

The puritan, and Wahhābī, propaganda left an unrelenting sense of alienation and illegitimacy. The books that one grew up reading, the music that accompanied the various stages of one's life, and the cloth that one's family and friends grew up wearing were declared part of the insignia that proclaims a person's lack of Islamicity. The puritans taught that, if one grew up listening to the Egyptian diva Umm Kalthoum, the whole foundation of one's upbringing was un-Islamic. If one grew up reading the books of Islamic theology and law, one had to contend with the realization that the juristic tradition, for the most part, was a corruption. Similarly, clapping the hands in public events, standing up to respect teachers or elders, shaking hands with women, drinking any liquid while standing up instead of sitting, socializing with family members

[12] See Muḥammad Nāṣir al-Dīn al-Albānī (d. 1999), *Ḥijāb al-Mar'ah al-Muslimah* (Cairo: al-Maktabah al-Salafiyyah, 1374 A.H); Abū al-Aʿlā al-Mawdūdī, *al-Ḥijāb* (Cairo: Dār al-Anṣār, 1977); Muḥammad Aḥmad Ismāʿīl al-Muqaddim, *ʿAwdat al-Ḥijāb* (Riyadh: Dār ayba, 1996). This later source is a three-volume work totaling about 2,000 pages on why Muslim women should veil themselves.

without segregating the men from women, reading novels, owning a razor blade, playing chess—all of this was considered a corrupt innovation (*bid'ah*). If one performed his prayers at home, that was considered insufficient and corrupt because all five prayers had to be performed in the mosque with a full congregation. Even the headscarf that one's mother, grandmother, and great grandmother wore, and the color of their clothing were all deviations from the true Islam. For instance, one of the noticeable developments in the history of contemporary Islam is the streamlining and standardizing of headscarf styles and colors of clothing throughout the urban centers of the Muslim world. Significantly, studying with Sufi scholars or Azharī jurists was considered a sign of indulging in superstition or succumbing to the temptations of disputation and scholasticism, both of which were considered deviations from the one and true Islam. The point is that it was becoming very difficult to be religious without having to justify and defend every culturally sanctioned practice. A religious person was forced to feel alienated from his culture, tradition, and the inherited wisdom of the generations. The only authenticity existed in books transmitting anecdotal reports about the Prophet and the Companions. But in order for this "authenticity" to remain pure and untainted, all forms of critical historical or contextual analysis had to be rejected. Context only interfered with the purity and intangibility of the vision of the true Islam—context forced the vision to deal with the messiness of history and tainted the purity of the ideal with the filth of reality. Ultimately, puritanism privileged itself with the knowledge of the true Islam and cast all else, including the juristic tradition, into the illegitimate other. In this sense, it is fair to say that the puritan experience, which continues to thrive to this day, like the Colonial experience has been quintessentially an experience of profound alienation from any sense of rooted identity.[13]

---

[13] The clash between Wahhābism and the juristic culture is well-exemplified in the controversy that ignited around Muḥammad al-Ghazālī's book, *al-Sunnah al-Nabawiyyah bayna Ahl al-Fiqh wa Ahl al-Ḥadīth* (Cairo: Dār al-Shurūq, 1989). Some jurists have addressed some of the phenomenon described above See Yūsuf al-Qaraḍāwī, *al-Imām al-Ghazālī bayn mādiḥīh wa nāqidīh* (Egypt: Dār al-Wafā', 1988); *idem, al-Ṣaḥwah al-Islāmiyyah bayn al-Juḥūd wa al-Taṭarruf* (Qatar: Kitāb al-Ummah, 1402 A.H.)

I came to the United States about twenty years ago. I was fortunate enough to have internalized an ethos that was quickly vanishing in the Arab world. This is not the place to engage in a full description of the nature of this ethos, except to say that it was, in part, apologetic. However, it was also immersed in the juristic tradition of disputation, opinions, and schools of thought. The jurists with whom I studied were masters of the dusty yellow-books (*al-kutub al-ṣafrā'*),[14] who, at the time, believed that the puritanism of the Wahhābīs was a marginal and passing phase. They were quite wrong. The ethos of which I speak celebrated and reveled in the search for the Divine Way. The search, the study—the process of pondering, weighing, and balancing was considered the ultimate act of worship (*'ibādah*). The engagement of the intellect in searching the Divine Way was invariably superior to the engagement of the body in treading the Divine Way. True piety manifested in the search for knowledge (*ṭalab al-'ilm*)—this piety is then affirmed by the physical acts of prayer, fasting, and so on. Importantly, finding the correct answer to any juristic problem was not considered a part of the act of worship (*'ibādah*). Finding the correct answer, if one existed, was considered a gift and blessing from God to be humbly enjoyed as long as it exists.

The United States, at least for me, represented a further opportunity for pondering, weighing, and balancing, and for exploring the outer limits of thought. The air of unfettered freedom to think and write in the United States, without fear of arrest or torture, was nothing short of exhilarating. Of course, in the same way that my teachers back home had underestimated the power of Wahhābism in the Arab world, I had over-estimated the commitment of the United States to freedom. But

---

14 The expression "yellow books" refers to the books of the classical Islamic tradition, which until the late 1970s were printed on cheap yellow paper. It was said that the yellowish color was easier on the eyes of the old sages. The covers of these books were pale blue, yellow, or green if paperback, or solid black if hardcover. By the 1980s the appearance of the printed classical books changed completely. They were printed on shiny white paper and their covers were lavishly decorated so that they would contribute to the appearance of the homes that they adorned. Another contemporary scholar of Islamic law has also remarked at the importance of these "yellow books" (*al-kutub al-ṣafrā'*). See Ṣubḥī Maḥmaṣānī, *Falsafat al-Tashrī' fī al-Islām,* 3rd ed. (Beirut: Dār al-'Ilm li al-Malāyīn, 1961), 10.

there was another reality that I had grossly misunderstood in the United States, and that is the role and reality of the Muslim movement in the United States. Naively, I had assumed that the freedoms afforded in the United States, and the relative absence of political persecution, would allow for a Muslim intellectual re-birth. After all, one grew up hearing his teachers repeat the vacuous statement, "In the Arab world there are Muslims but no Islam, and in the West there is Islam but no Muslims,"—meaning that the West lived by and implemented the core values of Islamic justice. Instead, what one found among Muslims in the United States was a remarkably arid intellectual climate. Far from freeing themselves from the burdensome baggage of their homelands, American Muslims reflected all the predicaments of their countries of origin, but in a sharply exasperated and pronounced form. By the 1990s, the same puritanism that was overcoming many parts of the Muslim world had become quite prevalent among American Muslims. For a variety of reasons, this puritanism was well suited for the American context—for a beleaguered minority searching for a sense of distinctiveness and autonomy, it provided a simple, straightforward, and aspirational dogma. Furthermore, it distracted this minority from its fears and worries about assimilation and loss of identity, with the comforting assuredness of privilege and distinctiveness. It dangled the ideal of the true, purified, and irreproachable Islam before the eyes of this minority, providing American Muslims with the means to escape confronting their intellectual and sociological insignificance. Furthermore, this ideal functioned as a tranquilizing narcotic, alleviating the anxieties of a minority living in a society that suffers from, what is at times, an intense Islamophobia. In addition, and perhaps most significantly, the Wahhābī brand of puritanism, in particular, has found a great deal of acceptance in a community that suffers from a fairly superficial knowledge of the Islamic intellectual tradition. The immigrant Muslim community in the United States is comprised largely of professionals who immigrated to the United States primarily for economic reasons.[15] There are no serious Muslim institutions of higher

[15] Yvonne Yazbeck Haddad, ed., *The Muslims of America* (Oxford: Oxford University Press, 1991), 4; Michael W. Suleiman, ed., *Arabs in America: Building a New Future* (Philadelphia: Temple University Press, 1999), 9. See also Kathleen M.

learning, and the field of Islamic Studies does not attract the brightest Muslims.[16] The few Muslims who do become accomplished in Islamic Studies are often perceived by the Muslim community to be a part of the secular paradigm, and are, therefore, alienated and marginalized.[17]

Moore, *Al-Mughtaribūn: American Law and the Transformation of Muslim Life in the United States* (Albany, N.Y.: State University of New York Press, 1995), 43-44, who indicates that the first wave of Muslim migration to the United States at the turn of the twentieth century was motivated by economic interests. Also see Yvonne Haddad, "The Dynamics of Islamic Identity in North America," in *Muslims on the Americanization Path?* eds. Yvonne Yazbeck Haddad and John L. Esposito (Oxford: Oxford University Press, 2000), 19-46.

16 This is partly because of the difficulty that Muslims experience in finding jobs in the field. A well-known joke in the field is that Near Eastern Departments ought to hang signs that say, "Muslims need not apply." See Edward Said, *Orientalism* (New York: Vintage Books, 1979), 284-328, on these dynamics.

17 Of course, the academic nature of the works of these Muslim scholars plays a role in limiting their impact upon the Muslim community. Nevertheless, the insights of these scholars do not filter into popular Muslim discourses in part because the works of these scholars are considered a part of the Western intellectual paradigm. I have in mind such Muslim scholars as the following: Afaf Lufi al-Sayyid Marsot, *A Short History of Modern Egypt* (1985; reprint, Cambridge: Cambridge University Press, 1994); *idem, Egypt in the Reign of Muhammad Ali* (Cambridge: Cambridge University Press, 1984); *idem, Women and Men in Late Eighteenth-Century Egypt* (Austin, Tex.: University of Texas Press, 1995); Fazlur Rahman, *Major Themes of the Qur'ān* (Minneapolis: Bibliotheca Islamica, 1994); *idem, Revival and Reform in Islam: A Study of Islamic Fundamentalism,* ed. Ebrahim Moosa (Oxford: Oneworld Publications, 2000); *idem, Islamic Methodology in History* (Islamabad, Pakistan: Islamic Research Institute, n.d.); *idem, Islam* (New York: Holt, Rinehart and Winston, 1966); Abdulaziz Abdulhussein Sachedina, *The Just Ruler in Shi'ite Islam: The Comprehensive Authority of the Jurist in Imamite Jurisprudence* (Oxford: Oxford University Press, 1988); *idem, The Islamic Roots of Democratic Pluralism* (Oxford: Oxford University Press, 2001); Khalid Yahya Blankinship, *The End of the Jihād State: The Reign of Hishām Ibn 'Abd al-Malik and the Collapse of the Umayyads* (Albany, N.Y.: State University of New York Press, 1994); Abdullahi Ahmed An-Na'im, *Toward an Islamic Reformation: Civil Liberties, Human Rights, and International Law* (Syracuse, N.Y.: Syracuse University Press, 1990); Mahmoud M. Ayoub, *The Qur'an and its Interpreters* (Albany, N.Y.: State University of New York, 1984); Amina Wadud-Muhsin, *Qur'an and Woman: Rereading the Sacred Text from a Woman's Perspective* (Oxford: Oxford University Press, 1999); Akbar S. Ahmed, *Postmodernism and Islam: Predicament and Promise* (London: Routledge, 1992); *idem, Toward Islamic Anthropology: Definition, Dogma, and Directions* (Ann Arbor, Mich.: New Era Publications, 1986); *idem, Discovering Islam: Making Sense of Muslim History and Society* (London: Routledge, 1988); Ebrahim Moosa, *Ghazali of Tus: His Life, Works and*

Once in the West, Muslims struggle to be rooted in a tradition, and Wahhābī puritanism offers a convenient, easy, and effective package. The package roots the Muslim in an irreproachable ideal that fits well in a social context that treats religious practice as an extracurricular activity.[18] One could be an objectified professional in the day practicing "real life" in one manner, and go to the mosque on the weekends to practice his extracurricular activity in an entirely different manner. Therefore, one could work and talk to non-Muslim women during the day, but insist that the voice of women should not be heard in an Islamic center[19] or that women sit behind a curtain when attending an Islamic lecture. Furthermore, a woman may sit in the front of the class when attending a lecture in her university, but must sit in the back of the room, if there is no curtain, when attending a lecture in an Islamic center. This bifurcated morality is partly facilitated by the Wahhābī perception that since Islamic law does not apply to non-Muslims, the corruptions and deviations of non-Muslims are not immoral.[20] Law defines morality, and since the law does not apply to non-Muslims, there is no morality that can be said to apply to them. Islamic law and morality, however, bind Muslims, and so what can be tolerated, when dealing with non-Muslims, cannot be

---

Teachings (Oxford: Oneworld Publications, 2000); Emad Eldin Shahin, *Political Ascent: Contemporary Islamic Movements in North Africa* (Boulder, Colo.: Westview Press, 1997); Shabir Akhtar, *A Faith for All Seasons: Islam and the Challenge of the Modern World* (Chicago: Ivan R. Dee, 1990); Hossein Modarressi, *Crisis and Consolidation in the Formative Period of Shi'ite Islam* (Princeton: Darwin Press, 1993).

[18] For an elaboration on this point, see Khaled Abou El Fadl, *Conference of the Books*, 287.

[19] I am referring here to the idea that *ṣawt al-mar'ah 'awrah*—the voice of a woman is considered akin to a private part that must be concealed, and thus it should not be heard except in cases of necessity. For a discussion on this topic, see Zayn al-Dīn b. Ibrāhīm b. Muḥammad Ibn al-Nujaym al-Miṣrī al-Ḥanafī, *Sharḥ al-Baḥr al-Rā'iq Sharḥ Kanz al-Daqā'iq* (Beirut: Dār al-Kutub al-'Ilmiyyah, 1997), 1:470-471; Muḥammad Amīn Ibn 'Ābidīn, *Hāshiyat Radd al-Muḥtār,* 2nd ed. (Cairo: Muṣṭafā al-Bābī al-Ḥalabī, 1966), 1:406.

[20] Arguably, Wahhābīs believe that such behavior is immoral, but tolerable. However, the problem is that in Wahhābī thought, law defines morality—there is no morality outside the law. Therefore, if Islamic law does not apply to non-Muslims, the morality of Islamic law does not apply either. Islamic morality, as defined by the law, is not relevant to anyone who is not bound by the law.

tolerated when dealing with Muslims. But more importantly, this bifurcation of ethos is further facilitated by the relatively undemanding standards for authoritativeness in Wahhābī thought, and by what might be called the accommodation of segmented thinking. Having, for the most part, freed itself from the Islamic intellectual heritage, the bar for inclusion in the realm of the authoritative is quite low in Wahhābī thought. All that is really needed to become authoritative is a working knowledge of the Qur'ān, a selective reading of some works on *ḥadīth* (the traditions attributed to the Prophet), and the internalization of the conceptual ideal of the "true" Islam. One need not think about such things as natural or inherent rights, or innate notions of dignity or common sense, because all the rights, dignity, and common sense to which one is entitled is given by Islamic law. Islamic law, which speaks for God, alleviates the need to burden oneself with such imponderables. But in a circular fashion, Islamic law is defined by reference to the ideal prototype of the true Islam. For instance, if a report states that the Prophet took a woman by the hand and sat with her on the side of the road, this necessarily clashes with the ideal. According to the ideal, the Prophet would not touch a woman and would not talk to her one on one. Therefore, either this report is unauthentic, or it was later abrogated by God, or the woman was not Muslim. An inquiry into the actual historical context is unnecessary and misleading because ultimately, it is a form of interpretive sophistry.[21] Thus, knowing the parameters of the prototype for the true Islam is necessary for candidacy in the realm of the authoritative. Furthermore, internalizing the relevant Qur'ānic verses and Prophetic traditions is crucial for attaining the qualifications for authoritativeness. Relevancy, of course, is defined in terms of the prototype of the true Islam—Qur'ānic verses or Prophetic traditions that destabilize the prototype are simply ignored. This amounts to a remarkably egalitarian rule of accessibility to moral authority—anyone with a minimal amount of study may easily become an authority in "true" Islamicity. Therefore,

[21] Interestingly, Wahhābism seems to have realized early on that all history is interpretation. If one must do away with interpretation, one must also do away with history. Wahhābī thought does not accept the idea that history is interpretation when it comes to the life of the Prophet and the Companions—the pietistic stories of their lives are taken as established facts.

becoming authoritative does not need specialization, and authoritativeness is attainable and exercisable as an extracurricular activity.

The second aspect, what I referred to as segmented thinking, is closely related to the first. The law, in Wahhābī thought, not only differentiates right from wrong, but it also defines beauty, common sense, reasonableness, and rationality. In many ways, the law does not define these values, but renders them redundant and unnecessary. By definition, what is required by Islamic law is reasonable, sensible, beautiful, and moral, and therefore, any independent inquiry into these values is redundant because if the inquiry does not reach the same conclusion that Islamic law reaches then the inquiry is flawed. For example, part of the Wahhābī conception of Islamic correctness mandates that if a husband asks his wife to make herself sexually available for his enjoyment, she must consent unless she is physically ill.[22] Therefore, according to the Wahhābī approach, this position is moral, beautiful, reasonable, and sensible by virtue of the fact that the law mandates it. Having precluded the need for an inquiry into normative values, each law or set of laws can create its own category of obligations without any regard to the overall coherence or reasonableness of a human being's life. In this context, segmentation means the dividing of the activities and feelings of a human being into neat and separate categories with each category creating a set of obligations and eliciting a set of responses without recognizing either the need nor the legitimacy of inquiring into the relationship between the various categories. One set of rules apply to being at work or school, a different set of rules apply to being in an Islamic center, and yet a different set of rules apply to dealing with one's family. There is no reason to inquire whether how one acts at work is consistent with how one acts in an Islamic center. Furthermore, one set of rules could apply to men and a very different set could apply to women.

22 Muḥammad al-Ṣāliḥ al-ʿUthaymīn, *Fatāwā al-Shaykh Muḥammad al-Ṣāliḥ al-ʿUthaymīn*, ed. Ashraf b. ʿAbd al-Maqṣūd ʿAbd al-Raḥīm (Riyadh: Dār ʿĀlam al-Kutub, 1991), 2:770. For a related *fatwā* concerning a woman's sexual obligations to her husband, see Ibn Fawzān, *al-Muntaqā*, 3:242-243. Incidentally, I am aware of the prophetic traditions used to support these *fatāwā*. However, this is not the appropriate place to engage a detailed study of those *ḥadīths*. For a discussion of these traditions, see Khaled Abou El Fadl, *Speaking in God's Name: Islamic Law, Authority and Women* (Oxford: Oneworld Press, 2001).

An inquiry into fairness, equality, consistency, decency, or compassion is futile and unnecessary. The law has already taken care of all of that.

One of the most noticeable effects of puritanism, especially of the Wahhābī variety, on Muslims in the United States has been its impact on Muslim women. The easiest and most effective way to prove one's legitimacy as an authority is to articulate rules that are restrictive for women. For instance, I recall that in one of the Islamic centers in the United States a fellow was invited to lecture to the congregation. The men were separated from the women with a wall. Before commencing his lecture, the fellow noticed that the door separating the women's quarter from the men's was open. Two women were in that quarter and unable to hear the lecture, so they opened the door and sat behind it so that they would not be visible to the men. Nevertheless, the lecturer insisted that the door be closed in order to foreclose any possibility of sexual enticement (*fitnah*). It is highly unlikely that this lecturer was actually sexually aroused, or that he thought that he might be aroused, by the idea of two veiled women sitting behind an open door. Furthermore, this lecturer and his congregation of men, who coincidentally agreed with him, lived, studied, or worked in the United States. Nonetheless, sexual enticement was not the issue—even these men are not so weak. The issue was an exercise of power to acquire authenticity and legitimacy according to the paradigms that puritanism sets as pertinent and relevant. Put differently, by making this statement, the lecturer instantaneously proved his impeccable legitimacy because he demonstrated vigilance in guarding the honor and modesty of women. But, of course, he gained this legitimacy entirely at the expense of women. Nonetheless, tormenting Muslim women is a low-cost proposition—Muslim women are like the proverbial punching bag upon which men can prove their power and worth. Having demonstrated his power and legitimacy, he conceded greater authoritativeness and privilege by the men—and perhaps even the whole community. Now, and this is the crucial point: it did not matter, and it does not matter, what legal evidence the lecturer is able or unable to offer in support of his closed-door policy. No one thought of asking about the legal basis for his determination, as if there were an assumption at work that this type of position is presumptively Islamic. Instead of this scenario, imagine if this speaker had commenced his talk by inviting the women in the secluded quarters to come forward and take the empty seats so that they might better hear the lecture. Having made this suggestion myself on several occasions, I am comfortable in surmising that 1) the rest of evening will be taken up by arguments about the legality of this suggestion; 2) women will play a very minor role in the debate, if at all; and 3) textual evidence that challenges the puritan paradigm will be waved away as the spin of a spin master.

Significantly, the anti-women discourses, as shown in this essay, find roots in the Islamic tradition. I am not claiming that the anti-women discourses are unauthentic while the pro-women discourses are rooted in Islamic authenticity. In fact, the extent to which contemporary discourses, consciously or not, are affected by pre-modern paradigms is, at times, surprising. But what is more surprising is the utter lack of historicity in dealing with the pre-modern tradition. For instance, I was attending a lecture in a mosque in North America when the *imām*, an engineer by training, advised the congregation that it is improper for men to sit where women once sat. He asserted that after a woman leaves a seat, men must wait until the woman's body heat dissipates before taking the same seat or, if they wish, they can fan the spot. The reason for this rule, the imām explained, is that the female body heat lingering in a seat is bound to cause *fitnah* (sexual seduction). I had never heard of such a rule despite having attended hundreds of lectures on Islamic conduct in many parts of the Muslim world. Furthermore, I had not encountered such a bizarre assertion in any classical or modern book. In fact, it seemed to me that a person who is sexually aroused by the lingering body heat of a woman on a chair is probably in need of professional attention. Years later, I found this same opinion attributed to the jurist Abū Ḥanīfah (d. 150/767), who reportedly recommended that men not take the seats of women until these seats lose their warmth.[23] I also located this same ruling attributed to the Prophet in the form of a *ḥadīth*. Reportedly, a woman sat down with the Prophet to discuss some affair with him. After she left, an unidentified man was about to take her seat when the Prophet instructed him not to sit in her

---

23 Ibn Aḥmad al-Makkī, *Manāqib Abī Ḥanīfah* (Beirut: Dār al-Kitāb al-ʿArabī, 1981), 132.

place until her body heat dissipated from the seat.[24] Importantly, this report is found only in classical texts that document fabricated traditions that were attributed to the Prophet. The report was fabricated and circulated by Shuʿayb b. Mubashshir, who alone reported this strange tradition. Apparently, the first appearance of this report was in the form of a tradition attributed to the Prophet, and later on, the report was circulated in the form of a legal ruling by Abū Ḥanīfah or, at times, Aḥmad b. Ḥanbal (d. 241/855). At any case, the classical jurists from all the different schools of thought, including the followers of Abū Ḥanīfah, dismissed this report in all its forms and refused to rely upon it in any determination. I am not sure if the above-mentioned engineering *imām* dreamt up the female body-heat ruling, or if he picked it up from one of the books on fabricated traditions. In either case, it is bewildering that traditions such as this would become buried and forgotten in Islamic history only to re-appear in one form or another centuries later. In re-appearing they draw legitimacy from an intangible abstractness called Islamic authenticity, but their re-appearance is not bounded and disciplined by a sense of historicity. A historical awareness would have easily deconstructed the discourse of the engineering *imām*, but instead his so-called Islamic ruling became a material proof of his piety and Islamicity. All the refuse that was once generated and soundly thrown out in Islamic history, now that the Islamic Civilization has crumbled, is once again accumulating. I fear that the infections and maladies that the Islamic Civilization in its prime was once strong enough to resist, now spread without a realistic hope of recuperation.

• • •

This is the context in which I wrote this essay. As noted above, a basketball player refused to stand up to the national anthem. The Islamophobics started ranting about the inability of Muslims to be loyal to the United States, and the dangers of Muslim intransigence.[25] Muslims conducted their own debates, often using rhetoric that gave

---

24 Abū al-Faraj ʿAbd Raḥmān b. al-Jawzī, *Kitāb al-Mawḍūʿāt* (Beirut: Dār al-Kutub al-ʿIlmiyyah, 1995), vol. 2, 162.

25 As recently as the year 2000, Daniel Pipes was still harping about this incident, see Daniel Pipes, "In Muslim America: A Presence and a Challenge," National Review, February 21, 2000, 40-1.

the Islamophobics many moments of delighted, "I told you so's." Some time during the debate, the Society for the Adherence to the Sunnah, which is Wahhābī and puritan, posted what it called a *fatwā* (legal *responsum*) regarding the issue. The invocation of the moral power of *Sharīʿah* had a stultifying impact on the debate, and most debaters fell silent. Frankly, I think it is quite appropriate for a Muslim to reflect upon the demands and imperatives of *Sharīʿah*. But the way in which *Sharīʿah* was invoked and the impact of that way upon the debate was symptomatic of a process that had become all too familiar. All the indicia of the arid process that desolates the richness of the heritage, the need for common sense or reasonableness, the use of methodology or reason, the inquiry into beauty or morality, and the appropriation of authenticity by the demeaning of women were all there. Provoked one too many times, I took the *responsum* to task.

There should be little doubt that there is a battle being waged over the very identity and character of the Islamic message. The battle includes fighting over the normative values, the ethics, and morals that the Islamic message is supposed to represent. There is also a battle over the relevance of the Islamic intellectual heritage, its role and character, and an intense battle over who gets to speak for Islamic law, how, and what ought to be said. In many ways, the arguments and struggles that rage in the United States about these issues is but a microcosm of the much larger reality of Islam. The struggles are more focused, intense, and polarized, but in the West, most of the ideological trends and ethnic identities and cultures are represented. I do not conceal the fact that this essay is part of this battle. Nonetheless, I do not side with an ethnic culture or particular identity. The purpose of this essay is far more modest. This essay attempts to challenge those who invoke the moral weight of Islamic law to their side as a way of foreclosing and ending the debate. Put in a blunt and uncouth fashion, the message of this essay is that: If you carry Islamic law as a weapon to silence others, you better know how to use it. However, at a more serious level, this essay attempts to resist the spread of what it perceives to be a puritan and despotic trend that is devastating the legacy of a very rich tradition. For instance, this trend has reached the point of banning books, such as *A Thousand and One Nights* and the poetry of Abū Nawwās (d. 198/814), texts that were preserved and transmitted in the Muslim Civilization for centuries. Furthermore, recently we have witnessed the phenomenon of publishing classical orthodox juristic texts but "cleansing" them of objectionable passages or ideas.[26]

This essay was initially published in an extremely modest form by a Muslim press. Next, a more earnest Muslim press that attempted to produce the text in better form adopted the book, and published the second edition. Dar Taiba, which later changed its name to Quill Publishers, complained that Muslim conferences and booksellers were refusing to carry the book. The real problems started when the book was translated to Arabic and several Arab presses attempted to print it. Three consecutive Arab presses accepted the book, signed a contract, and then reneged, complaining that publication of this book would endanger their business interests with some of the wealthy Arab countries. During this time, the publisher increasingly complained that although the sales of the English book were high, he was coming under pressure to stop distributing the text. Eventually, the publisher went out of business, I hope, for reasons unrelated to this text. Nevertheless, the existing copies of the book nearly sold out and its distribution has been surprising. At times, I got the sense that this essay was treated like a "dirty-secret"—many Muslims hesitated before admitting that they read it, but I received numerous messages expressing strong support. Considering the heart-wrenching betrayals of some friends and allies along the way, the hostility and defamation of opponents, and criticism of the protestors who wanted a more complex essay or who wanted a simpler essay, this work had worn me out, and I decided to close this chapter of my life. At this point, Professor Ebrahim Moosa and Oneworld Press of Oxford encouraged me to develop the ideas in this text into a more extensive work, and the result was a book entitled *Speaking in God's Name: Islamic Law, Authority and Women.*

Grace, my wife, refused to let bygones be bygones, and as if longing for the anxieties that this short essay had generated, she approached University Press of America with the idea of reprinting *The Authoritative and Authoritarian in Islamic Discourses*. In truth, I more than

---

[26] Abou El Fadl, *Conference of the Books,* 85-87.

welcomed the opportunity and resolved to bolster the argument in whichever way I could. Therefore, I added this lengthy justification hoping that it helps situate this essay in the subjective context of its author.

It is fitting to extend my first and foremost expression of gratitude to Grace. Furthermore, no words can express the extent of my debt to Professor Hossein Modarressi who is a true teacher, always authoritative but never authoritarian. Through my apprenticeship with him, I learned to become a loving and committed connoisseur of the Islamic juristic tradition. The encouragement of my mother, Afaf, father, Medhat, brother, Tarek, and sister, Eanas, through the ups and downs has kept me intact and sane. I also acknowledge my teachers in Egypt and Kuwait with overwhelming gratitude and humility. I am grateful to my students Anver M. Emon, Hisham Mahmoud, Anjum Mir, Mairaj Syed, and Jihad Turk for their competent and diligent assistance. I also thank the editor James Vowell for his rigorous work on this book. I thank Khalid al-Saleh for undertaking the publication of the Dar Taiba edition. I extend my sincere thanks to my colleagues Stephen Gardbaum, Stephen Bainbridge, Stephen Munzer, and Herbert Morris for their invaluable comments on this work. Mathew and Alaine Mengerink, the Institute for Usuli Thought, and Omar and Azmeralda Alfi supported my work in so many ways, and their support has made my scholarly life far less draining. I am indebted to them. As always, I am grateful to UCLA School of Law for its generous support of my work, and for providing me with a congenial and intellectually challenging environment in which to work.

II

The Problem of Authority

An Anecdotal Experience

I have always been intrigued by the Qur'ānic expression in the chapter known as *al-Muddaththir*, "And none can know the soldiers of God except God...."[1] The Qur'ān talks about nineteen angels guarding Hell, and Qur'ānic commentaries explain that this verse refers to the fact that only God knows why precisely nineteen angels (and not twenty or eighteen) guard Hell. Yet, the verse is phrased in the most interesting way. Only God can know God's soldiers. The language is expansive enough to express a general principle and is not necessarily limited to the matter of the nineteen angels guarding Hellfire. Furthermore, the verse is not necessarily limited to addressing why only God knows why nineteen angels guard Hell. Rather, the verse seems to be saying that only God knows who God's true or real soldiers are, and, by implication, that no one else can know who are God's true or real soldiers. If this is the meaning of the verse, then it is a magnificent negation of the authoritarian. One can aspire to be a soldier of God, and one can strive with the utmost exertion to achieve this status, but only God knows God's soldiers. Everyone has access to God's authority but no one is assured of receiving it.

[1] Qur'ān, 74:31.

Growing up in an Islamic religious culture, one is frequently reminded by his teachers that there is no church in Islam, and that no one embodies God's Divine authority. The picture conveyed and repeated is one of egalitarianism and the accessibility of God's Truth to all. Humans strive to discover the Divine Will, but no one has the authority to lay an exclusive claim to it. In this context, one often encounters the famous report attributed to the Prophet that every *mujtahid* (the person exerting an effort in deducing the law) is correct. If the *mujtahid* is correct in his or her *ijtihād* (judgment or determination as to the law), he or she receives two credits, and if he or she is wrong he or she receives one.[2] In other words, one must try to search for the law without fear of failure; one is rewarded for the success and the failure.

One also learns that when the ʿAbbāsid Caliph al-Manṣūr (d. 158/775) offered to implement the legal opinions of the jurist Mālik b. Anas (d. 179/796) as the uniform law of the Islamic nation, Mālik refused, arguing that there is no exclusive claim over the Divine truth.[3] One learns that Mālik insisted that there is no valid reason to impose one particular set of legal opinions as the law of the entire nation as opposed to any other set of legal opinions. The idea conveyed and constantly reinforced by one's teachers is that Islam rejects elitism and emphasizes that truth is equally accessible to all Muslims regardless of race, class, or gender. Furthermore, because accountability is individual and no one may carry the burden of another, the net result is diversity of consciences, beliefs, and actions. On the Final Day, each person will suffer only for his or her sins; no one will be made to suffer for the sins

---

[2] Narrated by al-Bukhārī, Muslim, Abū Dāwūd, al-Nasāʾī, Ibn Mājah, Aḥmad and others. See Muḥammad al-Shawkānī, *al-Qawl al-Mufīd fī Adillat al-Ijtihād wa al-Taqlīd* (Cairo: Maktabat al-Qurʾān, 1988), 89-91.

[3] See al-Shawkānī, *al-Qawl al-Mufīd*, 52; Aḥmad b. ʿAbd al-Raḥīm Shāh Walī Allāh al-Fārūqī al-Dahlawī, *al-Inṣāf fī Bayān Sabab al-Ikhtilāf fī al-Aḥkām al-Fiqhiyyah* (Cairo: al-Maṭbaʿah al-Salafiyyah, 1385 A.H.) 12; Jalāl al-Dīn ʿAbd al-Raḥmān b. Abī Bakr al-Suyūṭī, *Ikhtilāf al-Madhāhib*, ed. ʿAbd al-Qayyūm Muḥammad Shafīʿ al-Basṭawī (Cairo: Dār al-Iʿtiṣām, 1404 A.H.), 22-23; Yasin Dutton, *The Origins of Islamic Law: The Qurʾan, the Muwaṭṭaʾ, and Madinan ʿAmal* (Surrey: Curzon Press, 1999), 29; Patricia Crone and Martin Hinds, *God's Caliph: Religious Authority in the First Centuries of Islam* (Cambridge: Cambridge University Press, 1986), 86. Incidentally, there is a disagreement over whether the Caliph in question was al-Manṣūr or Hārūn al-Rashīd (r. 170/786 - 193/809).

of another.[4] In addition, potentially every Muslim may be the bearer of God's truth. The notion of individual and egalitarian accessibility of the truth results in rich doctrinal diversity.

One is taught that a major contributing factor to the diversity of Islamic theological and legal schools is the acceptance and reverence given to the idea of *ikhtilāf* (disagreement and diversity of opinions). One of the first books I read in Islamic law had the enchanting title, "*The Disagreement (ikhtilāf) of the Scholars Is a Mercy for the Nation.*"[5] This title, of course, is extracted from the famous *ḥadīth* (oral tradition) attributed to the Prophet providing that the disagreement of the *Ummah* (Muslim nation) is a source of mercy.[6] The book itself was a rather simplistic recounting of the positions of the different schools on a variety of legal issues. But the book and the traditions on which it relies reflect the fact that, in addition to the idea of accessibility, the expectation of disagreement is firmly supported by Muslim sources. Not only is disagreement to be expected, but it is actually a positive reality to be embraced and encouraged.

Yet these various egalitarian doctrines do not go unopposed. At the same time that one encounters the traditions and doctrines mentioned above, he also encounters a very different trend stressing the need for unity, uniformity, clarity, and simplicity. Often, the very same teachers who lectured on the doctrines of accessibility, egalitarianism, and diversity would lecture endlessly about the dangers of corrupt innovations (*bidaʿ*), *fitan* (sing. *fitnah*, discord or divisiveness) and the evils of intellectualism and theological disputations (*ʿilm al-kalām*). One is repeatedly reminded that Islam is simple and that the *Ummah* must reflect this simplicity. Often the same teachers who proudly asserted the absence of a church in Islam would insist that the doctrines of Islam are, for the most part, unitary, cohesive, and self-evident. In this context, those teachers would resort to invoking *ijmāʿ* (consensus) and argue that most of the doctrines of Islam are agreed upon and are well established. "*Al-*

---

4 See Qurʾān, 6:164, 17:15, 35:18, 39:7, 53:38.

5 Abū ʿAbd Allāh ʿAbd al-Raḥmān al-Dimashqī, *Raḥmat al-Ummah fī Ikhtilāf al-Aʾimma* (Kuwait: Maktabat al-Bukhārī, n.d.)

6 See Ismāʿīl al-Jirāḥī, *Kashf al-Khafāʾ wa Muzīl al-Ilbās* (Beirut: Muʾassasat al-Risāla, 1983), vol. 1, pp. 66-8.

Islām al-dīn al-samiḥ" ("Islam is the simple religion"), they proclaimed as they warned against the dangers of breaking with consensus or engaging in disputations.[7] At times, they would go so far as to declare that whoever violates a consensus is an apostate or unbeliever.[8]

There are numerous methodological problems with the doctrine of consensus. For instance, how does one verify a consensus, and whose consensus counts? Does the consensus of one generation bind subsequent generations? Is consensus limited by locale, or must it reflect the opinions of the scholars of the entire of nation? These and other issues surrounding the doctrine have been debated throughout Islamic history.[9] Therefore, it is doubtful whether the invocation of consensus can legitimately serve as a vehicle for the creation or enforcement of a simplistic uniformity. But there is a more fundamental problem with the whole notion of simplicity or "the simple religion." Simplicity is the

---

[7] "*Al-Islām al-dīn al-samiḥ*" or "*al-Islāmu dīnun samiḥ*" is based on *ḥadīths* reported in *Ṣaḥīḥ al-Bukhāri* and the *Musnad* of Aḥmad b. Ḥanbal. These *ḥadīths* state that the most beloved religion to God or the most authentic religion is the tolerant Ḥanīfiyyah. The Ḥanīfiyyah was an early monotheistic faith in the Arabian Peninsula prior to the revelation of the Qur'ān in Mecca. Aḥmad b. 'Alī Ibn Ḥajar al-'Asqalānī, *Fatḥ al-Bārī Sharḥ Ṣaḥīḥ al-Bukhārī*, eds. Muḥammad Fu'ād 'Abd al-Bāqī and Muḥibb al-Dīn al-Khaṭīb (Beirut: Dār al-Ma'rifah, n.d.), 1:116-118; Aḥmad b. Ḥanbal, *Musnad al-Imām Aḥmad b. Ḥanbal*, eds. 'Alī Ḥasan al-Ṭawīl, Samīr Ṭāhā al-Majdhūb, and Samīr Ḥusayn Ghāwī (Beirut: al-Maktab al-Islāmī, 1993), 1:293; Marshall G.S. Hodgson, *The Classical Age of Islam*, vol. 1 of *The Venture of Islam: Conscience and History in a World Civilization* (1974; reprint, Chicago, Ill.: University of Chicago Press, 1977), 160. Historically, the expression "*al-Islām al-dīn al-samiḥ*" meant Islam is the religion of ease, tolerance, or compassion. Co-opting the expression as an argument for a simple or simplistic religion seems to have taken place in the modern age, particularly by the Salafī school of thought.

[8] Although in the contemporary age it is commonly claimed that disagreeing with a consensus renders one an unbeliever, the pre-modern juristic tradition is very different. Most of the debate focused on whether it is a sin (as opposed to disbelief) to contravene the consensus. A large number of jurists held that opposing a consensus is neither disbelief nor a sin. See Ahmad Hasan, *The Doctrine of Ijma' in Islam* (Islamabad: Islamic Research Institute, 1978); Fakhr al-Dīn Muḥammad b. 'Umar b. al-Ḥusayn al-Rāzī, *al-Maḥṣūl fī 'Ilm Uṣūl al-Fiqh* (Beirut: Dār al-Kutub al-'Ilmiyyah, n.d.), 2:98-99; Sirāj al-Dīn Maḥmūd b. Abī Bakr al-Urmawī, *al-Taḥṣīl min al-Maḥṣūl*. ed. 'Abd al-Ḥamīd 'Alī Abū Zaynad (Beirut: Mu'assasat al-Risāla, 1988), 2:86.

[9] See Abū Bakr al-Jaṣṣāṣ, *al-Ijmā'*, ed. Zuhīr Shafīq (Beirut: Dār al-Muntakhab al-'Arabī, 1993), pp. 137-223.

antithesis of accountability, egalitarianism, and diversity. In fact, simplicity is the antithesis to the very notion of culture and civilization.[10] With diversity is born complexity and a pluralist reality. The more one emphasizes clarity, simplicity, and unity, the more one must reject ambiguity, complexity, and diversity. In order for things to be clear and simple, there must exist a unitary authority that resolves most disputes and settles most issues that might result in disagreement, essentially vitiating the accountability, egalitarianism, and diversity inherent to Islam. The simplistic response given to this dilemma is that the Qur'ān and *Sunnah* resolve most issues and disputes. Perhaps.[11] But Islamic history is the most profound testament that the Qur'ān and *Sunnah* inspired the greatest complexity in the Islamic heritage, namely the complexity of Islamic jurisprudence.

Anyone who has done even a minimal amount of research in Islamic law will be struck by the complexity of doctrines, diversity of opinions, and enormous amounts of disputations over a wide range of issues. Other than the main jurisprudential schools—the Ḥanafī, Mālikī, Shāfiʿī, Ḥanbalī, Jaʿfarī, Zaydī, Ibāḍī, and Ismāʿīlī—there are many extinct schools such as the schools of Ibn Abī Laylā (d. 148/765), Sufyān al-Thawrī (d. 161/778), al-Ṭabarī (d. 310/923), al-Layth b. Saʿd (d. 175/791), al-Awzāʿī (d. 157/774), Abū Thawr (d. 240/854), Dāwūd b. Khalaf (the Ẓāhirī) (d. 270/884) and many more. Even in one school, such as the Ḥanafī school, there could be several trends, such as the positions of Zafar b. al-Hudhayl (d. 158/774-775), Abū Yūsuf (d.

[10] The intended simplicity here is the normative orientation that endorses puritan visions of religion. The simplicity that I am referring to is the notion that Islam provides clear-cut, black-and-white, straightforward, and uncompromising mandates and prohibitions. This type of simplicity creates polarized and dichotomous visions of right and wrong. However, since right and wrong is manifested and practiced through human agency, the human agent, in order to give effect to this clear vision of right and wrong, must negate and exclude the dissenter. If right and wrong are always clear and precise, one is less likely to tolerate those who fail to see matters with the same of degree of clarity and precision.

[11] One way to look at this assertion is the following: Even if the Qur'ān and *Sunnah* resolve most issues and disputes, human beings also have the singular ability to derail and unsettle most resolutions. Since the Qur'ān and *Sunnah* speak only through human beings, the corruptability of what the Qur'an and *Sunnah* has to say is certain. Of course, I am not implying that the literal text of the Qur'ān is corrupted.

182/798), and al-Shaybānī (d. 189/804).[12] Furthermore, Muslim jurists often maintained that there is a long established tradition of disputation, debate, and disagreement that started from the age of the Companions of the Prophet and continued thereafter.[13] There is no doubt that Islamic jurisprudential history is complex and diverse. There is also no doubt that there are tremendous pressures in contemporary Islam to deny and negate this complexity.[14]

When studying Islamic law, one often asked his teachers about the proper balance to be struck between diversity and unity, or between dogma and discourse. The prompt, and quite typical, response was that Muslims disagree on the *furūʿ* (branches of religion) not the *uṣūl* (the basics or fundamentals). Therefore, Islamic legal schools, for example, may disagree on the *furūʿ* of Islam, but not the *uṣūl*. By itself, the dichotomy between *uṣūl* and *furūʿ* is not a tremendously useful distinction. It could mean that Muslims may disagree on everything except the basics or it could mean that Muslims only disagree on marginal and peripheral issues. In other words, one may define the *uṣūl* so expansively as to allow disagreements only on marginal and insignificant issues. Alternatively, one may define the *uṣūl* so restrictively as to open the gates for debate and disagreements on all types of material issues. The invariable trend in the contemporary age has been to limit the span

[12] The disagreements of the various jurisprudential schools of thought primarily related to systematic methodological principles that ought to guide the process of legal determination. The jurisprudential schools often disagreed on the admissibility and weight to be given to the different types of evidence that are relevant to determining the Divine law. Furthermore, the schools often disagreed on the general principles of law, and appropriate interpretive methods. These methodological differences frequently resulted in highly diverse affirmative legal determinations. For a discussion on methodological principles and disagreements, see generally, Ṣubḥī Maḥmaṣānī, *Falsafat al-Tashrīʿ fī al-Islām*, 3rd ed. (Beirut: Dār al-ʿIlm li al-Malāyīn, 1961); Muḥammad Abū Zahra, *Uṣūl al-Fiqh* (Cairo: Dār al-Fikr al-ʿArabī, n.d.); Muḥammad Bāqir al-Ṣadr, *Durūs fī ʿIlm al-Uṣūl* (Beirut: Dār al-Kitāb al-Libnānī, 1978); Mohammad Hashim Kamali, *Principles of Islamic Jurisprudence*, rev. ed. (Cambridge: Islamic Texts Society, 1991).

[13] See, for example, *Imām al-Ḥaramayn* Abū al-Maʿālī al-Juwaynī, *Kitāb al-Ijtihād min Kitāb al-Talkhīṣ* (Damascus: Dār al-Qalam, 1987), 43-4.

[14] As I noted in several parts of this book, contemporary Islam is plagued by a virulently puritan ideology.

of the *furūʿ* and to incorporate more and more *aḥkām* (positive commandments of law) within the scope of the *uṣūl*, thus limiting the possibility for diversity in discourse. The more issues injected into the purview of the *uṣūl*, the more one restricts the scope of legitimate disagreement and discussion.[15]

Muslim jurists have debated the definition of *uṣūl* and *furūʿ* for centuries. Significantly though, the historical debate, unlike the contemporary debate, has not been about which laws are among the *uṣūl* and which are among the *furūʿ*. Rather, the debate on *uṣūl* and *furūʿ* has been a debate about the use, authority, and interpretation of different sources of knowledge. The majority of the pre-modern authorities argued that the *uṣūl* are what is clearly proven by human reason (*ʿaql*) or by a textual source (*naṣṣ*). In the case of a textual source, it must be of definite authenticity, and of clear and precise meaning (*dalālah samʿiyyah wāḍiḥah*). Some pre-modern authorities have adopted a rather circular definition: *uṣūl* are whatever Muslims cannot and do not disagree upon. This is another way of saying that whatever Muslims unanimously agree upon is part of the *uṣūl*. Nonetheless, claiming unanimity on most issues historically remained problematic as long as there were learned challengers to an established dogma or doctrine. Alternatively, some jurists argued that the *uṣūl* are what have been clearly proven by human reason (*dalālah ʿaqliyyah wāḍiḥah*).[16] Consequently, they argued, the oneness of God or the attributes of God would be from the *uṣūl*.[17] However, the continued existence of different

[15] This issue is important because, in theory, any person who denies something considered to be part of the *uṣūl* is no longer a Muslim, and may be considered an apostate. In practice, matters were far more complex because of the historical reality of sectarianism in Islamic history. Considering that the punishment for apostasy and some forms of heresy could be death, the consequences of accusing a group of people of denying the *uṣūl* could be quite drastic. As a result, the practice of Muslim jurists in the various epochs of Islamic history was quite complex. Often, they avoided accusing a particular group or sect of denying an element of the *uṣūl*. See Khaled Abou El Fadl, *Rebellion and Violence in Islamic Law* (Cambridge: Cambridge University Press, 2001).

[16] This refers to the use of pure reason and not applied reason. Pure reason yields first principles such as the presumption of innocence or the presumption of continuity.

[17] See, on this issue, al-Juwaynī, *Kitāb al-Ijtihād*, 23-7.

theological schools of thought such as the Ash'arīs, Mu'tazalīs, Qadarīs, or Murji'īs rendered the reliance on self-evident or clearly proven reason problematic. In fact, Muslim theological schools never achieved consensus on issues such as God's attributes, pre-destination, the nature of evil and good, or the createdness or uncreatedness of the Qur'ān.[18]

Whatever the merits of the various positions, after concluding the discussion on the distinction between *furū'* and *uṣūl*, pre-modern Muslim jurists, typically, would next discuss whether the principle "every *mujtahid* is correct" applies to *uṣūl* and *furū'* or only *to furū'*. If one argues that this principle applies to *uṣūl* and *furū'*, then one admits the possibility of disagreements in the *uṣūl*. If one applies this principle only to *furū'*, then one is arguing that disagreements may occur only in the branches of law and not on the fundamentals of religion. But even in the field of *furū'*, Muslim jurists debated the meaning of the phrase "every *mujtahid* is correct." Does this mean that every *mujtahid* is potentially correct? Possibly, this phrase means that every *mujtahid* is potentially correct, but ultimately, only one *mujtahid* reaches the right answer—other *mujtahids* are ultimately wrong, but they are rewarded for trying anyway. Alternatively, this phrase could mean that truth is relative and every *mujtahid* is ultimately correct but in a very particular sense.[19] As discussed below, truth here relates to the object or purpose of the Divine Will. God, it is argued, does not seek an objective or singular truth. God wishes human beings to search for the Divine Will and seek it. Truth adheres to the search—the search itself is the ultimate truth. Consequently, correctness is measured according to the sincerity of the individual's search.

In this context, pre-modern Muslim jurists discussed whether the *taklīf* (legal or religious obligation or charge imposed on the *mujtahid*) is to find the truth or to simply perform the *ijtihād*. If one is obligated to perform the *ijtihād*, and is ultimately not responsible for missing the truth, then the emphasis is on the process and the results are left for God to assess and evaluate. Furthermore, if the emphasis is on the process,

---

[18] See, generally, Majid Fakhry, *A History of Islamic Philosophy,* 2nd ed. (New York: Columbia University Press, 1983), 205, 223.

[19] See al-Suyūṭī, *Ikhtilāf al-Madhāhib*, 21-39; Abū al-Ḥusayn Muḥammad b. 'Alī b. al-Ṭayyib al-Baṣrī, *al-Mu'tamad fī Uṣūl al-Fiqh,* ed. Khalīl al-Mays (Beirut: Dār al-Kutub al-'Ilmiyyah, 1983), 2:363.

then a duty of utmost diligence, exertion, and even exhaustion in investigating the sources is mandated. It is not sufficient that one happens to find the truth accidentally. Rather, one is evaluated on the sincerity of the attempt and the exhaustiveness of the search for the truth.[20]

Fundamentally, all of the above mentioned debates address the authority of Islamic sources, the nature and character of this authority, and who can represent, express, and direct it. In Islamic polemics, God is sovereign, but this sovereignty can only be exercised through human agents. The human agents, be they *mujtahids* or otherwise, are bound to faithfully execute the intent of the Principal (i.e., God) and can do so only through a set of written instructions. The instructions are in written form because revelation ceased with the death of the Prophet. The agents may not act *ultra vires* (outside the scope of their delegation) and, consequently, the agents must ascertain two issues. First, are the instructions, in fact, from God? Do these instructions truly come from the Principal? This is an issue of competence (i.e., authenticity). Second, what do the instructions say? This is an issue of meaning (i.e., interpretation).

---

20 See, on these issues, al-Suyūṭī, *Ikhtilāf al-Madhāhib*, 47-64; Abū al-Khaṭṭāb Maḥfūẓ b. Aḥmad b. al-Ḥasan al-Kalūzānī, *al-Tamhīd fī Uṣūl al-Fiqh,* ed. Muḥammad b. ʿAlī b. Ibrāhīm (Mecca: Markaz al-Baḥth al-ʿIlmī wa Iḥyāʾ al-Turāth al-Islāmī, 1985), 4:394; see Abū Isḥāq Ibrāhīm al-Shīrāzī, *Sharḥ al-Lumʿa,* ed. ʿAbd al-Majīd Turkī (Beirut: Dār al-Gharb al-Islāmī, 1988), 2:1043; Shams al-Dīn Muḥammad b. Mufliḥ al-Maqdisī, *Uṣūl al-Fiqh*, ed. Fahd b. Muḥammad al-Sadhān (Riyadh: Maktabat al-ʿUbaykān, 1999), 4:1469; Jamāl al-Dīn Abī Muḥammad ʿAbd al-Raḥīm b. al-Ḥasan al-Asnawī, *Nihāyat al-Sūl fī Sharḥ Minhāj al-Wuṣūl ilā ʿIlm al-Uṣūl*. ed. Shaʿbān Ismāʿīl (Beirut: Dār Ibn Ḥazm, 1999), 2:1025; Abū Ḥāmid al-Ghazālī, *al-Mustaṣfā min ʿIlm al-Uṣūl*, ed. Ibrāhīm Muḥammad Ramaḍān (Beirut: Dār al-Arqam, n.d.), 2:598; ʿAbd al-Majīd ʿAbd al-Ḥamīd al-Dībānī, *al-Minhāj al-Wāḍiḥ fī ʿIlm Uṣūl al-Fiqh wa Ṭuruq Istinbāṭ al-Aḥkām* (Binghāzī: Dār al-Kutub al-Waṭaniyyah, 1995), 2:345; Abū ʿAlī al-Ḥasan b. Shihāb al-Ḥasan al-ʿUkbarī, *Risāla fī Uṣūl al-Fiqh*, ed. Muwaffaq b. ʿAbd Allāh b. ʿAbd al-Qādir (Mecca: al-Maktabah al-Makkiyyah, 1992), 124; Muḥammad b. al-Ḥasan al-Badakhshī, *Sharḥ al-Badakhshī Manāhij al-ʿUqūl maʿa Sharḥ al-Asnawī Nihāyat al-Sūl* (Beirut: Dār al-Kutub al-ʿIlmiyyah, 1984), 3:260-261; Sayf al-Dīn Abū al-Ḥasan ʿAlī b. Abī ʿAlī b. Muḥammad al-Āmidī, *al-Iḥkām fī Uṣūl al-Aḥkām*, ed. ʿAbd al-Razzāq ʿAfīfī. 2nd ed. (Beirut: al-Maktab al-Islāmī, 1402 A.H.) 4:162; Fakhr al-Dīn Muḥammad b. ʿUmar b. al-Ḥusayn al-Rāzī, *al-Maḥṣūl fī ʿIlm Uṣūl al-Fiqh*, ed. Ṭāhā Jābir Fayyāḍ al-ʿAlwānī. 3rd ed. (Beirut: Muʾassasat al-Risāla, 1997), 6:6; Muḥammad ʿUbayd Allāh al-Asʿadī, *al-Mūjaz fī Uṣūl al-Fiqh* (n.p.: Dār al-Salām, 1990), 262; Abū Zahrah, *Uṣūl al-Fiqh*, 301.

Both competence and meaning implicate the issue of the sources or origins of the instructions, and also the authority of the instructions. What factors and elements must be considered in reaching a determination as to competence and meaning? This inevitably involves an intricate balance between the authoritativeness of the instructions and the authoritarianism of the agents. Since a human being is not the recipient of direct and personal communication from God, an individual must investigate the Divine Will through a medium. In Islamic jurisprudence the medium is most often a text.[21] But one must first establish that the text is a *bona fide* command from the Divine, and then investigate the precise meaning of the text. In reality, both the determination of the "*bona fidedness*" of the instructions and the meaning of those instructions are thoroughly dependent on human agency. Fundamentally, human agents negotiate the process of determining the authenticity and meaning of the text. In fact, the role of human agency in expressing the Will of the Divine is unavoidable.

In this negotiative process, one confronts two extremes. On one extreme, one might argue that no evidence or text concerning competence or meaning is excluded from investigation and nothing is predetermined by the Divine. But the risk run here is that one will have a religion that is entirely subjective, relative, and individual. One might risk undermining the very foundation of competence and meaning, and the very logic of authority. A religion that does not have any established dogma might defy being defined as a religion at all.[22] If all interpretations of a religious text, regardless of how idiosyncratic, unfounded, or

[21] I am not at all excluding the possibility that the medium could also be non-textual or ultra textual evidence of the Divine Will. For example, signs revealed through God's various creations and creatures could also be relevant. The past or present course of conduct of people or the habits and intuitions of human beings (*ṭabīʿat al-khalq* or *sharʿ man qablanā* or *ʿādat al-nās* or *sunat al-khalq*) or the laws of nature (*sunat al-kawn*) could all be relevant considerations in investigating the Divine Will. Furthermore, as noted earlier, Muslim jurists used pure reason to deduct relevant principles of law.

[22] By dogma, I mean presuppositions that are to be accepted without question, such as the existence and Oneness of God or the Prophethood of Muḥammad. In claiming authoritativeness, religious dogma mandates deference to these presuppositions that are taken as certain truths. Every religious system is founded on a bed of such presuppositions, which, in turn, define the essential character of the religion.

subjective they might be, are admitted, one runs the risk of diluting any authority a text might have. All texts are ultimately engaged, experienced, and understood by human beings. If one argues that all such experiences with texts, regardless of how subjective they might be, are equally valid, then one runs the risk of negating the value of the text as a source of authority. In doing so, one might invalidate the authoritativeness of religious textual sources.[23]

On the other extreme, one might argue that all issues of competence and meaning are decisively resolvable and that the agent need only worry about the faithful execution of the instructions. But the risk is a religion that is rigid, inflexible, and, ultimately, impractical and irrelevant. Even more, we risk a religion that, as defined by its agents, is not only authoritative, but also authoritarian. If one expands the realm of religious dogma and argues that the majority of religious texts have one possible meaning, then one might co-opt the authoritativeness of the religious text and transform it into a tool for human authoritarianism. Since the Islamic text is mediated through human agents, it would make little sense to speak of an authoritarian text.[24] Rather, it is the human agent who would transform the authority of the Islamic text into human authoritarianism. The agent takes the authoritativeness of the instructions and produces himself as authoritarian. Additionally, creating a defined body that represents and speaks for the text might

[23] I do not believe that the determination of meaning is accomplished solely by the reader. Rather, the determination of meaning is most often a product of the interaction between the objectivities of the text and subjectivities of the reader. Elsewhere, I argue that there ought to be a balancing process, an equilibrium of sorts, between the author, the text, and the reader. The three parties should attempt to negotiate meaning, fully realizing that the corruption of meaning ensues when one of the parties to the process dominates and negates the other.

[24] Here, I am talking about social authoritarianism not the authoritarianism of meaning. It is possible for a text to be so detailed, specific, and uncompromisingly particular so as to render the role of reader irrelevant. All readers who know the linguistic usage will probably come to a single conclusion as to the text's meaning and intent. Nevertheless, by making its reader irrelevant, the text has also become dull and boring. It has one thing to say, and it will say it again and again. In my view, such texts tend to condemn themselves to irrelevance in a fairly short time. If the Qur'ān and *Sunnah* are, in fact, not such texts, but a reader forces this precision and clarity upon them, I would argue that the reader has overstepped his or her bounds and despotically imprisoned the text.

institutionalize this authoritarianism.[25] The authoritarianism is manifested by the act of empowering oneself with the moral weight of religion in order to obtain unjustifiable deference from others. A person could appropriate a text with several possible meanings and recast it as a text with a single invariable meaning. Such a person could claim to be an authority vis-à-vis others because of his expertise and special competence in deciphering the Divine Will. Fundamentally, authoritarianism is an act of abuse of authority and a betrayal of the trust that is placed by others in the authoritative agent.[26]

While mediating the religious text through human agents, one faces the challenge of striking a balance between authoritativeness and authoritarianism. Ultimately, because religion, as doctrine and belief, must rely on human agency for its mundane existence, one runs the risk that those human agents will either render it entirely subjectively determined, or render it rigid and inflexible. In either case, one risks that the Divine will be made subservient to human comprehension and human will.

This essay focuses principally on the second phenomenon of the inevitable negotiation that must occur between the author, text, and the reader. In other words, it is a study of the authoritative and authoritarian in contemporary Islamic discourses. It is about how Muslims discourse about the Divine Will, and about how Muslims discourse about Islamic sources. As such, it is a work about how competence is determined and meaning is found. Using a case study method, this work presents an example of how the authoritative is co-opted and reconstructed into the authoritarian.

---

[25] Such as a church that knows the full and indisputable truth.

[26] For the purposes of this essay, I am assuming that the main medium for deciphering the Divine Will is a text or set of texts that are believed to embody the Divine Will. Effectively, a person who demands deference to his determinations or judgments, regarding the Divine Will, does so because of this purported competence in understanding and interpreting these texts. Lay individuals might defer to the judgments of such an authoritative person because they trust that this person is representing God's law. However, if the person who is considered by others to be an authority, misrepresents or conceals the evidence in order to obtain, for whatever reason, compliance with his determinations, this is an abuse of authority and breach of trust. The point at which such a breach becomes authoritarian is when the integrity and autonomy of the Divine or the text is negated. I elaborate upon this below.

• • •

Mohammed Arkoun has argued that Islamic culture has always suffered from the problem of the "unthought" and "unthinkable."[27] There are certain issues in Islamic culture, Arkoun argues, that remain unthought while other issues remain unthinkable. In other words, there are certain mental sets that prevent Muslims from entertaining certain thoughts or ideas. In this essay, we are not dealing with the "unthought" or the "unthinkable." As noted above, the authority, competence, and meaning of sources were debated frequently. With respect to Islamic discourses in the contemporary age, we have a new category to contend with, namely the category of the "forgotten." While in the pre-modern age the authority of the *mujtahid*, the authoritativeness of the source and its agent, and the risk of authoritarianism (*al-istibdād bi al-ra'y*) were debated vigorously, this discourse is now forgotten. This essay aspires to rekindle the debate and to remember an age-old discourse that has not outlived its usefulness.

This is not an academic essay. Nonetheless, it is scholarly and does, to the extent possible, attempt to maintain objective standards of analysis. In the past I have primarily published academic studies in academic journals where I problematized the authoritarian in Islamic sources. The method pursued in these studies was to stress the diversity of sources, understandings, opinions, and positions in Islamic jurisprudential history.[28] By presenting the diversity within the legal discourse, I hoped to demonstrate the inability of the authoritarian to dominate and establish uniformity over certain issues in Islamic legal history. This book

---

[27] See Mohammed Arkoun, *Rethinking Islam*, trans. R. Lee (Boulder, Colo.: Westview Press, 1994).

[28] See, for example, Khaled Abou El Fadl, "The Common and Islamic Law of Duress," *Arab Law Quarterly* 6, no. 2 (1991): 121-159; *idem*, "Legal Debates on Muslim Minorities: Between Rejection and Accommodation," *Journal of Religious Ethics* 22, no. 1 (1994): 127-162; *idem*, "Islamic Law and Muslim Minorities: The Juristic Discourse on Muslim Minorities from the 2nd/8th to the 11th/17th Centuries," *Journal of Islamic Law and Society* 1, no. 2 (1994): 141-187; *idem*, "Ahkam al-Bughat: A Study of Irregular Warfare and the Law of Rebellion in Islam," in *Cross, Crescent and Sword: The Justification and Limitation of War in Western and Islamic Tradition*, eds. James Turner Johnson and John Kelsay (Westport, Conn.: Greenwood Press, 1990), 149-176.

addresses the issue of authority directly. I have made an effort to be as succinct as possible and keep digressions to a minimum, and to make this study, to the extent possible, intelligible to the non-specialist.

Finally, I started this preface by a Qur'ānic verse that has engaged my thinking through the years. I should also give credit to a passage from Ibn Khaldūn's (d. 808/1406) *Muqaddima* that has equally engaged my thinking and heavily influenced my understanding of the method by which a source and its authority should be evaluated. The passage speaks for itself and is quoted below. Notably, it best represents the purpose of this essay.[29]

Ibn Khaldūn wrote:

> When it comes to reports, if one relies only on the [method] of transmission without evaluating [these reports] in light of the principles of human conduct, the fundamentals of politics, the nature of civilization, and the conditions for social associations, and without comparing ancient sources to contemporary sources and the present to the past, he [or she] could fall into errors and mistakes and could deviate from the path of truth. Historians, [Qur'ānic] interpreters and leading transmitters have often fallen into error by accepting [the authenticity of certain] reports and incidents. This is because they relied only on the transmission, whether of value or worthless. They did not [carefully] inspect [these reports] in light of [fundamental] principles [of historical analysis] or compare the reports to each other or examine them according to the standards of wisdom or investigate the nature of beings. Furthermore, they did not decide on the authenticity of these reports according to the standards of reason and discernment. Consequently, they were led astray from the truth and became lost in the wilderness of error and delusion.[30]

---

[29] As explained later in the essay and, as Ibn Khaldūn argues, reliance on the science of transmission (*'ilm al-riwāyah* or *'ilm al-ḥadīth*) alone is erroneous. Chains of transmission are only one of the factors to be evaluated in considering the authoritativeness of a tradition. *'Ilm al-riwāyah* cannot exclude *'ilm al-dirāyah* (the study of plausibility, weight, and implications of a tradition). *'Ilm al-dirāyah* must include evaluating the historical plausibility and social implications of a tradition. The fact that a particular tradition has an impeccable chain of transmission is only the first step in assessing its authenticity. Furthermore, even if a tradition's authenticity is probable, that fact standing alone is not probative as to the weight to be given to the tradition in making a legal determination.

[30] Abū Zayd 'Abd al-Raḥmān b. Muḥammad Ibn Khaldūn, *al-Muqaddima* (Beirut: Dār Iḥyā' al-Turāth, n.d.), 9-10.

III

The Text and Authority

بسم الله الرحمن الرحيم

A Case Study

Muslims in the United States are plagued by the problem of authority. By this I do not mean political or social authority—although that is a problem as well—but rather, textual authority. The problem is not so much the lack of an institutional framework to channel the authority of the text. Rather, the problem is developing the conceptual framework from which the text is approached, constructed, and presented. Muslims in the United States have not developed legitimate ways of understanding and interpreting Islamic texts. More importantly, they have not developed ways of evaluating the legitimacy or authoritativeness of the various ways according to which an Islamic text can be read and interpreted. The connections between the classical epistemological and hermeneutic heritage and Muslims living in the United States have been thoroughly severed. Muslims in the West are a disinherited bunch, and they are compelled to reinvent themselves without the collective wisdom of past Muslim generations. When it comes to making sense of Islamic texts, there is a remarkable vacuum—a vacuum that is often filled by authoritarian agents who are able to appropriate the Divine Will in order to proclaim the death of discourse. This fatality is proclaimed in the humble service of a despotic puritanism in order to impose a suffocating silence. The case study presented below is but one example of this process. However, before turning to discussing this process it is necessary to lay some foundation for our analysis.

Islam defines itself by reference to a book, and as such, it defines itself by reference to a text. In Islamic discourses, Muslims, as well as Christians and Jews, are described as the People of the Book. Therefore, the most basic frame of reference in Islam is a text. The text is endowed with a prominent degree of authority and reliability.[1] Significantly, the Islamic civilization has been marked by a prodigious literary production particularly in the field of *Sharīʿah*.[2] The factors contributing to this production are varied, but it is unmistakable that the text came to occupy a central role in constructing the basic frame of reference for religious and legal authority in Islam.

At the functional level, the text is represented by a reader or interpreter. The interpreter of the text speaks in its name; such an interpreter claims that the language of the text authorizes his or her understanding. But there is an inevitable tension between the text and its representative. The problem can be conceptualized in terms of the authoritative versus the authoritarian. Muslims in the United States are developing their own traditions on approaching, constructing, and presenting the Islamic text. The traditions being developed by them are not necessarily unique to the American context. In fact, many of the discourses and traditions developed by Muslims in the United States are borrowed from other cultures. Furthermore, the case examined in this book is not unique to the discourses of American Muslims.

[1] The definition of a text has been a subject of much debate. Jorge J. E. Gracia defines a text as: "Groups of entities, used as signs, that are selected, arranged, and intended by an author in a certain context to convey some specific meaning to an audience." Jorge J. E. Gracia, *Texts: Ontological Status, Identity, Author, Audience* (Albany, N.Y.: State University Press of New York, 1996), 3. I am using the word "text" in this study to mean the written sources of the Divine Will. This consists primarily of the Qurʾān and recorded traditions of the Prophet. The way the word text is used here leaves open the possibility that the text was not intended to convey a specific meaning to an audience.

[2] Johannes Pedersen has noted that: "the Arabic Book owes its origin to Islam." Johannes Pedersen, *The Arabic Book*, trans. Geoffrey French (Princeton: University of Princeton Press, 1984), 3.

Importantly, however, the case study presented here exemplifies the tension between the text and its reader, and between the authoritative and the authoritarian.

When considering this tension, one should first pose the question: What can be considered authoritative in the life of Muslims in the United States? To answer this question, we must reflect upon how the authoritative is understood and presented. And in presenting the authoritative how does one avoid establishing himself as the authoritarian? Significantly, is it possible for Muslim discourses to utilize the authoritative without indulging the authoritarian?

Defining "authoritative" is often an individual endeavor. One may know what is to be considered authoritative in one's life. For example, one may believe certain principles or texts to be authoritative. By authoritative, I mean principles, texts, or discourses that are considered binding or dispositive of an issue, or a set of issues in a person's life. The authoritative warrants deference—an individual will exclude the possibility of considering particular beliefs or courses of action in deference to what is perceived as authoritative. Different people regard different things as authoritative. Furthermore, people are not necessarily systematic in living by the dictates of what they consider authoritative. In other words, one may declare a certain source to be authoritative, but fail to give any effect to this declaration in his or her personal life. Nevertheless, whether one is consistent in following the dictates of the authoritative or not, one may wish to present or communicate his or her vision of the authoritative to other individuals. It is in this situation that one runs the very real risk of transforming that vision into an authoritarian discourse. For instance, a person may consider God's Word authoritative in the sense that this Word warrants deference. Whether or not that person is consistent in deferring to God's Word, he might attempt to convince others to show due deference to that Word. Furthermore, such a person might argue that others ought to defer to God's Word as he understands it. Therefore, that person will argue that if one is to properly defer to God's Word, one ought to believe such and such or do such and such.

Idiosyncratic and dogmatic visions of what is authoritative in a text risk becoming authoritarian. They risk becoming the exclusive and final word on what the authoritative text means or intends to say. If the presenter of the text is not disciplined, and does not follow a methodology by which he can identify and critically weigh countervailing pieces of evidence, the presenter might superimpose himself or herself upon the text. Furthermore, if the presenter of the text is unable or unwilling to distinguish between his or her subjective political or social preferences and the voice (or the possible voices) of the text, then the presenter might effectively replace the text.[3] Therefore, the authoritative text becomes limited by and subjugated to the presenter and his or her presentation of the text. In many ways, the authoritative text is hijacked by the presenter of the text; the authoritative yields to the authoritarian.

Assume, for instance, that person designated as X reads the Qur'ān to mean Y. Assume further that X refuses to look at any alternative interpretations and is not interested in any considering any view that contends that the Qur'ān means Z and not Y. In addition, assume that X said that the Qur'ān means Y for an entirely idiosyncratic reason—for instance, the Qur'ān means Y because my mother told me that the first symbolic association that springs to my mind is always correct. The more idiosyncratic and unverifiable X's opinion, the more inaccessible it is to others. Furthermore, the more insistent X is on not considering any competing view, the more idiosyncratic X's position becomes. By insisting that the text means Y and only Y, X is running the risk of rendering the text irrelevant. Since, thanks to X, the text says Y, and only Y, the determination of meaning (which is Y) overshadows the text, which, according to X, has nothing to say other than Y. The text's only role is to support the Y determination. Now, assume that, for whatever reason, other people consider X authoritative in the sense that they are willing to defer to his determinations. Effectively, X hijacked and nullified the text by violating the text's independence and integrity, and by rendering it

[3] The distinction is not between subjective and objective treatments of the text. Whether an objective treatment of a text is possible is problematic. Rather, the distinction is between subjective treatments of the text that exclude, ignore, or suppress alternative or variant voices of a text. In other words, the presenter, for various possible reasons, fails to consider or deal with evidence that suggests that the text may mean something other than the meaning chosen by the presenter. The presenter then asserts that the text only has the meaning he or she is giving to it.

entirely dependent on his determinations. What matters are X and Y, the text ceases to make a difference.[4] X has invoked the authority of the text to empower himself, and once duly empowered, X closed the process and rendered the text his captive or the captive of his determinations (i.e., of Y)—the text and Y have been fused into one. It is this act of transferring the authority of the text to oneself, and then condemning the text to irrelevance, that in this context, I am calling authoritarian.[5]

In the endless stream of dogma that one encounters in Muslim conferences, lectures, and publications, the Qur'ān and *Sunnah* are affirmed as authoritative. This is often presented as if it resolves all issues. However, in reality, this is only the beginning of the inquiry. Importantly, one must deal with who is presenting the Qur'ān and *Sunnah* and how they present these sources. Typically, a speaker addressing a particular issue in one of these publications or conferences will quote a couple of Qur'ānic verses or *ḥadīths* and perhaps an anecdotal story from the religious traditions. Nonetheless, quotations and anecdotes do not make an argument; they simply illustrate it. It is the speaker who makes the argument and it is the speaker who chooses the illustrative quotations or anecdotes. If the speaker is ill informed, simplistic, dogmatic, or ill-intentioned, he or she will seek to exclude the vast spectrum of authoritative texts and opinions in favor of his or her own authoritarianism. The speaker will assume that the text has a clear, precise, and singular meaning, while excluding all evidence to the contrary. Furthermore, after superimposing his or her understanding upon the text, the speaker equates himself or herself to the text. The authoritative text is subsumed into the speaker who, in turn, becomes the authoritarian. Effectively, the speaker approaches an open text—open because the text is accessible to all readers and interpreters—and closes

---

[4] In a sense, Y has become the new text that renders the old text irrelevant.

[5] What I am describing here is a form of literary authoritarianism, but the authoritarianism this essay is interested in is more than that. Authoritarianism is found not only in saying that the text means Y, and only Y, but also in representing to others that the text means Y while knowingly or recklessly ignoring other possibilities. In doing so, X is breaching his duties of honesty and diligence towards others by misrepresenting to them the potentialities of the text. In short, authoritarianism could be manifested in dealing with the text and in dealing with other individuals who are deferential to X.

it, rendering it inaccessible. The meaning of the text and the interpretive processes of the speaker become one and the same. The source is transformed from an open text to a closed text, and the text and speaker are fused as one.

In order to illustrate the problem, I will focus on a single example from contemporary Muslim discourses. This example is presented as a case study because it is representative of the current state of Muslim discourses. The example itself is fairly innocuous and if it were not for the fact that it represents how contemporary Muslims conduct their debates, it would not merit much attention. However, it is exactly because the example is fairly standard and unremarkable that it is important. It demonstrates a common discursive process among Muslims in the United States. The example involves a *fatwā* or religious *responsum* issued by an organization in the United States concerning a highly publicized event. Since the *responsum* claims to represent the law of God and does so by closing an open text, it is an apt example of the transformation of the authoritative into the authoritarian.

IV

The Case Study

بسم الله الرحمن الرحيم

The Fatwā[1]

In March 1996, while the national anthem was playing, Mahmoud Abdul Rauf, an African-American professional basketball player, refused to stand up. Abdul Rauf had signed a contract obligating him to play on a basketball team pursuant to certain terms and conditions, which presumably included joining his teammates in certain activities. However, Abdul Rauf argued that, as a Muslim, he may not stand up while the American national anthem is playing. His argument seems to have been that the national anthem of the United States represents a history of oppression and enslavement to African-Americans. Consequently, he found the act of standing up in respect to this symbol of oppression offensive to his Muslim sensibilities. The basketball league suspended Abdul Rauf, but after twenty-four hours, he decided to change his position.[2]

---

1 See Appendix for the full text of the *fatwā* issued by the Society for Adherence to the Sunnah (SAS).

2 Apparently, shortly after this controversy, Abdul Rauf migrated to a secular Muslim country, Turkey, where played basketball for several years. Reportedly, he has since returned to the United States where he continues to play in the NBA. At the time of publication, he plays for the Vancouver Grizzlies.

Let me state at the outset that I have no interest in defending or criticizing Abdul Rauf's decision. My interest here is in examining the process by which Islamic sources are used in contemporary American Muslim discourses. The Abdul Rauf matter might have ended quickly, but the event caught the attention of many Muslims as well as the American media. A large number of American Muslims debated the merits of the Abdul Rauf case, and several individuals addressed the event in Friday sermons, in letters to journals, in articles, and through the maze of electronic mail (e-mail). Many Muslims disagreed with Abdul Rauf, arguing that nothing in Islam precludes Muslims from standing up to the national anthem of their countries and that it is hypocritical to enjoy living in the United States yet refuse to respect the country's national symbolism. Other Muslims argued that the United States is a *kāfir* (infidel) country that has engaged in numerous acts of oppression, and that it is un-Islamic to stand for the national anthem or salute the flag. Most of these responses did not rely on any textual evidence, but were purely impressionistic, emotive, and even idiosyncratic. One response, however, published on e-mail by the "Society for Adherence to the Sunnah" (SAS), was particularly interesting. It is this response that will be the subject of this case study.

SAS's response illustrates the tension between the authoritative and the authoritarian and the process by which the authoritative is used to produce the authoritarian. Effectively, SAS's response in tone, style, and conclusion is modeled after a *fatwā* (legal *responsum*). It would not be an exaggeration to assert that SAS issued a *Sharʿī* (legal) *fatwā* regarding the Abdul Rauf issue. We do not focus on this *responsum* because of the political or social position of SAS. In all likelihood, the majority of Muslims have never heard of SAS or its *responsa*. Furthermore, we do not focus on SAS's response because of any inherent or unique quality in the *fatwā* itself. Rather, SAS's *fatwā* concerns us because in style and method it is fairly representative of the endemic quality of contemporary Muslim discourses. SAS's *fatwā* reads like numerous other *fatāwā* issued by a variety of religious organizations all around the Muslim world.[3]

[3] I have attempted to prove this point in *Speaking in God's Name*. Furthermore, as I note in the Afterthoughts section of this work, when prominent Saudi jurists considered whether it is lawful for students to stand up in honor of a teacher or whether it

SAS commences its response by asserting that a variety of organizations and individuals have debated the Abdul Rauf matter. It notes, however, that no one has sought out the ruling of *Sharīʿah* regarding this issue, and it then proceeds to establish the "true" rule of *Sharīʿah* on the matter. In style and method, SAS selectively employs the authoritative text and transforms itself into the voice of the authoritarian. SAS first defines *ʿibādah* (worship) as "all that Allah is pleased with from actions of the heart, tongue, or limbs." Having asserted that premise, SAS then relates four main points:

First, the *Sunnah* prohibits standing out of respect to anyone. SAS quotes two *ḥadīths* (Prophetic reports) to that effect:

> (a) 'Abd Allah b. Abd al-Rahman related that Anas said: No one was dearer to them (the Companions) than Allah's messenger (sallallahu 'alaihi wa salam) yet when they saw him they did not stand up because they knew of his dislike of that. (Narrated by al-Tirmidhi) [SAS's translation and transliteration]

> (b) Mahmoud b. Ghaylan related that Mu'awiyya came out so Abd Allah b. al-Zubayr and Ibn Safwan stood up when they saw him. Mu'awiyya said, "Sit down for I heard the Prophet say, 'Let he who is pleased by people standing up before him, await his place in Hell.'" (Narrated by Abu Dawud and al-Tirmidhi) [SAS's translation and transliteration]

Second, SAS states that it is narrated in al-Tirmidhī that the Prophet forbade bowing to anyone out of respect.[4]

Third, SAS quotes the following *ḥadīth*:

> Abu Hurayrah reports that when Muadh Ibn Jabal returned from Sham, he came to the Prophet (sallallahu 'alahi wa salam) and

is lawful to salute or stand up while honoring the flag, these jurists cited the same evidence and reached the same conclusions as SAS. This supports my argument that the SAS *responsa* is not an oddity in the modern Muslim world. ʿAbd al-ʿAzīz b. ʿAbd Allāh b. ʿAbd al-Raḥmān b. Bāz, *Majmūʿ Fatāwā*, ed. ʿAbd Allāh b. Muḥammad b. Aḥmad al-Ṭayyār (Riyadh: Dār al-Waṭan, 1416 A.H.), 1:286; *idem, Majmūʿ Fatāwā wa Maqālāt Mutanawwiʿah*, ed. Muḥammad b. Saʿd al-Shawīʿ (Riyadh: Maktabat al-Maʿārif lī al-Nashrwa al-Tawzīʿ, 1992), 5:349; *Fatāwā al-Lajnah al-Dāʾimah,* 1:144-148, 1:149-150; In one of these *responsa*, the official Saudi organ for the issuance of Islamic legal opinions held that standing up to meet someone is lawful, but to stand up in order to honor someone is unlawful.

4 Presumably, SAS is referring to the following *ḥadīth* that was narrated by al-Tirmidhī: "Anas reported that a man asked the Prophet, 'One of us may run into

> prostrated before him, saying that he had seen the people of Sham prostrating in respect to their monks, and that the Messenger (sallallahu 'alahi wa salam) deserved greater respect than what Muadh had seen the people of Sham give to their monks. The Prophet (sallallahu 'alahi wa salam) replied, "Were I to have commanded anyone to prostrate to anyone, I would have commanded the wife to prostrate to her husband." (Al-Tirmidhi) [SAS's translation and transliteration]

In each of these cases, SAS argues worship *per se* was not intended; yet, the physical act, regardless of intent, was prohibited. Consequently, SAS concludes, it must be that standing out of respect is at the very best *makrūh* (reprehensible) if not *ḥarām* (forbidden). Before bringing its *responsum* to a close, SAS argues that *walāʾ* (loyalty or fidelity) cannot be owed to non-believers. Presumably, standing in respect to anyone or anything is an act of *walāʾ* and hence, it is not allowable except to God, let alone non-believers.

The argument regarding *walāʾ* does not concern us here since, as stated above, my purpose is not to support or criticize Abdul Rauf's position. What is troubling is how Muslims in the United States employ the authoritative (in this case various *ḥadīth* accounts) and go about constructing the authoritarian. In other words, what is particularly problematic is the way Islamic sources are employed, explored, and recast in order to establish authority. The speaker, in this case SAS, invokes the authoritative text in a fashion that constructs the authoritarian. The speaker presents himself or herself as the embodiment of the text—the speaker and the text become inseparably attached as one. Ultimately, the speaker by the employment of the text becomes the voice of the authoritarian and the voice of Divine judgment. In order to illustrate this process, we will discuss several problematic areas in SAS's discourse. We will then relate these problems to the issue of the authoritative and authoritarian.

---

his brother or friend, may he then bow to him?' The Prophet said, 'No.' The man said, 'Should he then hold him and kiss him? ' The Prophet said, 'No.' The man said, 'May he then take his hand and shake it?' The Prophet said, 'Yes.'" Al-Tirmidhi reported this *ḥadīth* as *ḥasan*. Muḥammad ʿAbd al-Raḥmān b. ʿAbd al-Raḥīm al-Mubārakfūrī, *Tuḥfat al-Aḥwadhī bi Sharḥ Jāmiʿ al-Tirmidhī* (Beirut: Dār al-Kutub al-ʿIlmiyyah, n.d.), 7:425-426.

First, SAS overlooks a variety of complexities surrounding the *ḥadīths* it cites. Second, SAS ignores several *sharʿī* (legal) categorizations. We will take each of the *ḥadīth* cited by SAS and examine them in light of the complexity of the Islamic legal tradition.

Importantly, SAS does not make explicit its interpretive methodology or moral vision which, of course, it should and must do. Rather, it presents to us the rule of *Sharīʿah* (*ḥukm sharʿī*) as if the *ḥukm* (the positive rule or ruling) is not mediated through a subjective human agent—as if the Will of God and the will SAS are one and the same. In Islamic jurisprudence, when one addresses the law of God, one is bound by a heightened level of scrutiny and by the obligation of utmost diligence. Furthermore, part and parcel of the duty of diligence is the obligation to be clear and conscientious about one's method in deducing the legal ruling, and to evaluate and weigh all the relevant evidence for and against the possible ruling.[5]

The Anas Ḥadīth on Standing

SAS quotes the Anas *ḥadīth* on standing as if it were dispositive of the issue at hand. The implication here is that the existence of a reported *ḥadīth* on a point, any point, clearly resolves all issues. In fact, this is only the beginning of the inquiry, for we must discuss the authority and purpose of the *ḥadīth*. We must then consider the nature of the obligation, if any, that the *ḥadīth* creates and how that obligation is to be balanced against other *Sharīʿah* obligations and principles.

The first *ḥadīth* reported by Anas is narrated by al-Tirmidhī (d. 279/892-893). It is not included in any of the other collections, including those of al-Bukhārī (d. 256/870) and Muslim (d. 261/875).[6] How

[5] In the 1970s, Ḥasan Ayyūb dealt with the issue of standing in his *al-Sulūk al-Ijtimāʿī fī al-Islām* (Cairo: Dār al-Buḥūth al-ʿIlmiyyah, 1979), pp. 324-332. Ayyūb complains about the dogmatism of some Muslims who simplify Islamic legal discourses and adopt unreasonable positions. He argues that there are three categories of standing in Islamic law: clearly forbidden, clearly allowed, and disagreed upon. Ayyūb's categorizations are helpful, but they should not foreclose the discourse.

[6] However, the Anas *ḥadīth* is reported in a collection attributed to al-Bukhārī. See Muḥammad al-Bukhārī, *al-Adab al-Mufrad* (Beirut: Muʾassasat al-Kitāb, 1986), 202.

should we analyze this fact? The approach of *Ahl al-Ḥadīth* (a medieval school that emphasized the primacy of literal interpretations of *ḥadīth* as a source of law) has been to consider this fact inapposite. This school maintained that the fact that the *ḥadīth* is accepted only by al-Tirmidhī is irrelevant. The *ḥadīth* should still be granted full force. This approach might make sense when one is considering a *ḥadīth* that relates to *adab* (issues of etiquette and manners, sing. *adab*; pl. *ādāb*) in Islamic discourses, which have little impact on one's moral and ethical obligations. On issues relating to the heart of religious obligations (such as *wājibāt* and *furūḍ*, mandatory duties and obligations), however, one should not base fundamental theological imperatives on singular uncorroborated transmissions. The Uṣūlīs, the jurists belonging to a medieval approach that emphasized jurisprudential comprehension, did not consider an *āḥādī ḥadīth*, standing on its own, to be sufficient to establish a legal obligation unless it was supported by the totality of evidence.[7] We will return to a discussion of the probative value of *ḥadīth* of singular transmissions later.

Al-Tirmidhi cites the Anas ḥadīth in Kitāb al-Adab (the chapter on adab or good manners) and asserts that this ḥadīth is *"ḥasan ṣaḥīḥ gharīb min hādhā al-wajh."*[8] We must take note of two things:

1. This *ḥadīth* does not relate to the *ʿaqāʾid* or *ʿibādāt* (issues of belief or worship). It relates to matters of manners or etiquette.

---

[7] See Muḥammad al-Ghazālī, *Dustūr al-Wiḥdah al-Thaqāfiyyah Bayn al-Muslimīn* (Cairo: Dār al-Anṣār, 1981), 74, 79; Muḥammad al-Ghazālī wrote a powerful and polemic work emphasizing that the content (*matn*) of *āḥādī ḥadīth* must be evaluated according to rational principles and the totality of evidence. Al-Ghazālī argued that *āḥādī ḥadīth* that are not consistent with reason or Qurʾānic principles should be rejected regardless of the chain of transmission. Al-Ghazālī, *al-Sunnah al-Nabawiyyah,* 18, 29.

[8] Al-Tirmidhī often co-joined the category of *ḥasan* with *gharīb* in saying *ḥasan gharīb*. This expression is ambiguous. *Ḥasan* means a tradition that reaches us through a singular, but reliable, chain of transmitters. The initial narrator of the tradition is considered of just character, but not entirely reliable or considered a person who commits errors in narration. The chain transmitting the report, however, is acceptable. *Gharīb* means a tradition that is unique to a particular transmitter—others transmitters did not narrate the same version of the tradition. Al-Tirmidhī would say *ḥasan gharīb* meaning a tradition that has been narrated in the form of *ḥasan* and in the form of *gharīb*, or a tradition that has unique aspects to it.

2. A ḥadīth ḥasan ṣaḥīḥ gharīb, according to the particular language of al-Tirmidhī, is less than a *ṣaḥīḥ ḥadīth* (a tradition that is considered authentic).[9] In fact, in all likelihood, the other collections of ḥadīth do not accept the authenticity of this ḥadīth and hence, do not record it.

Nevertheless, in my opinion, there is a very good chance that the *ḥadīth* does in fact report an authentic state of affairs. As discussed below, others have reported that the Prophet did not want people to stand up upon seeing him, and the Prophet guarded against people sanctifying or immortalizing him.[10] However, what legal imperatives are to be drawn from this fact? Was this a matter of personal humility on the part of the Prophet, or was it a legal injunction that applies to all Muslims in all circumstances?[11] Al-Nawawī (d. 676/1277), the *muḥaddith* (transmitter of traditions) and jurist, comments on this *ḥadīth* by saying that the Prophet feared that the Companions would be afflicted by a *fitnah* (corruption) if they exaggerate in aggrandizing and honoring him. That is why the Prophet forbade the Companions from even praising him saying, "*lā taṭarūnī*" ("Do not praise me"). But other than that, al-Nawawī argues, the Prophet stood up out of respect for some of the Companions and they stood out of respect for each other in the Prophet's presence, and the Prophet did not forbid or criticize them.[12]

---

[9] See ʿImād al-Dīn Abī al-Fidāʾ Ismāʿīl b. Kathīr, *al-Bā'ith al-Hathīth Sharḥ Iktiṣār 'Ulūm al-Ḥadīth* (Beirut: Dār al-Kutub al-ʿIlmiyyah, 1983), 41. There is disagreement over the meaning of al-Tirmidhī's usage. See Subḥī Ṣāliḥ, *ʿUlūm al-Ḥadīth* (Beirut: Dār al-ʿIlm, 1991), 158; Nūr al-Dīn ʿItr, *Manhaj al-Naqd fī ʿUlūm al-Ḥadīth* (Damascus: Dār al-Fikr, 1981), 272.

[10] This methodological point is similar to the concept of *tawātur fī al-maʿnā* (corroborative meaning). See Kamali, *Principles of Islamic Jurisprudence,* 70. Fakhr al-Dīn al-Rāzī, *al-Maḥṣūl fī ʿIlm Uṣūl al-Fiqh* (Beirut: Dār al-Kutub al-ʿIlmiyyah, 1988) 2:184 notes that when various singular transmissions of *ḥadīth* agree in their purport, the substance of the *ḥadīth* can be considered *mutawātir*.

[11] Typical of *Ahl-al-Ḥadīth* methodology, Nāṣir al-Dīn al-Albānī in his *Silsilat al-Aḥādīth al-Ḍaʿīfah wa al-Mawḍūʿa* (Riyadh: Maktabat al-Maʿārif, 1988) 3:247, 635 argues that this is a distinction without a difference. Al-Albānī argues that whatever the Prophet did becomes a binding *Sunnah*.

[12] Aḥmad b. Ḥajar al-ʿAsqalānī, *Fatḥ al-Bārī fī Sharḥ al-Bukhārī* (Beirut: Dār al-Fikr, 1993), 12:322. (Hereinafter *Fatḥ al-Bārī*).

In the discourses on the Prophet's legacy (*sīrah*), not all of the Prophet's acts are of equal imperative value. Rather, their value is dependent upon their categorization. Some of the *Sunnah* is *tashrīʿiyyah* (intended by the Prophet to be legislative) and some constitutes *afʿāl jibilliyyah* (personal behavior not intended by the Prophet to be legislative). The non-legislative (*jibilliyyah*) category includes *Sunnah* that relates to specialized or technical knowledge on things such as medicine, commerce, agriculture, or war. It also includes matters that are peculiar to the person of the Prophet such as the number of his wives or *ṣawm al-wiṣāl*. The legislative (*tashrīʿiyyah*) is divided into matters relating to the Prophet's roles as a messenger of God or as head of state or as a judge.[13] Furthermore, the legislative acts of the Prophet could elucidate five or six different types of legal categories[14]—such acts could indicate an obligation (*farḍ*), duty (*wājib*), recommended (*mandūb* or *mustaḥabb*), permissible (*mubāḥ*), reprehensible or disapproved (*makrūh*), or forbidden (*ḥarām*). These injunctions could relate to matters of *ʿibādāt* (laws of worship regulating the relationship between humans and God), *muʿāmalāt* (acts relating to civil and commercial intercourse regulating the relationship between human beings), or *ādāb* (sometimes called *istiʾdhāniyyāt*—precedents that advise and educate on matters relating to manners and form). A specific system of analysis pertains to each category, and one must be very careful not to jump from one category to another without clear and persuasive evidence. For example, a *Sunnah* relating to *adab* (manners) cannot be used, by itself, to support an imperative ruling on *ʿibādāt* or *muʿāmalāt* (worship or civil interactions). However, an *ādāb Sunnah* may elucidate the proper etiquette in conducting business or performing *ʿibādah*. Consequently, a point of *ādāb* may relate to *adab al-muʿāmalāt* (the proper manners in undertaking civil interaction) or *adab al-ʿibādāt* (the proper manners in performing worship). This *Sunnah* is not a part of *ʿibādāt* or *muʿāmalāt* proper, but is a part of the proper etiquette to be

[13] See Kamali, *Principles of Islamic Jurisprudence*, 50-57.

[14] Since most jurists held that everything is permissible unless proven otherwise, jurists disagreed on whether permissibility is a legal category or just the natural order of things. Jurists also debated whether there is a difference between an obligation and a duty—*farḍ* and *wājib*.

followed in performing *muʿāmalāt* or *ʿibādāt*. An example will illustrate the point: it is part of the proper etiquette in conducting business to smile and shake hands.[15] Therefore, smiling and handshaking is part of the proper manners in conducting business (*adab al-muʿāmalāt*). However, the failure to smile or shake hands does not invalidate the contractual relationship to be established.

In any case, despite the fact that the *ḥadīth* under discussion is of singular transmission, is included in the *ādāb*, and, arguably, may be limited to how one should specifically deal with the Prophet, SAS, nevertheless, uses it in the context of its discourse on *ʿibādah* or acts related to the worship of God. This is not possible without careful and restrained analysis and strong evidence.[16] It should be recalled that SAS erroneously categorizes the issue of standing up as a matter relating to *ʿibādah*. Then SAS, without persuasive evidence, cites an *ādāb ḥadīth* in support of its "*ḥukm*" (ruling). This is problematic because it is a lapsing and confusing of categories.[17]

[15] On smiling and shaking hands generally, see Abū Zakariyyā al-Nawawī, *Riyāḍ al-Ṣāliḥīn* (Beirut: Dār al-Khayr, 1993) 292-3.

[16] Arguably, one could ask: Why should SAS be bound by these various categorizations? I deal with this issue in the Afterthoughts section of this book. However, in short, I would say that SAS claims to speak for *Sharīʿah*. At this point, *Sharīʿah* is defined by the juristic interpretive community and its various methodologies and determinations. Without the juristic tradition, the very idea of Islamic law would vanish. Having invoked this legal tradition as the basis for its legitimacy and authritativeness, SAS had become bound by sources that endowed it with authority. If SAS wishes to reform this legal tradition, it may do so as long as it discloses those reformative efforts so that others may decide whether they wish to continue deferring to SAS. If SAS rejects the legal tradition altogether, then it rejects Islamic law and it should make this point clear by asserting that it is not basing its decision on Islamic law, but basing it on some other source.

[17] Importantly, the collectors of traditions tended to include in the chapters on etiquette and manners (*ādāb* and *istiʾdhāniyyāt*) reports of dubious authenticity. This practice, known as *al-tasāhul fī al-ādāb*, meant that traditions that normally would not withstand scrutiny in any other area, would be accepted on the assumption that such traditions only relate to etiquette and manners. So, for instance, a report that is not sufficiently reliable to be included in the chapters on *ʿibādāt* or *muʿāmalāt* could be included in the chapter on *ādāb*. Put differently, a particular report would be accepted and documented in a book on traditions, but only on the assumption that it goes to the *ādāb* and nothing else. Therefore, a report that is not good enough for the

Interestingly, some books and commentaries on *ḥadīth* address the issue of standing up in respect to someone. Others, such as *Riyāḍ al-Ṣāliḥīn* (The Gardens of the Righteous), do not address the issue. However, books on law (*fiqh*) rarely discuss this matter at all. This is an indication that standing up in respect was not perceived to be a subject of legal inquiry. Islamic law books (*fiqh*) addressed issues considered central or even peripheral to *Sharī'ah*. Nonetheless, they would often omit the discussion of things relating to *ādāb* such as proper manners for eating or drinking. Political issues, if considered material to *Sharī'ah*, would be discussed in books of *fiqh*. Seemingly, the matter of standing up to persons, except on the occasion of funerals, was considered to be of no legal significance.

On a separate matter, whether or not the *riwāyah* (narration) of Anas relates to a matter of *'ibādah* or *ādāb*, can this *ḥadīth* be considered probative on whether one should stand up while a national anthem is being played? This could only be possible through a *qiyās adnā* or *khafiyy* (subtle analogy) because the operative cause in the reported actions of the Companions and the standing up during a national anthem is not the same (*li 'adam ittiḥād al-'illa*)—standing up to the Prophet (a person) and standing up to music are not the same things. A rule by analogy assumes that the effective or operative cause (*'illa*) in an old case and a new are the same.[18] Arguably, as legal elements a

'ibādāt or *mu'āmalāt*, might be good enough for the *ādāb*. This points to the risks that are inherent in the type of lapsing and confusing of categories performed by SAS. The collection and documentation of traditions in pre-modern Islam were performed within a context of particular categorizations and paradigms. The casual use of these reports, without a sufficient grounding in their historical contexts, results in confused and misdirected reinventions of the Islamic tradition. While the reinvention of tradition is not necessarily a bad thing, in this context, not being sufficiently grounded in the technical historical practices tends to endow secondary, and often pedantic, Prophetic traditions with a power and effect that is disproportionate to their reliability. In the end, one finds that ideas and doctrines that were always treated as peripheral and marginal, ascend to prominence, and even become central to a new understanding of Islam. Without a sufficient normative and moral direction, Islam becomes a religion of mindless pedantic practices.

[18] The operative cause (*'illa*) is the element that triggers the law into action. One can conceptualize it as the equivalent of the light switch that turns on the light. If the operative cause exists, the law is triggered into action and if it is absent the law remains dormant. Kamali, *Principles of Islamic Jurisprudence*, 206-214.

person and music or a person and the symbol for a nation are not equivalents and raise very different types of issues.[19] In order to make the connection between this *ḥadīth* and the Abdul Rauf situation, one must make several factual assumptions. First, one must assume that standing up for the national anthem is analogous to standing up for a person; second, that standing up to any person is analogous to standing up to the Prophet; and third, that the role of the Prophet is equal to or sufficiently similar to the function played by a national anthem. All of this can be reached only through *qiyās adnā* or *khafiyy*. According to the juristic tradition, this type of *qiyās* cannot be undertaken without explicit specification—i.e., a clear explanation of the methodology of the *qiyās* and its illustration.

A qiyās based on the similarity of purposes or objectives is called *qiyās ʿalā al-maqṣad* (or *maqāṣid*) or *ḥikmat al-ḥukm*. This type of qiyās would not focus on the operative or effective cause of the ḥukm but on the purpose or reason behind the reported prohibition against standing up in respect. This, in turn, depends on what the stated purpose of the rule, if any, is and how one identifies the purpose. As noted, the operative cause of a ruling (*ʿilla*) is the trigger that fires the law into action. For example, the operative cause for the prohibition against drinking alcohol is that it is an intoxicant. The *maqṣad* or purpose of the ruling is several: because intoxicants hamper consciousness and negate responsibility, because intoxicants spread corruption, because intoxicants prevent one from knowing what he or she is saying in prayer, etc. If one extends the law according to a unity of operative causes any intoxicant would be prohibited. On the other hand, if one extends the law according to the unity of purposes, anything that hampers consciousness or spreads corruption would be prohibited. In any case, as explained below, a *qiyās ʿalā al-maqāṣid* is not appropriate in the context of the Abdul Rauf issue.

---

[19] Similar issues are posed by practices such as standing up for the national anthem in the Olympics, saluting military superiors, and standing up when a judge enters the courtroom. One suspects that SAS is sufficiently dogmatic and puritan to condemn all of these practices as a heretical innovation (*bidʿah*).

The Muʿāwiyah Ḥadīth

The Muʿāwiyah *ḥadīth* is narrated by Abū Dāwūd (d. 275/889) and al-Tirmidhī (d. 279/892-893) through Abū Mijlaz from Muʿāwiyah. Again, the *ḥadīth* occurs in the section on *adab* or *istiʾdhān*, consequently, much of the above analysis applies here with equal force. Furthermore, there is an important discrepancy that occurs in the various transmissions of this *ḥadīth*. Abū Dāwūd reports that when Muʿāwiyah emerged, Ibn ʿĀmir stood up and Ibn al-Zubayr remained sitting. Consequently, Muʿāwiyah told Ibn ʿĀmir to sit down and recited the *ḥadīth* attributed to the Prophet. According to the al-Tirmidhī version, when Muʿāwiyah emerged both Ibn al-Zubayr and Ibn Ṣafwān stood up. Ibn ʿĀmir is not mentioned at all. So there is disagreement as to who exactly stood up and who remained sitting.

Additionally, most of the transmitted versions of this *ḥadīth* go back to Abū Mijlaz. Not much is recorded about this *rāwī* (transmitter of *ḥadīth*). His full name was Lāḥiq b. Ḥumayyid al-Sadūsī al-Baṣrī and he lived in Basra. He seems to have been employed as a treasurer and was appointed to some official tasks by the Caliph ʿUmar b. ʿAbd al-ʿAzīz. Some said he died in 106/725 or 109/728 or before either date. While he did live at the time of Muʿāwiyah, he was fairly young. More significantly, Abū Mijlaz lived in Basra not Damascus, where Muʿāwiyah lived and ruled. Abū Mijlaz did not transmit much, and no one else seemed to have witnessed the event that is recounted in this narration.

In a different version of this narration, Ibn Barīdah reports that his father entered upon Muʿāwiyah, who said that the Prophet said, "Whoever likes men to stand before him let him await his place in Hell." This version is not accepted by any of the main six books on *ḥadīth*.

Significantly, there are two essential problems with all versions of this narration. First, this type of narration might fall in the category of "political narrations," which renders it problematic.[20] It is well known

[20] This point is not without precedent. In the context of sectarian debates, *ḥadīths* with sound chains of transmission were rejected because they favored one faction or another. See ʿIzz al-Dīn Balīq, *Minhāj al-Ṣāliḥīn* (Beirut: Dār al-Fatḥ, 1978), 38; Muhammad Zubayr Siddiqi, *Hadith Literature* (Cambridge: Islamic Texts Society, 1993), 113.

that Muʿāwiyah (r. 41/661-60/680), the first Umayyad Caliph, and ʿAlī Ibn Abī Ṭālib (r. 35/656-40/661), the Prophet's cousin and fourth Rightly-Guided Caliph, found themselves locked in a political conflict. This conflict led to the Battle of Ṣiffīn (37/657), the infamous arbitration attempt and, eventually, to Muʿāwiyah's coming to power. The narration discussed above portrays Muʿāwiyah in a positive political light. ʿAlī consistently accused Muʿāwiyah of political opportunism and of unjustly seeking power. This narration casts Muʿāwiyah in a very different light. Not only is Muʿāwiyah not a political opportunist, but he does not even desire the vestiges of power. One cannot exclude the possibility that the supporters of Muʿāwiyah put this narration into circulation.

Second, even if one accepts the authenticity of this narration, al-Ṭabarī (d. 310/923) and al-Nawawī (d. 676/1277) consider the *ḥadīth* inapposite. According to al-Ṭabarī and al-Nawawī, the *ḥadīth* does not prohibit standing up or not standing up. Rather, it says that whoever is pleased with people standing up for him is doomed. In other words, the prohibition applies to the person being stood up for, not the person doing the standing up. The *ḥadīth* calls for the humility of leaders but says nothing to the followers.[21]

In reality, there are a variety of other *ḥadīths* that could have been cited by SAS in the discussion on standing up. For instance, Abū Dāwūd (d. 275/889) narrated that Abū Umāmah al-Bahlī reported that the Prophet came out to the believers leaning on a cane. Upon seeing him, the believers stood up. So the Prophet said, "Do not stand up as the *aʿājim* (non-Arab unbelievers) stand up for each other." However, al-Ṭabarī argued that this *ḥadīth* is weak due to problems in its chain of transmission.

In another transmission, again through Ibn Barīdah from Muʿāwiyah, it is reported that the Prophet said, "Any man that likes men to stand at his head [i.e., stand before him] as litigants multiply before him will not enter Heaven." In another *ḥadīth* reported through Jābir, it is related that the Prophet felt ill during prayer so he sat down. But the believers continued to stand. The Prophet saw them and signaled them to sit down. After prayer was completed the Prophet said,

[21] Ibn Ḥajar al-ʿAsqalānī, *Fatḥ al-Bārī* (1993), 12:318, 322.

"You were about to do as the Persians and Byzantines do. They stand while their kings sit down. Do not do that!" In another *ḥadīth*, Anas related that the Prophet said, "Those before you have been ruined by the fact that they have glorified their kings by standing up as their kings sit down."[22] Additionally, Mālik ruled that a woman may not remain standing before her husband.[23] Hence, other than the *ḥadīth* cited by SAS, there are several reports that relate to the issue of standing up.

Possibly, one could argue that regardless of the specific problems that might plague any single transmission, it is clear that there is a concurrence of transmissions on a central theme. Arguably, regardless of the probative value of any individual transmission, if one puts all the transmissions together, a clear rule prohibiting standing may emerge. Generally, I think this approach has some appeal. Arguably, the collective memory of the believers recalled that the Prophet took some issue with standing up before him.[24] However, in this case, this approach is not tenable.

The problem here is one of conflicting evidence. For example, Abū Dāwūd narrates that Aḥmad b. Yūnus reported that the Companions kissed the Prophet's hand. Al-Tirmidhī (d. 279/892-893) narrates that Abū Kurayyib reported that two Jews kissed the Prophet's hands and feet. Notably, Abū Dāwūd (d. 275/889), al-Bukhārī (d. 256/870), Muslim (d. 261/875) and al-Bayhaqī (d. 458/1065) narrate, through a variety of transmissions, that the Prophet told the Companions to stand up for Sa'd b. Mu'ādh (d. 5/626).[25] According to these reports, after Sa'd's judgment was accepted by Banū Qurayẓa (a Jewish tribe), Sa'd returned to the Prophet and the Companions. Upon seeing him the

---

22 See al-Bukhārī, *al-Adab al-Mufrad*, 202.

23 Ibn Ḥajar al-'Asqalānī, *Fatḥ al-Bārī* (1993), 12:319.

24 I am referring here to the idea of *tawātur al-ma'nā* or *tawātur bi al-ma'nā*—the establishment of a particular meaning by cumulative evidence. Kamali, *Principles of Islamic Jurisprudence,* 70. The main problem with this type of evidence is that the substance of a report that originated from a singular transmission could have become widespread in early Islam. Such a report does not prove that it originated with the Prophet, but only proves that the substantive message of the report became widely dispersed in early Islam.

25 Al-Bukhārī, *al-Adab al-Mufrad*, 202.

Prophet exclaimed, "*qūmū ilā sayyidikum*" ("Stand up for your master").[26] It is also narrated by Abū Dāwūd (d. 275/889) that Abū Hurayrah (d. 59/679) reported that when the Prophet would stand up to leave, the Companions would stand up and remain standing until he left the mosque. Furthermore, in *Fatḥ al-Bārī* there is a discussion as to whether the Prophet's standing up to greet Fāṭimah (d. 11/632) or ʿIkrima b. Abī Jahl or the Prophet's suckling brother is relevant to this issue.[27]

It is also reported by al-Tirmidhī (d. 279/892-893) and al-Nasāʾī (d. 303/915) that the Prophet would stand up when he would see a passing funeral. In one famous incident, the Prophet stood up for a Jewish woman's funeral. When told that the deceased was Jewish, the Prophet was reported to have commented, "But isn't she a soul!" Nonetheless, Muslim jurists have debated whether this rule on standing up for funerals has been abrogated. Mālik (d. 179/796), Abū Ḥanīfah (d. 150/767), and Muḥammad b. Idrīs al-Shāfiʿī (d. 205/819-820) said that standing up for funerals is abrogated. Aḥmad b. Ḥanbal (d. 241/855), Ismāʿīl b. Isḥāq (d. 282/896) and other Mālikīs said it is a matter of personal choice. Al-Nawawī (a Shāfiʿī) (d. 676/1277) said that standing up for funerals is not preferred. Other Shāfiʿī jurists said standing is recommended. Al-Sanadī said sitting down is permissible but standing is preferred.[28]

These various reports and the dilemmas they pose have existed in Islamic history for a long time. There is extensive jurisprudential literature on these reports. Despite the anti-historical and anti-jurisprudential attitude of some contemporary Muslims, one is well-advised not to reinvent the wheels of jurisprudence. One should learn from the discourse and efforts of our ancestors. Precedent has probative value and it is imperative that jurisprudential precedent be considered and

---

26 Al-Albānī insists that the reason the Prophet told the companions to stand up was so that they may assist Saʿd off his horse saddle. See al-Albānī, *Silsilat al-Aḥādīth al-Ḍaʿīfah*, 3:637; *idem*, *Silsilat al-Aḥādīth al-Ṣaḥīḥah* (Beirut: al-Maktab al-Islāmī, 1972), 1:103-106. The version of the *ḥadīth* that al-Albānī relies on is not mentioned in *al-Adab al-Mufrad* or in *Fatḥ al-Bārī*.

27 Ibn Ḥajar al-ʿAsqalānī, *Fatḥ al-Bārī* (1993), 12:321. Also see al-Bukhārī, *al-Adab al-Mufrad*, 201-2.

28 Jalāl al-Dīn al-Suyūṭī, *Sharḥ al-Suyūṭī ʿalā Sunan al-Nasāʾī* (Beirut: Dār al-Qalam, n.d.), 2:43-44.

weighed. The existence of jurisprudential precedent is not dispositive of an issue; nevertheless it is probative. If necessary, precedent could be abandoned after proper evaluation. But it ought not be ignored.

As to the issue of standing, the question then becomes: How did the earlier Muslims reconcile the various reports? How did they understand them or discourse about them? Muslim jurists have adopted various positions depending on how they understood and interpreted the injunctions. Al-ʿAynī (d. 855/1041), the author of *ʿUmdat al-Qārī fī Sharḥ al-Bukhārī* said that no set rule was reached on the issue of standing because of the disagreements on the matter.[29] Ibn Ḥajar al-ʿAsqalānī (d. 852/1449), the author of *Fatḥ al-Bārī,* agreed with this assessment. He argued that no final rule was reached because of disagreement.[30] However, Ibn ʿAbd al-Salām (d. 661/1262) and Ibn Ḥajar al-ʿAsqalānī add that if the failure to stand up will result in insult or create a *mafsada* (corruption) then it becomes forbidden not to stand up. Both Ibn ʿAbd al-Salām and Ibn Ḥajar al-ʿAsqalānī rely on the logic of priorities in *Sharīʿah*—the regulations as to standing up are low-order priorities in *Sharīʿah* and they may not be indulged if doing so will violate a higher *Sharīʿah* value.[31]

We already mentioned al-Nawawī's view that the prohibition applies to the person who demands and enjoys people standing in his presence. As to the person doing the standing, al-Nawawī relied on the principle that people should be given their rightful place (*bi ʿumūmiyyāti tanzīl al-nāsi manāzilihim*). This means, according to al-Nawawī, that one should stand up before one's elders and the wise.[32]

---

29 Badr al-Dīn Maḥmūd b. Aḥmad al-ʿAyīnī, *ʿUmdat al-Qārī bi Sharḥ Ṣaḥīḥ al-Bukhārī* (Beirut: Dār al-Fikr, n.d.), 11:251.

30 Ibn Ḥajar al-ʿAsqalānī, *Fatḥ al-Bārī* (1993), 12:317.

31 Ibid., 323. Similarly, Ibn Ḥajar al-Haytamī asserts that in his day and age, it has become customary to stand up out of respect for certain people. He argues that if one would refuse to stand up, this would lead to people taking offense, and to hostility and enmity between Muslims. Therefore, he concludes, that standing up has become recommended, if not mandatory, in order to achieve social harmony and to avoid unnecessary conflicts. Al-Haytamī indicates that this matter is not a priority in Islamic law and, therefore, concessions to social practices is acceptable. Ibn Ḥajar al-Haytamī, *al-Fatāwā al-Kubrā al-Fiqhiyyah* (Beirut: Dār al-Kutub al-ʿIlmiyyah, 1983), 4:247-8.

32 Ibid., 321.

Ibn Ḥajar al-ʿAsqalānī, al-ʿAynī, and others held that it is recommended that one stand up for the leader, a just ruler (*imām*), an elder, or knowledgeable person. Al-Baghawī (d. 510/1117), in his *Sharḥ al-Sunnah*, al-Bayhaqī (d. 458/1066) and al-Ghazālī (d. 505/1111) said that standing up out of compassion or respect is permissible.[33] Al-Mundhirī (d. 656/1258) maintained that what is prohibited is for one to remain standing while the other remains sitting. Al-Ṭabarī argued that it all depends on the intention. If one stands up to promote arrogance and conceit, then standing is prohibited. If one is merely showing respect, then it is permitted. Ibn Kathīr (d. 774/1373) argued that what is prohibited is imitating non-Muslims, but standing up to one who arrives from travel, or to a governor in his place of governorship is permitted. Ibn al-Qayyim (d. 751/1350) and Ibn al-Ḥājj (d. 785/1383) disagreed and argued that standing up in all circumstances is reprehensible because one can never know whether the one you stand up for is truly pious or knowledgeable or not. Ibn Rushd (d. 520/1122) argued that standing up is of four types:[34]

1. It is prohibited for one to arrogantly and self-conceitedly want others to stand up in his presence.
2. It is reprehensible to stand up to one who is not conceited or arrogant, but of whom it is feared that he or she will become conceited or arrogant when people stand in his or her presence.
3. It is permissible to stand up as a sign of respect before someone who you do not fear will become arrogant.
4. It is recommended that one stand up to greet someone who arrives after traveling.[35]

---

[33] Ḥusayn b. Masʿūd al-Baghawī, *Sharḥ al-Sunnah* (Beirut: Dār al-Fikr, 1994), 7:213; Ibn Ḥajar al-ʿAsqalānī, *Fatḥ al-Bārī* (1993), 12: 320, 323.

[34] Ibn Ḥajar al-ʿAsqalānī, *Fatḥ al-Bārī* (1993), 12:320.

[35] Al-Albānī in his *Silsilat al-Aḥādīth al-Ḍaʿīfah*, 3:637-8, discusses the authenticity of some of the *ḥadīth* on standing. He vehemently attacks those who endorse standing for anyone. Strangely, he also endorses Ibn Rushd's categorization but adds that only the Prophet is immune from conceit or arrogance. Thus, he implies that standing is not permissible.

As should be apparent, the issue of standing up is susceptible to reflection and complex analysis.[36] The Abdul Rauf situation added significant factors that further complicated the analysis. The standing here is being done before a national anthem and not a person. The standing is being done in the context of a sports event and not in the context of standing up before a political figure. The standing is incumbent upon everyone without exception. In other words, no specific person is being honored or stood up for. The standing is taking place in the context of a non-Muslim country. Additionally, failure to stand up might subject Muslims to derision or contempt by the non-Muslim majority. Finally, the standing up implicates the specific history of a specific country. In this context, standing up could have a symbolic meaning that needs to be considered on its own merit.

The Abdul Rauf situation is further complicated by the fact that Abdul Rauf signed a contract with the sports authorities. Possibly this poses a problem of conflicting *Sharīʿah* obligations (*ḥālat tazāḥum*). On the one hand, the *Sharīʿah* demands that promises (i.e., contracts) be fulfilled; on the other hand, a provision of this contractual obligation might arguably violate a *Sharʿī* (legal) rule. In this type of situation one must engage in a priorities analysis (*baḥth fī awlawiyyāt al-Sharīʿah*). Can a point of *adab* (matters relating to proper Islamic manners) void a provision of a contract while upholding the legality of the overall contract? As is well-known, the Qurʾān demands that Muslims discharge their contractual obligations. This obligation is a strict *wājib* (duty). But what if, after the fact, one becomes convinced that a provision of the contract violates the *Sharīʿah*? The point here is whether a point of *adab* is sufficient to vitiate the duty of fulfilling contractual obligations.[37] And even

[36] The Mālikī jurist al-Shāṭibī (d. 790/1388) states that the custom of standing up out of respect to greet someone is consistent with *Sharīʿah*, i.e., it is lawful. Interestingly, he asserts that under the Caliph ʿUmar b. ʿAbd al-ʿAzīz (r. 99-101/717-720), it had become an established practice. This established practice, he argues, was consistent with the precedent set by the Prophet because the Prophet rose to greet his cousin Jaʿfar. See Ibrāhīm b. Mūsā al-Shāṭibī, *al-Muwāfaqāt fī Uṣūl al-Sharīʿah*, ed. ʿAbd Allāh Darrāz (Cairo: Dār al-Fikr al-ʿArabī, n.d.), 3:64-65.

[37] In the discourses of classical Muslim jurists, the purpose of *Sharīʿah* law is to fulfill the *maṣlaḥah* (pl. *maṣāliḥ*, good and well-being) and avert the *mafsadah* (pl. *mafāsid*, wrongfulness, harm, and hardship). The objectives of the law are divided

if a point of *adab* can override the duty to discharge contractual obligations, is the remedy that one unilaterally declare this provision void, or alternatively must one void the entire contract and re-negotiate an altogether new contract?

All of this creates a very different situation and context than that which is directly addressed by the reports attributed to the Prophet. As stated above, if SAS thought that a *ḥukm qiyāsī* (rule by analogy) was appropriate in this situation, there are strict methodologies for *qiyās* that ought to be followed.[38] *Qiyās* cannot be assumed but must be argued and proven.

The important point is not whether Abdul Rauf was right or wrong. One must respect his convictions and principled stand. But *Sharīʿah* analysis must be undertaken pursuant to an equally principled methodology of inquiry. *Sharīʿah* analysis must not be susceptible to the self-righteous or dogmatic treatment that some contemporary Muslims afford it. In contemporary Muslim discourses, it has become common for one to read a few *ḥadīth* and declare oneself qualified to render judgment on an issue that has engaged Islamic thinking for centuries.[39] This

---

into necessities, needs, and luxuries or perfections. Within each category, there are higher ranking and lower ranking priorities. Juristic practice seeks to insure that jurisprudential theory systematically guards the higher order objectives in order to achieve an overall just balance in the production and application of the law. One of the best works produced on this subject by a classical jurist is al-Shāṭibī, *al-Muwāfaqāt*, 2:176-300. In the particular case at hand, regardless of the conclusions that one ultimately reaches, engaging in this type of inquiry is essential. A comprehensive and systematic balancing between the values of *Sharīʿah* is crucial, otherwise the practice of Islamic law in the contemporary age is bound to fall prey to the sensationalism of demagogues.

[38] Again, the "ought" here is based on the fact that SAS claimed to speak for Islamic law. Islamic law is essentially a juristic tradition. For instance, the very notion of rule by analogy is a juristic creation. If a person invokes a category or methodology created by the juristic tradition, but wishes to ignore the parameters and limitations expounded by this tradition, such a person should make this point clear. For instance, if I will claim that I am speaking of American Constitutional law, but I wish to ignore the existence of *dictum* in Supreme Court opinions, I should make this point clear and justify my decision. Furthermore, I cannot ignore the jurisprudence of *stare decisis* in American Constitutional law without explaining why I think the concept of *stare decisis* is not relevant to analyzing American Constitutional law.

[39] Muḥammad al-Ghazālī has dealt with this problem over the course of several books. His position is best stated in his *al-Sunnah al-Nabawiyyah*.

is hardly a methodology; rather, it is an authoritarian construction based on *hawā* (caprice or whim). In this specific case, either SAS was not aware of the complex discourse on this issue or it was aware and chose not to present it. In either case, SAS violated the most basic requirements for issuing a *fatwā* and denied the text its authoritativeness.

Ḥadīth Methodology and The Prostrating Ḥadīth[40]

In addition to citing *ḥadīths* on standing, SAS also cited a *ḥadīth* about women prostrating before their husbands. The citation of this *ḥadīth* in this context poses several significant methodological issues. Other than the problem of the relevance of such a *ḥadīth* to the issue of standing, what is the probative value of this report? Furthermore, what factors are to be considered in evaluating the value of such a report? Importantly, without careful analysis, reports such as the prostrating *ḥadīth* easily lend themselves to the construction of the authoritarian.

One must admit it is difficult to understand why SAS quoted the prostration *ḥadīth*, cited above, in this context. SAS seems to be arguing that the Prophet did not accept that a person prostrate before him. Evidently, SAS is drawing an analogy between prostrating and standing. This is another unspecified *qiyās*. In all the sources consulted on the issue of standing, no one dared draw such an analogy.[41] The reason no one drew such an analogy is because there is neither a unity of purposes

[40] Much of the analysis concerning the prostrating *ḥadīth* applies to the *ḥadīth* forbidding one person from bowing to another. There are several material points concerning the prostrating *ḥadīth*: One, the *ḥadīth* is narrated by al-Tirmidhī and designated as *ḥasan* and not *ṣaḥīḥ*. Two, the *ḥadīth* relates to *adab* and not to *ʿibādāt* as SAS assumes. Three, the *ḥadīth* is inapposite to the issue of standing up before a flag because of different operative causes. Four, the historical context of the *ḥadīth* is not clear because Anas reports that a man asked the Prophet "such and such." We do not know who this man is. Furthermore, the *ḥadīth* seems to forbid bowing to or kissing a man, which contradicts other reports and practices from the *Sunnah*.

[41] The use of an unspecified *qiyās* by mixing and confusing issues is, unfortunately, not uncommon in contemporary Muslim discourses. Especially in the United States and Europe, enthusiasts or activists who do not have a basic familiarity with Islamic sources and who have no legal training represent the cause of Islamic law.

(*maqāṣid* or *ḥikmat al-ḥukm*) in the two *ḥadīths* nor of operative causes (*ittiḥād al-ʿilal*). The symbolic meaning conveyed by standing is different than that conveyed by prostrating before a person. This means that there is no unity of purposes between the prohibition against standing and that of prostrating. Even if there were a unity of objectives or purposes between the two types of *ḥadīths*, the vast majority of jurists would not permit a *qiyās* based on *ittiḥād al-qasd*. Furthermore, since most jurists opposed analogy through the unity of purposes, such an analogy needs to be justified and defended.

Basing laws on *ittiḥād al-qasd* could lead to over-extending the application of many laws. For example, as noted earlier, the operative cause in prohibiting the consumption of alcohol is that it is an intoxicant. The purpose or objective in prohibiting the consumption of alcohol could be to control crime, allow for concentration in prayer, promote moral responsibility, or increase social productivity. If one extends laws through analogy by searching for unity of operative causes, then any intoxicant other than alcohol may be prohibited. However, if one extends laws through analogy by searching for unity of objectives, then anything that promotes crime, vitiates moral responsibility, decreases social productivity, or decreases concentration in prayer may also be prohibited. The second case will lead to a sweeping extension of laws; therefore, it must be approached cautiously and judiciously.

The prostrating *ḥadīth* has serious social and moral implications. Therefore, the *ḥadīth* itself must be approached with great caution, let alone used to extend the law through analogy. This *ḥadīth* is narrated in a variety of forms and through a variety of transmissions by Abū Dāwūd (d. 275/889), al-Tirmidhī (d. 279/892-893), Ibn Mājah (d. 273/886-887), Aḥmad (d. 241/855) in his *Musnad*, al-Nasāʾī (d. 303/915) and Ibn Ḥibbān (d. 354/965).[42]

In one version, Maḥmūd b. Ghīlān reports that Abū Hurayrah said that the Prophet said: "If I would have ordered anyone to prostrate to anyone, I would have ordered a wife to prostrate to her husband."[43] This

[42] See, generally, Abū al-Faraj b. al-Jawzī, *Kitāb Aḥkām al-Nisāʾ* (Beirut: Muʾassasat al-Kutub al-Thaqāfiyyah, 1992), 136-9; Muḥammad al-Shawkānī, *Nayl al-Awṭār* (Cairo: Dār al-Ḥadīth, n.d.), 6:207-8.

[43] Al-Mubārakfūrī, *Tuḥfat al-Aḥwadhī*, 4:271.

version also occurs by the way of Fadl b. Jubayr from Abū Umāmah al-Bahlī.

In another version, Abū Bakr b. Abī Shaybah reports that ʿĀʾishah said that the Prophet said: "If I would have ordered anyone to prostrate to anyone, I would have ordered a wife to prostrate to her husband. If a man orders his wife to move [a load] from a red mountain to a black mountain and [again] from a black mountain to a red mountain it is incumbent upon her to obey."[44]

In a related version, ʿĀʾishah is reported to have said that the Prophet was standing among a group of Muhājirūn (native Meccans who migrated to Medina with the Prophet) and Anṣār (native Medinian converts) when a camel came and prostrated to the Prophet. The Companions said, "O' Prophet the cattle prostrate before you; are we not more deserving [of such an honor]?" (meaning: "Shouldn't we prostrate to you?"). The Prophet said: "Worship your God and honor your brothers..." The balance of the *ḥadīth* is the same as above.[45]

Another version comes from Azhar b. Marwān. He reports that when Muʿādh b. Jabal returned from Shām he prostrated to the Prophet. The Prophet said, "What are you doing Muʿādh? " Muʿādh said, "I was in Shām and I saw that the people there prostrated to their priests and clergy and I wished we could do the same for you. " The Prophet said, "If I would have ordered anyone to prostrate before anyone but God, I would have ordered a woman to prostrate to her husband. By God, a woman cannot fulfill her obligations to God until she fulfills her obligations to her husband and if he asks for her [i.e., for sex] while she is on a camel's back, she cannot deny him [his pleasure]."[46]

---

44 Abū ʿAbd Allāh Muḥammad b. Yazīd al-Qazwīnī Ibn Mājah, *Sunan al-Ḥāfiẓ Ibn Mājah*, ed. Muḥammad Fuʾād ʿAbd al-Bāqī (Cairo: ʿĪsā al-Bābī al-Ḥalabī, 1972) 1:595.

45 Ibn Ḥanbal, *Musnad*, 6:89.

46 Ibn Mājah, *Sunan*, 1:595. Some versions of this report state, "on the back of a mount" (*ʿalā ẓahr baʿīr*). Other versions state on a "*qatab*" or saddle. The significance of the word "*qatab*" employed in some traditions, was debated by jurists. Some stated that the use of saddle refers to submission while mounting an animal. Others argued that it is referring to a type of seat used to facilitate birthing. The second usage is intended to signify the importance of sexual compliance; even if a woman is in the process of birthing, she ought not refrain from fulfilling her husband's sexual desires. This, of course, is an exaggeration, but the point of the exaggeration is to

Another version has Muʿādh returning from Yemen, not al-Shām, and asking the Prophet if Muslims should prostrate to him. The Prophet's reply is the same as above without the addition about having sex on a camel's back. In yet another version, it is Qays b. Saʿd b. ʿUbādah who is returning from Ḥīra. The same scenario then takes place as above.[47]

In a final version, Anas b. Mālik reports that the Prophet said, "No human may prostrate to another, and if it were permissible for a human to prostrate to another I would have ordered a wife to prostrate to her husband because of the enormity of his rights over her. By God, if there is an ulcer excreting puss from his feet to the top of his head, and she licked it for him she would not fulfill his rights."[48]

According to scholars of ḥadīth, the authenticity of these *ḥadīths* range from *ḍaʿīf* (weak) to *ḥasan gharīb* (good). All of them are *aḥādī*

---

emphasize that even if a woman is pre-occupied with some immediate task or is in pain, she must fulfill her husband's sexual desires. See Abū ʿUbayd al-Qāsim b. Salām al-Harawī, *Gharīb al-Ḥadīth* (Beirut: Dār al-Kutub al-ʿIlmiyyah, 1986), 2:361; Abū ʿAbd Allāh Muḥammad al-Ḥakīm al-Tirmidhī, *Nawādir al-Uṣūl fī Maʿrifat Aḥādīth al-Rasūl* (Beirut: Dār Ṣādir, n.d.), 176; Abū al-Qāsim Sulaymān b. Aḥmad al-Ṭabarānī, *al-Muʿjam al-Kabīr*, ed. Ḥamdī ʿAbd al-Majīd al-Salafī (Beirut: Dār Iḥyāʾ al-Turāth al-ʿArabī, 1985), 5:200, 208; 8:334; Abū al-Saʿādāt al-Mubārak b. Muḥammad Ibn al-Athīr al-Jazrī, *al-Nihāyah fī Gharīb al-Ḥadīth wa al-Athar*, ed. Abū ʿAbd al-Raḥmān b. ʿUwīḍah (Beirut: Dār al-Kutub al-ʿIlmiyyah, 1997), 4:10.

47 See Ibn al-Jawzī, *Kitāb Aḥkām al-Nisāʾ*, 137.

48 Ibn Ḥanbal, *Musnad*, 3:200. Some versions of this genre of reports state that even if the husband's nose is oozing with puss and blood, and his wife licks it, she will not do him justice. ʿAlāʾ al-Dīn ʿAlī al-Muttaqī b. Ḥusām al-Dīn al-Burhān Fawzī al-Hindī, *Kanz al-ʿUmmāl fī Sunan al-Aqwāl wa al-Afʿāl* (Beirut: Muʾassasat al-Risāla, 1985)16:338; ʿAbd Allāh b. Muḥammad b. Abī Shaybah, *al-Muṣannaf fī al-Aḥādīth wa al-Āthār*, ed. Saʿīd al-Laḥḥām (Beirut: Dār al-Fikr, 1989), 3:399. In my view, the graphic and repulsive nature of these reports is evidence of the fact that they were produced in the context of highly contentious social dynamics. Their wording and style seem intended to shock, challenge, and frustrate a particular social strata or set of interests. They appear to proclaim the futility of resisting patriarchy by invoking sexually sadistic images. There is a certain deviant eroticism in the image of a woman submissively licking the excretions of a man. Therefore, these traditions appear to be rather "kinky male erotic projections. The mere fact that these reports zealously pander to the male ego and libido make them inherently suspect. These traditions must be subjected to the most strict and uncompromising moral and evidentiary scrutiny. In my view, these traditions fail to pass on both counts, and ought to be rejected as corruptions.

ḥadīth (*ḥadīth* of singular transmissions) not reaching the level of *tawātur* (*ḥadīth* of several transmissions).[49] These *ḥadīths*, although not legal because they do not specify a particular legal obligation, do explicate a fundamental principle that is supposed to impact upon all marriages. While the physical act of prostration to the husband is not permitted, the moral substance of prostration does apply through such *ḥadīths*. The clear implication of the *ḥadīths* is that a wife owes her husband, by virtue of him being a husband, a heavy debt. The husband is owed the utmost degree of respect and even servitude. It is not an exaggeration to say that, according to these *ḥadīths*, the wife lives as the husband's humble servant; she is to submit sexually on the back of a camel and lick his puss-filled ulcers if need be.[50] Consequently,

[49] The technical definition of *aḥādī ḥadīth* is that which has not reached the level of *tawātur*. The definition of *tawātur*, in turn, depends on the school of thought defining the term. Generally, however, *mutawātir* means that the *ḥadīth* or narration was transmitted throughout the first three generations of Muslims by such a large number of transmitters that it is highly unlikely that the *ḥadīth* is fabricated. Opinions differ as to the number of transmitters in each generation that is required for a *ḥadīth* to attain the level of *tawātur*. Some say seven, some say forty, some say seventy, and some say more than that. *Aḥādī ḥadīth* are those transmitted in the first three generations by a number less than that of the *mutawātir* category. Generally speaking, in the *mutawātir* category it is fairly certain that the Prophet uttered the *ḥadīth*. In the *āḥād* category there remains the suspicion that the *ḥadīth* is not authentic. Kamali, *Principles of Islamic Jurisprudence,* 68-70, 71-78. All the prostration traditions and the traditions mentioning sexual submission, even on the back of a camel, contain individuals, such as Ayyūb b. ʿUtbah, Muḥammad b. Jābir, and Ṣadaqa b. ʿAbd Allāh, whose credibility is suspect. This has led many scholars to question the authenticity of these reports. Abū Aḥmad ʿAbd Allāh b. ʿUdayy al-Jurjānī, *al-Kāmil fī Ḍuʿafāʾ al-Rijāl*, eds. ʿĀdil Aḥmad ʿAbd al-Mawjūd and ʿAlī Muḥammad Muʿawwaḍ (Beirut: Dār al-Kutub al-ʿIlmiyyah, 1997), 2:13; 3:139; 4:332; 5:117.

[50] In fact, after citing the prostration *ḥadīth*, Ibn al-Jawzī (d. 597/1201) concludes that a wife is to consider herself, for all practical purposes, the husband's slave. Ibn al-Jawzī states: "It is incumbent upon a woman to know that it is as if she is owned (*ka'l mamlūka*) by her husband, therefore she may not act upon her own affairs or her husband's money except with his permission. She must prefer his rights over her own and over the rights of her relatives, and she must be ready to let him enjoy her through all clean means. She must not brag about her beauty and must not taunt him about his shortcomings... It is incumbent upon a woman to endure her husband's mistreatment as a slave should [endure]. We have seen that the virtues of a slave woman were described to al-Mālik b. Marwān. When she was presented to him, he asked her about her affairs. She said, 'I cannot forget who I am. I am your slave.' So

these *ḥadīths* seem to have rather grave theological, moral, and social consequences.[51]

Structurally the *ḥadīths* are interesting. In most reports, the Prophet is asked about whether it is permissible to prostrate to him, the Prophet. To this he is supposed to have answered, "No! But actually if a human could prostrate to a human it would be the wife to a husband." Such a fundamentally revolutionary view is expressed out of context. Basically, according to these reports, the Prophet volunteers this injunction although that is not what is being asked. In most versions, the one doing the asking is a man and the response is given to a man or men. Although the *ḥadīths* have a profound impact upon women, this advice is supposed to be enunciated before an audience of men. This is quite a

---

[al-Mālik] said, 'This covered [woman] is worth her price. '" Ibn al-Jawzī, *Kitāb Aḥkām al-Nisā'*, 139-140. It is significant that Ibn al-Jawzī engages in this largely chauvinistic and, possibly, immoral discussion after citing several versions of the prostration *ḥadīth*.

51 Upon the publication of the second edition of this book, some tunnel visioned and shamelessly apologetic individuals argued that these traditions are metaphorical and not literal. They claimed that no one would sensibly argue that the Prophet actually meant that women should literally lick ulcers, and that the Prophet is simply exaggerating to make a point. Likewise, they argued, the Prophet said if one would carry his mother on his back while performing *ṭawāf* around the Ka'bah, he would not fulfill his mother's rights over him. In response, I would make the following points: 1. A metaphorical exaggeration is employed in order to emphasize and clarify a point. I am not interested in whether wives ought to lick ulcers, or anything else; my focus is on the moral message conveyed by these reports. For instance, if I tell someone, "You can lick my shoes," surely, I can think of better ways of polishing my footwear, but my intention is to insult and degrade. Regardless of the mental gymnastics that appeal to some people, and whichever way you look at it, these traditions are degrading to women; 2. In fact, it is quite conceivable that one would have to carry his mother on his back in *ṭawāf*. Anyone that has been to Ḥajj knows that there are men and women who are carried on the shoulders during Ḥajj. Normally, they are carried by hired help because they are too weak to withstand the exertion in Ḥajj. But if help cannot be found, they should and would be carried on the shoulders of their children. Do the apologists want to argue that wives should and would lick their husbands' ulcers? 3. The very image invoked by these traditions is contrary to Islamic morality. The fact that the traditions are supposedly *majāzī* instead of *ḥaqīqī* is entirely irrelevant. Why are husbands, by virtue of being husbands, entitled to such reverence and honor? Mothers and fathers are exalted in the Qur'ān because they raise and nurture their children. What is Qur'ānic evidence that husbands are entitled to share the status of God in the world of metaphor and symbolism? Furthermore, this symbolism is powerful in conveying meaning and creating law. For instance, the influential Abū Ḥāmid

casual way of delivering advice that will have profound social and theological implications upon women in particular. Furthermore, as a matter of symbolic discourse, an unjustifiable nexus is created between the Prophet and husbands. The question posed to the Prophet is about the respect that is owed the Prophet. The response addresses the respect that is owed husbands. A powerful symbolic association is created between the status of the Prophet and the status of husbands.

The context and structure of the *ḥadīths* makes them suspect. It is highly unlikely that the Prophet in such an unsystematic, haphazard, or casual fashion would address Islamic theological questions. Furthermore, any *ḥadīth* that draws an association between the status of the Prophet and the status of a human being is inherently suspect. Under all circumstances, if a *ḥadīth* has serious moral and social implications, it should meet a heavy burden of proof before it can be relied upon. But even more, if a *ḥadīth* is suspect because of a contextual or structural defect, among other reasons, then there should be a presumption against its authenticity. The evidence supporting the authenticity of the *ḥadīth* should be conclusive.

In the case of the prostration *ḥadīths*, the evidence thus far considered suggests that the *ḥadīth* cannot be relied upon. Additionally, considering the way the Prophet treated his wives, it is not possible that the Prophet would have made such a problematic theological association in this casual fashion. For example, al-Bukhārī narrated that ʿUmar's wife while arguing with ʿUmar told him, "You reproach me for answering you! Well, by God, the wives of the Prophet answer him, and one of them might even desert him from morning until night."[52] In al-Ṭayālisī's report, one of the Prophet's wives might argue with him until she angers him.[53] These reports cast an image of the Prophet as a husband that is

al-Ghazālī, like Ibn al-Jawzī, relying on these traditions, reaches the conclusion that a wife is a "sort of" slave to her husband, and therefore, she must obey all his commands as long as he does not command her to perform a sinful act. See Abū Ḥāmid al-Ghazālī, *Iḥyāʾ ʿUlūm al-Dīn* (Cairo: Dār al-Maʿrifah, n.d.) 2:56. Furthermore, relying on these types of traditions, al-Ḥakīm al-Tirmidhī asserts that a woman must submit to her husband's sexual desires whether she feels like it or not, and even if doing so would cause her hardship. See al-Tirmidhī, *Nawādir al-Uṣūl*, 176.

52 Ibn Ḥajar al-ʿAsqalānī, *Fatḥ al-Bārī* (1993), 10: 347.

53 Ibid., 352.

very different from the image advocated by the prostrating *ḥadīth*. The point, again, is not whether these reports, even if in *Ṣaḥīḥ al-Bukhārī*, have legal imperative value. The point is that the Prophet, as the most elementary reading of the *sīrah* (Prophet's legacy) would reveal, was not a dictator within his family. For the Prophet to announce a foundational principle that has profound theological and social implications in this casual manner is suspect.

The approach advocated here requires that the totality of circumstances be considered in evaluating reliance on a *ḥadīth*. There should be a proportional relationship between the theological and social implications of a *ḥadīth* and the burden of proof it should satisfy. If a *ḥadīth* with serious theological and social implications is suspect for any reason, then it should not be relied upon unless its authenticity can be conclusively established. Besides scrutinizing the theological and social implications of a *ḥadīth*, the approach advocated requires that a *ḥadīth* undergo a substantive evaluation.

In response, one might argue that it is wrong to look to issues relating to the substance (*matn*) and that the only relevant issue in studying *ḥadīth* is the chain of transmission (*isnād*). If the chain of transmission is sound, then the *ḥadīth* is declared *ṣaḥīḥ* (authentic) and that would be the end of the inquiry. One might further argue that context or implications of a *ḥadīth* must not be evaluated and that the only relevant point is authenticity. In other words, in evaluating issues of authority, one should not think about how or why something was said, but only about what was said and who said it.

Matn or substantive analysis is not a novelty in Islamic history.[54] According to *ʿilm al-ḥadīth* (the science of *ḥadīth*), and particularly the field of *ʿilal* (defects), a report with an impeccable chain of transmission may be rejected because the text of the *ḥadīth* is not sound. Such a *ḥadīth* would be rejected either because it contains grammatical or historical errors, or because it contradicts the Qurʾān, or because the text is contrary to the laws of nature, common human experience, or the

[54] In the contemporary age, Muḥammad al-Ghazālī was an advocate of *matn* analysis. Many of his writings focused on the need to evaluate the substantive plausibility of *āḥādī ḥadīth* regardless of the structure of the chain of transmission. See al-Ghazālī, *al-Sunnah al-Nabawiyyah*, 18-29; *idem*, *Dustūr al-Wiḥda*, 67-87.

dictates of reason.[55] *Ḥadīth* scholars would declare a *ḥadīth* suffering from these defects, or others, to have *ʿilal qādiḥa fī al-matn* (an effective defect in the content).[56]

However, the field of *ʿilal al-matn* is fraught with ambiguities, and not much has been written about it. *Ḥadīth* scholars often stated that *ʿilal al-matn* is a mysterious science into which only the most learned scholar can delve. After studying the totality of issues surrounding a particular *ḥadīth*, a scholar would make a judgment about the existence of an effective defect in the *ḥadīth*.[57] Effectively, that meant that the methodologies of the field were elusive, and the judgment reached was

---

[55] See Siddiqi, *Hadith Literature*, 114; Balīq, *Minhāj al-Ṣāliḥīn*, 36-9.

[56] Abū ʿUmar Ibn al-Ṣalāḥ, *ʿUlūm al-Ḥadīth* (Damascus: Dār al-Fikr, 1986), 91-2; See Abū Muḥammad al-Rāzī, *ʿIlal al-Ḥadīth* (Beirut: Dār al-Maʿrifah, 1985).

[57] Ṣāliḥ, *ʿUlūm al-Ḥadīth*, 179-187; ʿItr, *Manhaj al-Naqd*, 447-454. Although it could be argued that *matn* analysis elevates human reasoning above revealed truth, and thus commits the sin of self-idolatry, I believe that this argument is unfounded. The relationship between reason and revelation is complex, and classical scholars ranging from Ibn Rushd II to Ibn Taymiyyah have written on it. See Abū al-Walīd b. Rushd, *Faṣl al-Maqāl fī mā bayn al-Sharīʿah wa al-Ḥikmah min al-Ittiṣāl*, ed. Muḥammad ʿImārah, 2nd ed. (Cairo: Dār al-Maʿārif, 1983); Taqī al-Dīn Abī al-ʿAbbās Aḥmad b. Taymiyyah, *Darʾ al-Taʿāruḍ al-ʿAql wa al-Naql ʾaw Mawāfaqat Ṣaḥīḥ al-Manqūl li Ṣarīḥ al-Maʿqūl*, ed. Muḥammad Rashād Sālim (Riyadh: Dār al-Kunūz al-Adabiyyah, n.d.); *idem, al-Qaḍāʾ wa al-Qadar,* ed. Aḥmad ʿAbd al-Raḥīm al-Sāyiḥ and al-Sayyid al-Jamīlī (Beirut: Dār al-Kitāb al-ʿArabī, 1991). Although this matter warrants a separate book, I would like to mention in brief five main points. First, text is not the only way of knowing the Divine or the Divine Will. One can develop a knowledge of God through other manifestations of the Divine such as nature, history, prayer, and supplications. *Matn* analysis seeks to balance between textual and non-textual means of knowledge. Second, *matn* analysis seeks to evaluate the authenticity of text in light of other competing texts. For example, the Qurʾān could say X, and a report of singular transmission could say Y. *Matn* analysis would allow a person to accept X and reject Y because the authenticity of the Qurʾān is higher than any singular transmission. Third, *ʿādah* (the physical rules of nature) is considered a part of the Divine law. *Kharq al-ʿādah* (the breaching of the physical rules of nature) is accepted only through authentic revelation. Reports that are of probable, and not certain, authenticity cannot establish a case of *kharq al-ʿādah.* Fourth, *matn* analysis is not applied to texts of certain authenticity; it is applied to traditions of doubtful or probable authenticity as part of the overall evaluation in order to determine the weight to be given to a particular report. The weight given to a report could be sufficiently minimal, to the point that the report is dismissed as the equivalent of an inadmissible report. Finally, and perhaps most importantly, in Islamic theology, truth is not established by revelation alone. Pure reason and

fairly subjective. Furthermore, most of the efforts of past scholars of *ḥadīth* were directed at authenticating the *isnād* of *ḥadīth*. *Matn* analysis remained undeveloped and under-utilized.[58] Even more, the science of *ḥadīth* did not correlate the authenticity of *ḥadīth* with its theological and social ramifications. The scholars of *ḥadīth* did not demand a higher standard of authenticity for a *ḥadīth* that could have sweeping theological and social ramifications. Additionally, as the quote from Ibn Khaldūn in the introduction implies, *ḥadīth* scholars did not engage in historical evaluation of *ḥadīth* or examine its logical coherence or social impact. Consequently, *ḥadīth* scholars often accepted the authenticity of *ḥadīth* with problematic theological and social implications.

Take, for example, a *ḥadīth* narrated by Abū Dāwūd (d. 275/889), al-Tirmidhī (d. 279/892-893), Ibn Mājah (d. 273/886-887), Ibn Ḥibbān (d. 354/965) and al-Ḥākim al-Niysābūrī (d. 405/1015): Umm Salamah reported that the Prophet said, "Any woman who dies while her husband is pleased with her enters Heaven." This *ḥadīth* is of the same degree of authenticity as the *ḥadīths* on prostration. The commentators on *Riyāḍ al-Ṣāliḥīn* say that this means only if the woman is pious and her husband is pleased with her will she enter Heaven.[59] This is, of course, read by implication (*mafhūm al-naṣṣ* or *mīthāq al-naṣṣ* or *maḍmūn al-naṣṣ*). The literal text does not say a pious woman; it says any woman who dies with

---

revelation are considered equally valid methods of uncovering the Divine Will. In case of a clear and unavoidable conflict, revelation is accepted over pure reason. However, since pure reason can yield certainty, only revelation that has been established as authentic as a matter of certainty can trump pure reason. I submit, however, that the proportionality requirement advocated in this essay would make a *matn* analysis necessary in all circumstances. As I argue later, the counting of the number of transmitters by itself is not particularly probative. It is important to correlate between the certainty of the Divine Command and the impact of this command. Arguably, God clearly and unequivocally establishes the general and basic principles of the religion. All lesser order principles must be evaluated in light of the higher principles. Essentially, this is an evaluative process, and will not yield singular and uniform determinations.

58 See Rahman, *Islam,* 64-67; *idem, Islamic Methodology,* 27-82.

59 Muṣṭafā al-Khann, Muṣṭafā al-Baghā et. al, *Nuzhat al-Muttaqīn Sharḥ Riyāḍ al-Ṣāliḥīn* (Beirut: Mu'assasat al-Risāla, 1987), 1:289. See generally on this *ḥadīth*, ʿAbd al-Karīm Zīdān, *al-Mufaṣṣal fī Aḥkām al-Marʾah wa al-Bayt al-Muslim* (Beirut: Muʾassasat al-Risāla, 1994), 7:274-5; al-Shawkānī, *Nayl al-Awṭār*, 6:207-210; al-Mubārakfūrī, *Tuḥfat al-Aḥwadhī*, 4:272-1.

her husband pleased with her will enter Heaven.[60] This is problematic because it makes God's pleasure contingent on the husband's pleasure. But even if we say the *ḥadīth* only applies to pious women, it is still problematic because God's pleasure is still contingent on the husband's pleasure regardless of how impious the husband might be. The wife might be pious and the husband impious, and, yet, the husband's pleasure matters. Then we are forced to read a further implication; this *ḥadīth* applies only if the husband is pious and the wife is pious. But even then it is still problematic because what if the wife is more pious than the husband? What if the husband is spend-thrifty or ill-mannered or ill-tempered or violent or cowardly or stupid or lazy? Yet, despite any occasionality, God's pleasure would be contingent on the husband's pleasure. This is a revolutionary concept with profound theological and social implications. Before this *ḥadīth* can be recognized as setting a theological foundational principle, it must be of the highest degree of authenticity, which it is not.

Another version of this *ḥadīth* provides that it is reported that Anas b. Mālik reported that the Prophet said: " If a woman prays five [times

---

[60] After the second edition of this book was published, *ḥadīth* apologists argued that many traditions are elliptical and that such traditions must be understood within a context. Therefore, it should be understood that the Prophet, in effect, was saying, "If a woman is pious and devout and dies with her husband pleased with her, provided that the husband, himself, was pious and devout, she will enter Heaven." I think this argument strains to make sense of the non-sensical. First, it is odd that puritans of Islam, who pride themselves on being literalists, find themselves in a position in which they are forced to understand the text in a contextual and non-literal fashion. Second, if their argument is correct, then the tradition is too ambiguous and indefinite to serve as the legal source for any normative obligation. Third, once again, we have no sense of why the pleasure of a husband is one of the preconditions for entering Heaven. Assume that the wife and husband are equally pious, but the wife dies with her husband displeased with her because, for instance, she did not support his decision to take a second wife, does this mean that the wife will not enter Heaven? The *ḥadīth* apologists seem to argue that a wife owes her husband a duty of blind obedience as long as the husband is not commanding something that is contrary to God's law. This is exactly what I find so objectionable—the *ḥadīth* apologists ignore the fact that God's law is not always determinable, that people become pleased or displeased due to matters involving preference, taste, and personality, that other than the technical legalities there are things such as sagacity and wisdom, and, most importantly, that a woman could be wiser, more sagacious, more balanced, more reasonable, and more knowledgeable than her husband. If that is the case, why is the pleasure of husbands an element in achieving the Divine pleasure?

a day], fasts Ramadan, obeys her husband, and guards her chastity, she will enter Heaven."[61] Arguably, this version explains or specifies (*takhṣīṣ*) the earlier version. So, it is not simply any woman that obeys her husband who will enter Heaven; rather, it is only a woman who obeys, prays, fasts, and guards her chastity. However, there are several problems with this logic as well.[62] First, fewer narrators than the first accept this version. Second, one of the individuals in the chain of transmission of this version is Ibn Luhay'a, who is not trustworthy.[63] Third, this version does not at all avoid the ambiguities of the first version. For example, what happened to the duty of paying *zakāh* (prescribed alms) or performing *ḥajj* (pilgrimage to Mecca)? Perhaps this is relegated to the financial abilities of the husband. But what if the wife is rich and the husband is poor? Additionally, what if the wife prays, fasts, protects her chastity, and obeys her husband but is despicable otherwise? What if she backbites, slanders people, beats her children, steals from the neighbors, tortures her cat, and mocks the poor? Is she still entitled to enter Heaven? The only way we can give a negative response to this question is by imputing different meanings to the *ḥadīth* than the apparent meaning of the words.

The difficulty with this genre of traditions is that they promote a formalistic obligation of obedience to husbands while ignoring all

---

61 This version is narrated by Aḥmad b. Ḥanbal, Ibn Ḥibbān and al-Ṭabarī.

62 There are several *ḥadīths* attributed to the Prophet that assert that a woman's prayer or worship will not be accepted by God if she upsets or disobeys her husband. Other *ḥadīths* assert that the angels will curse any woman who upsets her husband by refusing him conjugal relations. See al-Shawkānī, *Nayl al-Awṭār*, 6:209-210. I would argue that these *ḥadīths* are inherently suspect since God's pleasure is contingent upon the husband's. A similar type of tradition provides, "There is an hour every Friday when all prayers will be answered except the prayers of a woman if her husband is upset with her." This tradition has been declared fabricated by the majority of scholars. See Ibn al-Jawzī, *Kitāb al-Mawḍū'āt*, 1:77.

63 Ibn Ḥajar al-'Asqalānī claims that he is *ṣadūq* (truthful). See Ibn Ḥajar al-'Asqalānī, *Taqrīb al-Tahdhīb*, ed. 'Abd al-Wahhāb 'Abd al-Laṭīf (Cairo: n.p., 1975), 1:444; However, Ibn Luhay'a's reliability was contested. It is reported that he became mentally unstable after his books burned in the year 170. Some considered him unreliable after that event. Others refused to transmit or accept *ḥadīth* from him before or after that event. See Muḥammad Ibn Ḥibbān, *al-Majrūḥīn min al-Muḥaddithīn wa al-Ḍu'afā' wa al-Matrūkīn* (Ḥalab: Dār Wa'y, 1397 A.H.), 2:11-16.

competing moral values in Islam. For instance, several traditions attributed to the Prophet dictate that husbands ought to be obeyed even if they are unjust or oppressive.[64] One such tradition asserts that a wife ought to appease her husband even if he is unfair or unjust to her. If the husband unfairly rebuffs her efforts to appease him, she has done her duty and will be rewarded by God.[65] The import of the tradition is that as long as the husband has not commanded his wife to perform a sinful act, he is entitled to deference and accommodation. This stance is reinforced in a tradition that is absurdly formalistic, and immoral. According to this report, a husband lived with his wife in a two-story house—the wife's father lived on the first floor of the same house while the couple lived on the second. Before leaving on a business trip, for some unstated reason, the husband ordered his wife not to leave the second floor of their home. Pursuant to the husband's instructions, the woman could not visit her father on the first floor, or anyone else for that matter. After the husband left, the wife's father fell gravely ill. The wife wanted to see her father before he died, but she did not wish to disobey her husband. Consequently, she sent to the Prophet asking him if she may visit her father. The Prophet replied that she may not do so because she must obey her husband's commands. The father soon died, and the woman again sent to the Prophet to ask if she may leave the second floor before her father's burial. However, again, she received the same response commanding her to obey her husband. After the father was buried, without the presence of his daughter, the Prophet sent for

---

64 For the different versions of this tradition, see Ibn Abī Shaybah, *al-Muṣannaf*, 3:396-397; Abū ʿUmar Yūsuf b. ʿAbd Allāh b. Muḥammad b. ʿAbd al-Barr al-Nimrī, *al-Tamhīd li-mā fī al-Muwaṭṭaʾ min al-Maʿānī wa al-Asānīd*, eds. Muṣṭafā al-ʿAlawī and Muḥammad al-Bakrī (Morocco: Maktabat Faḍālah, 1982), 1:229-231; Abū Bakr Aḥmad b. al-Ḥusayn b. ʿAlī al-Bayhaqī, *Kitāb al-Sunan al-Kubrā* (Beirut: Dār al-Maʿrifah, n.d) 7:291-293; Jalāl al-Dīn al-Suyūṭī, *al-Jāmiʿ al-Ṣaghīr min Ḥadīth al-Bashīr al-Nadhīr*, ed. Muḥammad Muḥyī al-Dīn ʿAbd al-Ḥamīd (Cairo: Dār Khadamāt al-Qurʾān, n.d.), 1:507-508; ʿAlāʾ al-Dīn ʿAlī al-Muttaqī b. Ḥusām al-Dīn al-Burhān Fawzī al-Hindī, *Kanz al-ʿUmmāl fī Sunan al-Aqwāl wa al-Afʿāl* (Beirut: Muʾassasat al-Risāla, 1985) 16:339. Interestingly, in some versions of this report, a woman asks the Prophet about the duties of a wife towards her husband. When she is informed that, right or wrong, her husband is entitled to obedience, she declares that she will never marry as long as she lives.

65 Al-Bayhaqī, *Kitāb al-Sunan*, 7:293.

the woman, informing her that God has forgiven her father's sins because she faithfully obeyed her husband.[66] Although most classical jurists seem to have dismissed this tradition as unreliable, it exemplifies the immoral and absurd logic that is inherent in the principle of blind obedience to any human being. Furthermore, this report also demonstrates that the principle that a husband will not be obeyed if he commands a sin is an insufficient guard against despotism and ill-character. People can stay within the bounds of the law and still remain despicable human beings. Unless we infuse the notion of legality with a moral conscience, legality will constitute the beginning of morality and not its complete fulfillment. In addition, the realm of sin in this earthly life is contested, debated, and negotiated. It is not possible for a married couple to reduce all of their interactions to a legal rule.

All of the traditions noted above do not explain the reason for this fatuous adulation of husbands. In fact, this preeminence given, in these traditions, to the whims and desires of husbands is contrary to Islamic principles that dictate that the merit of a person is defined by his or her piety and good deeds. Furthermore, these traditions are not consistent with the Qur'ānic conception of the marital relationship. The Qur'ān states: "From His signs is that He created mates for you from yourselves so that you may find repose and tranquility with them and He has created love and compassion between you."[67] The Qur'ān also describes spouses as garments for each other.[68] In *Sūrat al-Nisā'*, the Qur'ān provides: "Men are the support (*qawwāmūna*) of women as God gives some more means than others, and because they spend of their wealth (to provide for them). So women who are virtuous are obedient to God and guard the hidden as God has guarded it."[69]

The *ḥadīths* discussed above set foundational principles and the Qur'ānic verses quoted above set foundational principles as well. With a minimal amount of reflection one can see a conflict between the foun-

---

[66] This report has a defective chain of transmission. See Abū Ḥāmid al-Ghazālī, *Iḥyā'*, 2:57; al-Tirmidhī, *Nawādir al-Uṣūl*, 176.

[67] Qur'ān, 30:21.

[68] Qur'ān, 2:187.

[69] Qur'ān, 4:34.

dational principles set by the Qur'ān and *ḥadīth.* The Qur'ān talks of love, compassion, friendship, and virtuous women who are obedient to Allāh. Arguably, compelling your wife to have intercourse on the back of an animal or demanding unquestioning reverence is not conducive to love, compassion, friendship, virtue or obedience to Allāh. One cannot command reverence, but rather must earn it. But in that case, the wife is equally qualified to earn reverence as well as the man. The Qur'ānic conception of marriage is not based on servitude but on compassion and cooperation, and the Qur'ānic conception of virtue is not conditioned on the pleasure of another human being, but on piety and obedience to God.

If there is a conflict between the sources, one has a duty to reconcile them. This is a well-established principle in Islamic jurisprudence. But one should ask the following methodological question: Should *ḥadīths* of divergent versions, of *āḥādī* nature, which do not reach the highest level of authenticity, and which have suspect theological logic and profound social implications, be allowed to conflict with the Qur'ān in the first place? In fact, and more importantly, should *ḥadīths* with the qualities described above be recognized as establishing laws, let alone foundational principles, for something as essential as marriage? I propose that only those *ḥadīths* of the highest degree of authenticity be recognized as foundational in matters of crucial religious or social implications.

As a final example, let us consider three further *ḥadīths*. In the first *ḥadīth*, it is reported that Abū Mūsā said the Prophet said, "Three [types of people] will pray and their prayers will not be answered: 1. A man married to an ill-mannered woman and he does not divorce her. . . ."[70] In the second *ḥadīth*, it is reported that Thawban said the Prophet said, "Any woman who asks her husband for a divorce without suffering

[70] The full text of the *ḥadīth* states: "Three [types of people] will pray and their prayers will not be answered: (1) A man married to an ill-mannered woman and he does not divorce her. (2) A man who refuses to testify against another because he owes him money. (3) A man who gives his money to someone who is of poor judgment because God has said, 'Do not give your properties to those who are of weak judgment (Qur'ān, 4:5).'" Al-Ḥākim al-Niysābūrī, *al-Mustadrak 'alā al-Ṣaḥīḥayn* (Beirut: Dār al-Ma'rifah, n.d.), 2:302. I am concerned here only with the first part of the *ḥadīth,* although I would argue that the full *ḥadīth* is problematic.

hardship will not enter Heaven."[71] In the third *ḥadīth*, it is reported that Ibn ʿUmar reported that the Prophet said, "If the end of time comes and the people of whims fall in disagreement [and conflict], follow the religion [i.e., religious views] of the people of the desert and the religion of women."[72] All three *ḥadīths* are of singular transmission, and all three have profound theological and social implications. The first *ḥadīth* might lead to an explosion in the number of divorces. Proper manners are often a matter of subjective contention and depend on one's social and cultural context. Ill manners could range from sinful acts to moral defects such as insensitivity, a short-temper or argumentativeness. Yet, in order to avoid the risk that your prayers would not be answered, suspecting that one's wife is ill-mannered would compel one to divorce her. The second *ḥadīth* would seem to negate the Islamic legal procedure of *khulʿ* in which a wife returns her dowry or abandons all financial claims in return for a no-cause divorce. The third *ḥadīth* has obvious theological implications, and, in fact, seems to contradict the first *ḥadīth*. One might ask: How does one follow the religion of Bedouins and women? Which Bedouins and which women? What if the Bedouins and women disagree? What if the women disagree with each other?[73]

Fundamentally, in light of the obvious grave religious and social consequences that would follow from these three *ḥadīths*, one must ask: Should these *ḥadīths* be given legal force? And if yes, how? Since these *ḥadīths* are of singular transmission, and the circumstances surrounding these *ḥadīths* are suspect or unclear, despite what *Ahl al-Ḥadīth* contend, one cannot be sure that the Prophet, in fact, uttered them. Consequently,

---

[71] This tradition has been narrated by Aḥmad b. Ḥanbal, Abū Dāwūd, al-Tirmidhī, Ibn Ḥibbān, Ibn Mājah, and al-Ḥakīm al-Niysābūrī. It has been reported through several chains of transmission, all considered weak or problematic. See al-Jurjānī, *al-Kāmil fī Ḍuʿafāʾ al-Rijāl*, 4:31.

[72] Al-Ḥakīm al-Niysābūrī and al-Daylamī, in his *Musnad al-Firdaws*, reported this tradition. See al-Jurjānī, *al-Kāmil fī Ḍuʿafāʾ al-Rijāl*, 4:249; 6:462; Ibn al-Jawzī, *Kitāb al-Mawḍūʿāt*, 2: 177.

[73] This report is contradicted by several equally problematic traditions providing: Consult with women and do the opposite; a man who follows the capriciousness of women will be thrown in Hell; and obedience to women will bring only regret and sorrow. See al-Jurjānī, *al-Kāmil fī Ḍuʿafāʾ al-Rijāl*, 4:249; 6:462; Ibn al-Jawzī, *Kitāb al-Mawḍūʿāt*, 2: 177.

it is reasonable to deny them any theological or legal force. They are to be left to the individual believer to evaluate their worth according to the dictates of his or her conscience, as the case may be. The individual worshipper may read them for whatever spiritual persuasiveness they may have, but never to support a mandatory obligation. In other words, they belong to the realm of private conscience, but not the realm of religious, social, or political obligations.

The *Ahl al-Ḥadīth* have argued that an *āḥādī ḥadīth* creates certain knowledge (*yaqīn qaṭʿī*) and, hence, could support a binding rule not only in *ʿibādāt* and *muʿāmalāt,* but also in *ʿaqāʾid* (the basic tenets of belief). The other schools of thought disagreed, some arguing that *āḥādī ḥadīth* do not yield knowledge at all and may not be used to support legal imperatives. The majority, however, held that such *ḥadīth*, while not leading to certain knowledge, do lead to probability (*ẓann*). Furthermore, the majority of jurists argued that *aḥādī ḥadīth* can support legal imperatives in the field of *furūʿ* (branches of religion), but not *uṣūl* (fundamentals of religion). The majority then disagreed amongst itself: Some argued that *āḥādī ḥadīth* can establish a legal imperative in the branches of religion as long as it does not contradict the Qurʾān or *mutawātir ḥadīth*; others argued that *āḥādī ḥadīth* cannot contradict the practice of the people of Medina; others argued that *āḥādī ḥadīth* cannot contradict a *qiyās* and others asserted that *āḥādī ḥadīth* cannot support independent legal imperatives but only support an exception or a specification to a general rule.[74]

Other than those of the *Ahl al-Ḥadīth*, it is clear that the vast majority of Muslim jurists wanted to limit the scope of *āḥādī ḥadīth*. Since *āḥādī ḥadīth* cannot lead to certain knowledge of the Prophet's utterances, they cannot be relied upon to the same extent as *mutawātir ḥadīth*. *Āḥādī ḥadīth*, the majority argued, could be used to establish branches of the religion but not the fundamentals. Although the majority

---

[74] See ʿAlī al-Āmidī, *al-Iḥkām fī Uṣūl al-Aḥkām*, ed. Sayyid Jamīlī (Beirut: Dār al-Kitāb al-ʿArabī, 1984), 2:48, 62-66; Fakhr al-Dīn al-Rāzī, *al-Maḥṣūl* (1988), 2:184, 215; Aḥmad al-Sarakhsī, *Uṣūl al-Sarakhsī* (Beirut: Dār al-Kutub al-ʿIlmiyyah, 1993) 1:321, 333; *Imām al-Ḥaramayn* al-Juwaynī, *al-Burhān fī Uṣūl al-Fiqh* (Cairo: Dār al-Anṣār, 1400 A.H.), 1:606. See also the useful discussion in Bernard Weiss, *The Search for God's Law* (Salt Lake City: University of Utah Press, 1992), 293-94, 299-300.

of jurists struggled with the distinction between fundamentals and branches, the fact remains that they did not consider *āḥādī ḥadīth* of sufficient probative value to establish matters that are essential to religion. Therefore, it makes perfect sense to argue for a proportional relationship between the authenticity of *ḥadīth* and its effective legal scope. Even though the majority of jurists did not explicitly phrase their arguments in these terms, proportionality is the clear import of their debates on *āḥādī ḥadīth*.[75] However, to limit the logic of proportionality to the dichotomy between *uṣūl* and *furūʿ* is not plausible. As noted in the introduction to this book, the distinction between *uṣūl* and *furūʿ* is itself problematic.[76] It is not at all clear how one defines *uṣūl* or *furūʿ*. More importantly, the issue is not whether a problem could be technically classified as part of *uṣūl* or *furūʿ*. Rather, the issue is proportionality

[75] For instance, al-Shāṭibī (d. 790/1388) divided sources of the law into those that articulate universals and those that articulate particulars. This means that there are legal provisions that establish general foundational principles and others that establish particulars that are designed to be an affirmation and fulfillment of the universals. The status of legal evidence (*dalāʾil* or *adillah*) depends on its relationship to the universals or particulars. Evidence that corresponds to the universals is considered certain, and evidence that corresponds to the particulars is considered probable. In most cases, this will mean that evidence that contradicts the Qurʾān or the *mutawātir* traditions will not be considered certain. However, it is possible for particular Qurʾānic verses or *mutawātir* traditions to deal with particulars and not universals. Consequently, evidence that corresponds with this genre of Qurʾānic verses and traditions will not yield certainty. Effectively, al-Shāṭibī, like many other classical jurists, affirms the existence of an evidentiary hierarchy based on a hierarchy of values. The particulars cannot negate the universals, and if need be, the universals could void the particulars. Importantly, inconsistency between the evidentiary universals and particulars will result in downgrading the authority and reliability of the particulars. See al-Shāṭibī, *al-Muwāfaqāt*, 3:15-26.

[76] The confusion surrounding *uṣūl* and *furūʿ* is aptly demonstrated in the debate over the *ḥijāb* (veil) of the Muslim woman. The majority of Muslim writers argue that the issue of *ḥijāb* is not open to debate or discussion. According to them, a Muslim woman must cover all her body and hair except her face and hands. See al-Albānī, *Ḥijāb al-Marʾah;* al-Mawdūdī, *al-Ḥijāb*. Effectively, these writers are arguing that the *ḥijāb* is among the *uṣūl* of religion and, therefore, no disagreement may be tolerated. Other writers have argued that the *ḥijāb* is an appropriate subject for debate. See Hāshim Sharīf, *al-Marʾah al-Muslimah Bayn Ḥaqīqat al-Sharīʿah wa Zayf al-Abāṭīl* (Alexandria: Dār al-Maʿrifah al-Jāmiʿiyyah, 1987); Fatima Mernissi, *The Veil and the Male Elite* (New York: Addison-Wesley Publishing Company, 1991). I would argue that whether *ḥijāb* is a part of *uṣūl* or *furūʿ*, it is an appropriate subject

between our knowledge of the source of a text and the impact of the text. The greater the potential impact of a textual source, the more one should insist on its authenticity, i.e., that it comes from an authoritative source. *Mutawātir* traditions lead to greater certainty as to their authenticity and, therefore, could possibly be relied upon to establish legal imperatives with far-reaching theological, social, or political implications. Nevertheless, the analysis should not simply be limited to whether a tradition is *mutawātir* or *aḥādī*. Whether a *ḥadīth* is *mutawātir* or *aḥādī* is only the beginning of the inquiry. Relying solely on the counting of the number of early transmitters will yield little benefit. The point is not only how many people from the first generations of Muslims transmitted a *ḥadīth*. Rather, when a *ḥadīth* has serious social, theological, or political implications, the inquiry should be whether the totality of the evidence can provide us with certain knowledge that the Prophet did, in fact, say or do what is attributed to him. The totality of evidence would include the authenticity and trustworthiness of the transmitters, the number of transmitters from the early generations, the number of versions of the *ḥadīth*, the factual contradictions between the different versions, the substance of the *ḥadīth*, the relation between this *ḥadīth* and more authentic or less authentic reports from the *Sunnah*, the Qur'ānic evidence (in terms of contradictions or consistencies), the historical context of the *ḥadīth*, and the practices of the Prophet and companions in related contexts. By their very nature, *mutawātir* traditions will be able to withstand greater scrutiny than their *āḥādī* counterparts.

One might argue that the approach advocated here will not lead to definitive results, and that too much uncertainty will engulf the *Sunnah*. Different scholars will assess the above-mentioned factors differently, and some scholars will conclude with certainty that a specific *ḥadīth* is from the Prophet while others will disagree. Furthermore, the jurists will disagree on the proper weight to be given to the various traditions.

for debate. However, whoever claims that the *ḥijāb* is a part of the fundamentals of religion bears a heavy burden of proof. Essentially, nothing is excluded from debate. Rather, in my view, the distinction between *uṣūl* and *furūʿ* delineates different burdens of proof whose weight depends on whether one claims an issue to involve an *uṣūl* or *furūʿ*.

Consequently, we are bound to end up with different *Sharʿī* (legal) rules on the same issues depending on the individual *ijtihād* of each scholar. This criticism is not compelling.

The history of Islamic law and the development of a variety of jurisprudential schools in Islamic history is the greatest confirmation of the validity of this approach. Different jurists are bound to assess the same evidence differently and come to different conclusions as to the authenticity and the meaning of the evidence. Through this process, a discourse on the authoritative is created and an authoritarian conclusive voice is never established. Even a temporary *ijmāʿ* might not be able to establish the authoritarian. For one, the requirements for *ijmāʿ* are quite difficult to fulfill. Two, different schools have different rules for *ijmāʿ*.[77] Three, the burden of proof is always on the one claiming that an *ijmāʿ* exists on a certain issue, and is a burden that might never be met. In sum, even the institution of *ijmāʿ* should not be able to establish the authoritarian and silence the discourse.[78] The discourse symbolizes the

[77] For instance, some jurists, such as al-Shāfiʿī, argued that the *ijmāʿ* must include the lay people. Effectively, under this view, *ijmāʿ* becomes restricted to matters such as the five daily prayers, fasting, the *zakāt*, etc.

[78] On the issue of *ijmāʿ* generally, see al-Jaṣṣāṣ, *al-Ijmāʿ*, 137-223; Maḥmaṣānī, *Falsafat al-Tashrīʿ*, 159-162; Hasan, *Doctrine of Ijmaʿ*. Importantly, most jurists agreed that one who challenges or violates a presumed *ijmāʿ*-based ruling is not a *kāfir*. For instance, Abū Bakr al-Sarakhsī (d. 483/1090) argues that because *ijmāʿ*, as a source of law, is clear and certain (*qaṭʿī*) proof for a *ḥukm*, any violation of an *ijmāʿ*-based ruling is tantamount to *kufr*. Abū Bakr Muḥammad b. Aḥmad b. Abī Sahl al-Sarakhsī, *al-Muḥarrar fī Uṣūl al-Fiqh* (Beirut: Dār al-Kutub al-ʿArabiyyah, 1996), 1:238-240. Fakhr al-Dīn al-Rāzī, on the other hand, argues that the ontological authority of *ijmāʿ* is not certain, but rather, probable (*ẓannī*), and that there is an *ijmāʿ*-based ruling which holds that one who opposes or violates a rule based on *ẓannī* proof is not a *kāfir*. Furthermore, he also argues that *ijmāʿ* is not essential or fundamental to religion. Fakhr al-Dīn al-Rāzī, *al-Maḥṣūl* (n.d.), 2:98-99. See also al-Urmawī, *al-Taḥṣīl*, 2:86. Others such as al-Zarkashī and al-Āmidī argue that failure to adopt an *ijmāʿ*-based ruling on a fundamental matter of faith constitutes *kufr*, whereas a violation of a lesser matter does not. Shams al-Dīn Muḥammad b. ʿAbd Allāh al-Zarkashī, *al-Baḥr al-Muḥīṭ* (Cairo: Dār al-Ṣafwā, 1988), 4:524-528; Sayf al-Dīn Abū al-Ḥasan ʿAlī b. Abī ʿAlī b. Muḥammad al-Āmidī, *al-Iḥkām fī Uṣūl al-Aḥkām* (Cairo: Muḥammad ʿAlī Sābī, 1968), 1:209. Other jurists held that denial of *ijmāʿ*, as a source of law, constitutes *kufr*, but that rejection of a specific *ijmāʿ*-based ruling does not. ʿAbd al-ʿAzīz b. Aḥmad al-Bukhārī, *Kashf al-Asrār* (Beirut: Dār al-Kitāb al-ʿArabī, n.d.), 2:479-480. On the other hand, jurists like *Imām al-Ḥaramayn*

human search for the Divine Will, but no single or collective human voice is ever allowed to become the exclusive representative of the Divine Will.

al-Juwaynī disagreed with the claim that the rejection of *ijmā*ʿ as a source of law led to disbelief and *kufr*. Rather, al-Juwaynī argued that only if one accepts the ontological value of *ijmāʿ*, but subsequently rejects a particular *ijmāʿ*-based ruling, then he would be engaged in an act of *kufr*. Al-Juwaynī, *al-Burhān*, 1:280. Al-Juwaynī's student, Abū Ḥāmid al-Ghazālī, states that it is *ḥarām* (prohibited) to oppose an *ijmāʿ*-based ruling or to engage in what the *ummah* has prohibited. However, he does not suggest that violating an *ijmāʿ*-based ruling is tantamount to *kufr*. Abū Ḥāmid al-Ghazālī, *al-Mustaṣfā*, 1:198.

V

The Construction of the Authoritarian

A reader interprets a text by constructing its meaning. Assuming that the author of the text intends a specific meaning, the reader's construction may or may not coincide with the specific meaning intended. In fact, there is a perpetual state of tension between the reader and the text. If the author is alive, present, and accessible, the tension may ultimately be between the author and the reader.[1] If, however, the author is not accessible or does not directly refute the reader then the tension is between the text and the reader. In a sense, the reader directly negotiates meaning with the text.

A reader, for example, may approach the Qur'ānic verse stating that, "There is no compulsion in religion."[2] The reader must decide on the meaning of the text. Arguably, this verse means that no one should

[1] I am no longer persuaded of the validity of this point. Even if the author is alive, the text, with its system of symbolic significations, attains a certain degree of autonomy. The author may object to how her text is being read, but the author cannot control the interpretive process. Therefore, the tension between the reader and text exists regardless of the author. This does not mean that the author's intent is irrelevant to the process of determination of meaning. In fact, the author's intent, the text, and the reader become engaged in a tri-polar dynamic of negotiating meaning.

[2] Qur'ān, 2:256.

be forced to become a Muslim. Alternatively, this verse could mean that while one may be forced to become Muslim, one could not be compelled to believe. The verse could also mean that one may not be forced to pray, fast, or wear the *ḥijāb* (woman's veil). Possibly, the verse also means that one may not be punished for apostasy. Furthermore, one might argue that since there is no compulsion in religion, there should be no compulsion as to anything else. Therefore, one may conclude that contracts entered into under compulsion are invalid. One may further argue that free consent is necessary for a marriage contract. Arguably, one may extend this logic to invalidate contracts of adhesion.

In each of these steps, the reader is constructing the meaning of the text. A reader approaches a text and decides how to read it. The text only states that there is no compulsion in religion. It may or may not have intended to address prayer, *ḥijāb*, apostasy, marriage, or contracts of adhesion. Since the text does not address any of these issues directly, it is the reader who has to construct the meaning for the audience. A state of tension exists between the reader and the text because the reader may be entirely wrong in understanding the text as the author intended it.[3]

The reader approaches the text because it is authoritative. The text is authoritative because of its origin. In the case above, the authority of the text is derived from its divine origin. If the reader cites the text and then states a rule, the reader has unified himself with the text. The reader becomes one with the text and stands suspended, untouchable, and transcendent. The text and the construction the reader has given it become one and the same. Effectively, the text remains authoritative but the reader becomes authoritarian. Truth is only presented through the reading the reader chooses for the text. No other readings are possible; or at least, this is how the reader phrases the discourse to his audience. The text is rendered subservient to the reader and, effectively, the

---

[3] The author's intent is also negotiated through the medium of the text and language. The author might intend X, but once X goes through the medium of language, that intention becomes translated as Y. Of course, when dealing with the Qur'ān, one must assume that God expressed God's self perfectly, and that whatever ambiguities exist in the text are intended. This could mean that God intended that the reader have a liberal negotiative space within the text.

reader is substituted for the text. In many ways, the reader has not only attempted to construct the meaning of the text but has gone beyond that and constructed the text itself.

Importantly, the reader also constructs the meaning of the text, and possibly the text itself, by choosing which parts of the text to present to an audience. The reader may subvert the authoritativeness of the text by selectively choosing the text. So, for example, when dealing with the issue of compulsion in religion, if one cites the above-quoted verse and no other relevant text, then one has replaced the authoritativeness of the text with his or her own authoritarian choice. Alternatively, one may present a full array of texts and evidence—all conflicting and competing. The reader then analyzes the texts or evidence and then distances his interpretation from the text. The reader creates the distance by using such terminology as "I propose" or "arguably" or "seemingly," etc. The text remains authoritative—it cannot be embodied or represented by any single reader. The reader is authoritative as well because he argues a case and does not state facts. The reader should not say, "This is what the rule of *Sharīʿah* is." Rather, the reader should say, "from all the evidence presented . . . ," or "in my view . . . ," or "in my school . . . ," or "in my understanding . . . ," "the rule of *Sharīʿah* is . . . ."[4]

Only through a two-prong methodology of diligence and self-restraint may the authoritarian be avoided. The reader must exercise the utmost diligence in searching for and analyzing textual sources. Additionally, the reader must exercise self-restraint in representing the meaning of such sources. This point is well illustrated in a quote by *Imām al-Ḥaramayn* al-Juwaynī (d. 478/1085). He states: "If the *mujtahid* is not negligent in his research and is diligent in his search for sources and does not find them then the law of God, as to him, is according to his *ijtihād*."[5]

---

[4] Of course, the issue is not simply to insert qualifiers before one's interpretive determinations. Rather, it is the internalization of the realization that the reader does not have the right to "lock" the reading of the text upon a particular determination and reject all others without consideration. Furthermore, the authoritarian is thwarted when the authoritative reader is honest with others about the highly contingent nature of his determinations.

[5] Al-Juwaynī, *Kitāb al-Ijtihād*, 64.

In researching *Sharīʿah* issues, there is a duty of intellectual and investigative diligence (*badhl al-naẓar wa jahd al-qarīḥah*) in presenting the full array of relevant text on a specific issue. Furthermore, the reader must exercise self-restraint by realizing that although the text might embody the Divine Will, the reader does not. Although the reader negotiates the meaning of the text, the reader must maintain a distance between himself or herself and the text. The material point is not whether the reader accurately represents the true intention of the author of the text. Rather, the material point is whether the reader sufficiently respects the text by trying to understand but not replace it. In this sense, the highest morality is the morality of the discourse and not necessarily correctness.

As noted in the introduction, Muslim jurists frequently debated the meaning of the phrase "Every *mujtahid* is correct."[6] In its essence, this debate related to the negation of the authoritarian in Islamic discourses. At the heart of the debate was what "correctness" means. This, however, begged the question: What does the author of the text ultimately want? If the author of the text wants us to reach a "correct" understanding then how could every reader or *mujtahid* be correct?

Muslim jurists dealt with whether or not a Muslim is charged with the duty to find the correct answer to a textual problem. This, of course, depended on whether there is ultimately a correct answer. To put it differently, does the author of the text intend a specific result, and is the reader charged with the duty of discovering it? In responding to this issue, Muslim jurists disagreed. The vast majority of Muslim jurists agreed that as long as the reader exercises due diligence in searching for the Divine intent, the reader will not be held liable nor incur a sin regardless of the result. Some jurists argued that, ultimately, there is a correct answer to every textual problem. However, only God knows what the correct response is, and it will not be revealed until the Final Day. In this sense, the author of the text does have a specific intent but one can never conclusively establish whether one correctly understood the author. In this sense, every *mujtahid* is correct in trying to find the answer. However, one reader might reach the truth while the others

[6] In this context, Muslim jurists also debated a report attributed to the Prophet in which he says, "Whoever performs *ijtihād* and is correct will be rewarded twice and whoever is wrong will be rewarded once." See al-Suyūṭī, *Ikhtilāf al-Madhāhib*, 38.

mistake it. God, in the Final Day, will inform all readers who was right and who was wrong.[7]

Jurists such as *Imām al-Ḥaramayn* al-Juwaynī, Jalāl al-Dīn al-Suyūṭī (d. 911/1505), Ḥāmid al-Ghazālī (d. 505/1111), and Fakhr al-Dīn al-Rāzī (d. 606/1210) argued that there is no correct answer.[8] They argued that if there were a correct answer, God would have made the textual evidence conclusive and clear. God cannot charge human beings with the duty to find the correct answer when there is no objective means to discovering the truth about a textual problem. Human beings are charged with the duty to diligently investigate a problem and then follow the results of their own *ijtihād.* Al-Juwaynī explains this point by asserting, "The most a *mujtahid* would claim is a preponderance of belief and a balancing of the evidence. However, certainty was never claimed by any of them... If we were charged with finding [the truth], we would not have been forgiven for failing to find it."[9] According to al-Juwaynī, what God wants or what the author of the text intends is for human beings to search. Al-Juwaynī explains that it is as if God has said: "My command to my servants is in accordance with the preponderance of their beliefs. So whoever preponderantly believes that they are obligated to do something, acting upon it becomes My command."[10] God's command to human beings is to diligently search. God's law is suspended until a human being forms a preponderance of belief about God's law. At that point, as to that individual, God's law becomes in accordance with the preponderance of belief formed.[11]

What if two individuals, each with their own preponderance of belief, have a conflict of interest? What is the law of God then? Al-Juwaynī argues that the law of God for each individual is the

---

[7] This school of thought is known as the *mukhaṭṭiʾah.* See sources cited below.

[8] This school of thought is known as the *muṣawwibah.* See al-Bukhārī, *Kashf al-Asrār,* 4:18; Abū Ḥāmid al-Ghazālī, *al-Mankhūl min Taʿlīqāt al-Uṣūl* (Damascus: Dār al-Fikr, 1980) 455; , *al-Mustaṣfā,* 2:550-1; Fakhr al-Dīn al-Razī, al-*Maḥṣūl,* 2:500-8.

[9] Al-Juwaynī, *Kitāb al-Ijtihād,* 50-1.

[10] Ibid., 61.

[11] Abū al-Ḥusayn al-Baṣrī, *al-Muʿtamad,* 2:363, argues that as long as one is exhaustive and diligent, any result reached is correct.

preponderance of his or her belief. However, in relation to each other, the law of God is suspended until there is a formal legal adjudication between the competing interests.

Al-Juwaynī demonstrates this argument through two interesting examples. Assume there is a Shāfiʿī husband who in a moment of anger yells at his Ḥanafī wife, "You are divorced." Since the husband is Shāfiʿī, he might believe that since the pronouncement of divorce was uttered in anger, it is ineffective and his wife is still his wife. However, since the wife is Ḥanafī, she might believe that a divorce pronounced at a moment of anger is effective. In another example, al-Juwaynī assumes a Ḥanafī wife who marries without the permission of her guardian. Since she is Ḥanafī, she might believe that it is her right to marry whomever she wants. Meanwhile, the woman's guardian (presumably her father), who happens to be a Shāfiʿī, marries her off to a second husband. Since the guardian is a Shāfiʿī, he might believe that it is his right to marry his daughter to whomever he wants, with or without her permission. Al-Juwaynī poses the question: What is the law of God in these situations? Al-Juwaynī argues that the command of God as to both of them accords with their sincere beliefs. However, since there is a conflict of interests among the different parties, the law of God becomes one of suspension until a judge decides the matter. In other words, since the different parties have conflicting interests, the law of God is suspended until the matter is referred to a judge. The judge's verdict will then be the law of God. However, the judge's verdict is not the law of God because it is more correct than any other alternative ruling. Rather, it is the law of God as a matter of procedural justice.[12]

[12] Al-Juwaynī, *Kitāb al-Ijtihād*, 36-8. Al-Juwaynī is not arguing that the only morality is the morality of the process, or that there are no ultimate truths. It should be recalled that he argues that as to the fundamentals or *uṣūl*, there are ultimate truths. As to the *furūʿ*, the ultimate morality is that of the process. I disagree with al-Juwaynī's definition of *uṣūl* and *furūʿ*. Nonetheless, this should be left to another study. Furthermore, I admit that I find the notion of God's law, as a matter of procedural justice, troubling. Under the first school of thought discussed above, a judgment is potentially God's law until human beings are able to determine whether the judgment is correct or incorrect. However, human beings will realize the correctness or error of their judgments in the Hereafter. Under the second school of law, a determination is God's law only if the individual conscience accepts it as such. The judgment of a court or the legislation of the state is obeyed, not because it substantively correct,

Al-Juwaynī's approach effectively distinguishes sin from legal liability. Sin is only incurred for failure to diligently investigate the evidence and not for any result reached. Legal adjudication arises from the necessity of resolving conflicting interests. But at the same time, no one can claim to have reached the only possible right answer. In the absence of legal adjudication, one is bound to follow the result of his or her own *ijtihād*.[13]

---

but because of the priority of stability and order. It would seem to me that a court judgment (or any legislation) is not God's law, but state law. Once a law becomes the law of the state, it would seem implausible to describe it as God's law—it is the law of order, of necessity, or convenience. It is also potentially God's law. But whether this potentiality is realized or not depends on the individual conscience. It seems to me that to speak of a state-enforced Divine law is incoherent.

[13] In both examples discussed above, I believe that proper moral and legal analysis would vindicate the interests of the woman involved. Al-Juwaynī does not deal with a situation in which a person might believe that his or her conviction is fundamental to his or her conception of religion. For instance, the woman in the examples above might believe that her right to choose her husband is fundamental to her understanding of Islam. Consequently, she might refuse the order of a judge if it is in favor of the father. This would be a case of conscientious objection to the law. I would argue that in this situation, it would be religiously incumbent upon the woman to disobey the order of the judge. I would further argue that under the circumstances, the woman should be legally treated as a rebel (*baghī*). See, on the law of rebels, Abou El Fadl, *Rebellion*; *idem*, "Ahkam al-Bughat," 149-176. I should note that under the classical law, arguably, this woman would be declared a *nāshiz* (disobedient or defiant). See, for instance, Abū ʿAbd Allāh Muḥammad b. Aḥmad al-Anṣārī al-Qurṭubī, *al-Jāmiʿ li Aḥkām al-Qurʾān* (Beirut: Dār al-Kutub al-ʿIlmiyyah, 1993), 5:112. If one rejects the Shāfiʿī doctrine of *ṭāʿah*, which could compel this woman to return to her husband's household, this woman might be entitled to a *khulʿ* (a form of divorce according to which she returns her dowry or pays a sum of money in return for divorce). However, classical jurists disagree on whether the consent of the husband is necessary in order to obtain a *khulʿ*. Furthermore, the husband, according to some schools, may demand a higher amount than the amount of the dowry. Abū Muḥammad ʿAbd Allāh b. Qudāmah, *al-Mughnī* (Beirut: Dār Iḥyāʾ al-Turāth al-ʿArabī, n.d.), 7:51-53; Abū al-Walīd Muḥammad b. Aḥmad b. Muḥammad b. Aḥmad Ibn Rushd, *Bidāyat al-Mujtahid wa Nihāyat al-Muqtaṣid* (Beirut: Dār al-Kutub al-ʿIlmiyyah, 1997), 2:114-118; Judith E. Tucker, *In the House of the Law: Gender and Islamic Law in Ottoman Syria and Palestine* (Berkeley and Los Angeles: University of California Press, 1998), 95-100; Susan A. Spectorsky, trans., *Chapters on Marriage and Divorce: Responses of Ibn Ḥanbal and Ibn Rāhwayh* (Austin, Tex.: University of Texas Press, 1993), 50-52. For the sake of argument, I am assuming that this woman would not be entitled to *khulʿ*—an assumption that, I think, is consistent with the position of most classical schools of thought.

The effect of al-Juwaynī's approach is to preserve the integrity and authoritativeness of the text. Since discourse is a moral value in itself, the construction of the authoritarian is avoided. Even in the case of a legal adjudication, one may continue to believe and argue that the positive law has misconstrued the Divine text. Even a judge must be cognizant of the fact that he or she represents only an opinion about the Divine law and not the Divine law itself.

Each religion espouses certain basic values or fundamentals. This is what Muslim jurists described as the *uṣūl* or certain truths. Muslim jurists argued that as to these fundamentals, the ultimate value is not the discourse but the fundamental or certain truth itself. Admittedly, the distinction between a fundamental and non-fundamental truth is elusive. Therefore, in my view, discourses on the purported fundamentals should not be censored. However, when one claims to deal with a fundamental or certain truth of Islam, one must meet a heightened duty of diligent scrutiny and self-restraint. The burden of proof is much higher and the duty of exertion in research is much more demanding.

Anything that is susceptible to textual interpretation is not among the fundamentals. Muslim jurists argued that anything that is not a certain truth is to be considered among the branches or non-fundamentals of religion (*furūʿ*). Arguably, it is a certain truth that the preservation of human life is a value. God said: "Do not take a life which God has forbidden unless for some just cause."[14] Elsewhere, the Qurʾān states: "And do not kill yourselves."[15] What constitutes "just cause" is susceptible to debate. Furthermore, perhaps whether smoking is a form of killing oneself is among the branches. As to the branches, the ultimate value is the value of the search. The search for the Divine law is an object in itself because the ultimate value is for human beings to live a life in the service of the Divine. The Divine, however, is not serviced by following specific laws. Rather, the Divine is serviced by living a moral life and by the absorption of the intellect and soul in the endless search for that life. In many ways, God rewards the sincerity of efforts, not the results.

---

[14] Qurʾān, 6:151.

[15] Qurʾān, 4:29.

One of the often repeated phrases in Islamic discourses is the statement: "*Allāhu aʿlam,*" ("God knows best"). This formula is supposed to act as a reminder that regardless of the circumstances, no one can guard against error or ignorance. However, it is also supposed to act as a reminder that one must do everything possible to guard against error or ignorance. This means one is bound by a duty of diligence. This formula also signifies that human knowledge is separate and apart from the Divine knowledge. No one can represent or embody the Divine Will. This means that one must exercise self-restraint in arguing the Divine Will. It has become customary for Muslims in the United States, and elsewhere, to end their speeches and writings with the pronouncement: "And God knows best." The only condition, however, is that, at the very minimum, it not be recited pro-forma but that it be sincerely meant.

VI

Publication Afterthoughts

بسم الله الرحمن الرحيم

The most sensible afterthought is an apology. Every text set in motion by a writer inevitably becomes a source of embarrassment for its author. This is not because the author always has more to offer than his or her text, but because every author wants to believe that the text betrayed him somehow. Unless the author is intent on silence, there is always the wishful belief that a text situated in the past has failed, and that the text to come will prove a decisive improvement. But, of course, it is the author who fails the text, and so it is fair to say that every author owes his text an apology.

On the third re-print of *The Authoritative and Authoritarian in Islamic Discourses*, I am painfully aware of the ways that I have failed this book. There are many issues that deserve elaboration and development—this book is entitled to richer treatment of several matters that were flagged but not developed. There is the strong temptation to remedy these shortcomings by substantially revising many parts of the book, but it is a temptation that I resist. If I instituted the contemplated revisions, the old book would die and a new book would be born. But I realize with a certain degree of humility that a book renders its author irrelevant, and that this book has acquired rights to an autonomous existence that I am loathe to ignore. I have already revised many of the ideas expressed in this book and these ideas now appear in an entirely new work.[1] However, this does not mean that I have the right to sentence the present work to death, or that I can seek comfort in the idea that the latest work voids everything that preceded it. Put simply, I preserved *The Authoritative and Authoritarian*, for the most part, unchanged or unrevised, because I cannot be the one to judge whether my later ideas are demonstrably superior to my earlier ideas. The reader may find certain disparities between what I expressed in *The Authoritative and Authoritarian* and my later works. Nevertheless, the reader will have to be the ultimate judge of which set of ideas are more persuasive or useful.

Authority and the Determination of Meaning: One God, One Book, and One Meaning

Among the issues not adequately developed in *The Authoritative and Authoritarian* are those pertaining to the text and the determination of its meaning. While I believed then, as I continue to believe now, that meaning is determined through a complex engagement between author, text, and reader, I chose not to explain or develop this point. Furthermore, I did not address the issue of the objectivity of meaning in the text or how one might differentiate between reasonable readings and abusive readings of a text. I failed to delineate the boundaries between the authority of the reader, author, and text in the determination of meaning. Arguably, if any of the parties to the dynamic that determines meaning exceeds its proper bounds the result could be a hermeneutic of despotism. I also failed to address the rather challenging issue of who authors a text. Texts could have a single or multiple authors, but the list of authors is not necessarily limited to those individuals whose names appear on the cover of a book. Especially when one deals with an oral tradition, such as the *Sunnah* of the Prophet, one must confront the very real possibility that an authorial enterprise, and not a single author, stands behind the text. In addition, even in the case of a text that is signed by a single author, although attributed to this

[1] Abou El Fadl, *Speaking in God's Name.*

single author, in reality it is produced by the many intellects and normative social values that shaped that author's thinking.

Related to the issues of determination of meaning and the roles of the author, text, and reader is the challenging notion of authority. There is a material difference between coercive authority and moral authority. Coercive authority, such as the authority of a policeman, does not necessarily rely on persuasion to obtain deference or consent. Instead, it relies on the threat of some harm to be inflicted if deference or consent is not granted. Moral authority obtains deference through some form of persuasion that induces an individual to prefer particular courses of belief or action to the exclusion of other possibilities. Of course, *The Authoritative and Authoritarian* primarily deals with moral authority, but I did not attempt to develop a systematic conception of authority in this work. I believe that any relationship of legitimate authority, coercive or otherwise, relies on a set of representations manifested in claims—for instance, claims of power, delegation, knowledge, or entitlement. The party that concedes to this authority relies on these representations whether such representations are made explicitly or implicitly. When I go to my doctor who happens to have an office in a hospital, wears the typical white coat, and calls himself M.D., I rely to my detriment on these representations. I am willing to forgo the possibility of going to an herbalist or my mother for a remedy because of these representations of authority. These representations, for a variety of reasons, persuade me that the M.D. knows better, and is able to perform the tasks that are socially presumed to be within the competence of medical doctors. But these representations of authoritativeness, and the ensuing relationship, are founded on an assumption of a set of duties. If these duties are breached the parties to the relationship have a good reason to complain. Authoritarianism in this type of dynamic is manifested in the type of breach that can be described as abusive. Put differently, authoritarianism invariably involves an abuse of authority that violates the conditions upon which deference is granted. In this book, I did not develop the conditions that could be said to govern the relationship between a Muslim scholar and those who rely on his opinions to their detriment.

Issues related to the determination of meaning and the concept of authority are compelling, and are directly relevant to evaluating the authoritarian as opposed to the authoritative in any discourse. However, as I noted in the introduction to this work, I very much wanted to produce a work that is accessible to the common Muslim living in the West, and to situate this work squarely within the Islamic tradition. Discussions involving matters of literary criticism and conceptions of authority tend to become quite abstract, and are largely alien to contemporary Muslims in the West. It took me a few years after writing *The Authoritative and Authoritarian* to develop a framework that hopefully would be accessible and palpable to contemporary Muslims.[2] In this book, I limited the idea of authoritarianism to the act of usurping the authority of the Divine. If I am a paralegal working in a law firm but I pretend before clients to be the attorney in charge of a case, arguably I exceeded my bounds and usurped the attorney's authority. I did not usurp it in the sense that I transferred it to me and denied the attorney of it, but I usurped it in the sense that I appropriated an authority that I am not entitled to possess. But there are other more subtle forms of usurpation of authority. If, as a member of the law faculty, I pretend to have the power to make decisions that properly belong only to the dean of the school, I have appropriated an authority that I have no right to claim. In doing so, I do not have to pretend to be the dean; it suffices that I claim to have powers that I do not in fact possess in a situation where I can reasonably know that some people will rely on my representations to their detriment.

One's relationship to the Divine Will raises similar issues. Since I cannot ask God directly about the His expectations and demands upon me, and since I do not have the time, desire, or capacity to uncover the Divine Will, I might seek out the specialists in studying this Will. For instance, if I am contemplating a divorce and I want to conduct this divorce pursuant to the Divine Will, I might conclude that the divorce

[2] I deal with these issues in *Speaking in God's Name*. Interestingly, one of the common complaints communicated to me about *The Authoritative and Authoritarian,* even in its present form, is that it is too abstract and inaccessible. I do not believe, however, that I have the ability to further simplify this work without rendering it into an ineffectual and meaningless work.

ought to be conducted according to the dictates of Islamic law. I might call up the dean of my law school to ask him but this would seem absurd unless I have good reason to believe that the dean knows the laws for an Islamic divorce. In the alternative, I might go to the mosque and ask the first person that I meet there. Unless I have good reason to believe that every person on the premises of the mosque has studied the Divine Will, my behavior would be unreasonable. Alternatively, I might approach a person who manifests all the insignia of a Muslim scholar,[3] and ask him instead. My behavior would remain unreasonable unless I have good reason to believe that individuals who wear the insignia are, in fact, knowledgeable about the Divine Will. Insisting on discovering the Divine Will as it relates to my divorce, I might approach a man with the insignia and ask him whether he is knowledgeable in this field. Assuming that the man responds in the affirmative, I present my questions and receive the necessary answers. What if it turns out later that the man advised me on the laws of divorce in the Justinian Code of Roman law without bothering to disclose this fact? It is plausible to conclude that since the man with the insignia could have foreseen that I would reasonably assume that the laws he is elucidating are Islamic laws, this man has abused his moral authority over me. I thought that I would learn Islamic law but I learned Roman law instead without being informed of this fact. This, in its basic form, is what I mean by authoritarianism. Assume that the man with the insignia is not insane, rather he relied on Roman law simply because he knows Roman law and knows next to nothing about Islamic law. However, he found it convenient to presume that all law is the same—if Roman law says something, there is no reason to think that Islamic law would say anything materially different. To make this example more realistic, we could assume that the man with the insignia instead of Roman law relied on Egyptian law instead, or perhaps he relied on what Urologists told him about Islamic law, or he simply relied on what makes sense to him. These might all be legitimate sources of knowledge, but it is not what I asked about, and this is not what I would have reasonably presumed to be the reliable sources for discovering the Divine Will. If I

[3] The person, for instance, wears a beard and robe, and leads prayer in the mosque.

have reason to know that people in the relevant community consider Urologists to be the authoritative voice of God, it is difficult to argue that this man breached his duty to me. He might have breached his duty to God, and by relying on him, I might have done so as well, but since this fellow did not misrepresent his qualifications or defraud me he has not acted in an authoritarian fashion vis-à-vis me.

Moral authoritarianism, at least in all the examples that I have been able to think of to date, invariably involves some form of misrepresentation or fraud. More basically, it involves a lie—a lie that induces some type of false reliance. In the context of Islamic legal practice, authoritarianism involves the invoking of God's authority in a process that ultimately makes light of God's authority. It is not that the authoritarian necessarily involves the misrepresentation of the Divine Will, but it misrepresents the process that results in the determination of the Divine Will. The issue, in a sense, is what type of assumptions are implicated in inquiring about the Divine Will? If I ask someone about the rule of Islamic law, I am not posing this question in a vacuum. There is a relevant community that gives meaning to this question and to any response that I might receive. Hence, when I pose the question, I am assuming the relevance of the Qur'ān, the *Sunnah*, and the juristic tradition to the question and response. I am assuming that the person who claims to be competent in Islamic law is going to base his or her response on sources recognized as legitimate and persuasive in the relevant community of interpretation. Unless I belong to a community of interpretation that considers intuition or unbounded reason to be determinative of the Divine Will, I will not expect a response simply based on intuition or reason. Nonetheless, as long as there are the necessary disclosures, a response based on intuition or reason is not necessarily authoritarian. What is authoritarian is to explicitly or implicitly claim that a response is based on the Qur'ān, *Sunnah,* and juristic tradition when, in fact, it is not. The reason this is authoritarian is that it arrogantly presumes the Qur'ān, *Sunnah,* and juristic tradition to necessarily be in accord with one's intuition or reason. Furthermore, this type of misrepresentation does not afford the questioner the necessary respect and concern in generating a response that the questioner might consider legitimate. I am not arguing that reason or intuition have no role to play in Islamic law—far from it. I am simply calling for conscientiousness and honesty in the use of culturally informed assumptions, intuition, or reason in representing the Divine Will.

Apart from the duties raised by the existence of presumed communities of interpretation, there are ethical obligations that bind the conduct of a person who assumes a position of moral authority. Let us call this person X. Again, if I ask X about God's law, I have a sincere desire to obey a law that is attributable to God. At a minimum, I am presuming X does not believe himself to be God. Even more, I am expecting that he does not believe himself to be Divinely inspired, and if he does, in fact, believe himself to be Divinely inspired, I would expect to be informed of this conviction. In the context of Islamic theology, these assumptions would be reasonable, if not necessary. In addition, I would expect that X would exercise conscientious restraint in differentiating between his whims and desires, and what he thinks the objective evidence mandates. I would expect that X will exercise the necessary restraint so that he does not negligently become a Divine pretender. Furthermore, I will have a reasonable expectation that when X represents the Divine law, he will do so only after exercising due diligence in investigating the totality of the evidence that is pertinent to the question posed.[4] Similarly, if I consult a doctor about a medical problem, I expect that this doctor will be restrained in his representations and assurances to me, that he will diligently investigate all the evidence relevant to my medical condition, including all the appropriate medicines, and that he will exercise his judgment in a responsible and reasonable fashion, so that he does not use me as a test case for experimental treatments without my consent. The failure of X to discharge these obligations violates his duties towards me, and if the breach is sufficiently deceptive, the relationship between X and me becomes abusive.

Abusive relationships are often despotic, but abuse by itself does not create the authoritarian. For the authoritarian to exist, the abusive must necessarily involve the misrepresentation that a matter that is open for inquiry and investigation is conclusively resolved. For

[4] In *Speaking in God's Name,* I argue that five factors, honesty, self-restraint, diligence, comprehensiveness, and reasonableness, guard the relationship between the person claiming moral authority and the person conceding to this authority.

instance, I might ask X about an issue designated as Z. X responds that Z is clearly and decisively resolved in Islamic law and that Z is forbidden. If in fact Z is not as clearly resolved as X claims it to be, this is what I describe as authoritarian. Effectively, X has attempted to end the autonomy of the Divine Will by derailing the living process by which that Will manifests itself. X has taken a work in progress and declared the work to be finished, and by doing so X has claimed to himself something that only God is authorized to do. If God leaves an issue open to human inquiry, how could a human being have the authority to declare it closed? Whether X closes the issue because of arrogance, dishonesty, or negligence is beside the point. To bring an ongoing discussion to an arbitrary halt is authoritarian regardless of the reasons.

Although the above mentioned is abstract, it is well grounded in the Islamic tradition.[5] Since this is the whole point behind this work, this elaboration, I believe, is justified. Interestingly, upon the publication of this book, I noticed that in several Islamic conferences and events, a good number of speakers started describing such and such speaker, argument, or position as authoritarian. Perhaps this was an indication that *The Authoritative and Authoritarian* did reach a broad audience. However, I also noticed that the various speakers were describing positions that they found objectionable or speculative as authoritarian. This perhaps was an indication of my failure to make my ideas clear—an indication of the ways I failed the text. An argument that confesses its status as an argument, and that does not present itself

---

[5] Many sources and reports have emphasized that jurists speak on God's authority and must discharge his or her obligations conscientiously and diligently. Jurists obtain their authoritativeness from the claim that they are qualified to represent God's Will, and therefore, they are to be held liable before God if they abuse this authority. In this context, the sources emphasize the uncompromising obligations of knowledge and due diligence. A jurist must not speak out of ignorance and must investigate God's law with the requisite amount of exhaustiveness. Misrepresenting God's law because of ignorance, whimsicalness, or laxity is a grave sin. See Ibn Qayyim al-Jawziyya, *I'lām al-Muwaqqi'īn*, 4:172-5, 217-219; Abū Zakariyyā Muḥyī al-Dīn b. Sharaf al-Nawawī, *al-Majmū' Sharḥ al-Muhadhdhab* (Cairo: Dār al-Fikr, n.d.) 1:40-41; Aḥmad b. Ḥamdān al-Ḥarrānī, *Ṣifat al-Fatwā wa al-Muftī wa al-Mustaftī*, ed. Muḥammad Nāṣir al-Albānī (Damascus: al-Maktab al-Islāmī, 1380), 46. On the sin of those who speak on God's law without knowledge, see al-Hindī, *Kanz al-'Ummāl*, 10:193; Abū 'Abd Allāh al-Ḥākim al-Nīsābūrī, *al-Mustadrak*, 1:103.

as an authoritative determination or adjudication of an issue, in my view, cannot be described as authoritative. An opinion on a matter that presents itself as a point of view and that acknowledges that other points of view are possible is not authoritarian. An argument or opinion could be fraudulent, dishonest, or negligent, but if it does not claim to be decisive and conclusive, I hesitate in describing it as authoritarian. Of course, it is possible for an opinion to be presented under a set of circumstances that are sufficiently oppressive that it would have to be described as authoritarian. For example, I might be advising a group of recent converts to Islam who do not know Arabic and have little recourse but to come to me. In this situation, unless I inform this group of the alternative points of view, effectively they might have no recourse but to accept my representations as final and conclusive. Depending on the circumstances, and also depending on the way that I present my opinions, the situation could be of such a nature that the predictable affect of my behavior would be to usurp and foreclose the process that is necessary for searching for the Divine Will.

Choosing a Case Study: Pick on Someone Your Own Size

A book such as this was bound to raise some controversy, and I am grateful for that since I learned a great deal from the various criticisms. Some of the criticisms were simply silly. For instance, some called the author an Uncle Tom or wondered why the author is picking on SAS. As I made abundantly clear, this book is not about SAS, and I have very little interest in this organization as an organization. Several individuals questioned why I chose to focus on an e-mail *responsum* issued by a relatively unknown organization. But to my mind, this is exactly the point of this work. I was not focused on analyzing the discourses of elite organizations or examining the debates of scholars. The whole point is that the discourses of organizations such as SAS, in popular forums such as the one chosen by SAS, suffer from an authoritarianism that is embedded in the popular culture of Muslims in United States. It is the manifestation and acceptance of authoritarianism in

Muslim popular culture that I find problematic. Another aspect of the SAS *responsum* that attracted my attention is its off-handed and derogatory attitude towards women. My experience in the United States has led to the firm conviction that the role and position of women is one of the most problematic issues for American Muslims. In Muslim conferences, journals, and mosque practices, the treatment and attitude towards women has become nothing short of psychotic. I have noticed that in numerous situations discussions that are seemingly unrelated to matters of gender roles become transformed into a forum to deprecate women. Whether the discussion is focused on the availability of parking around a mosque or keeping the bathrooms clean, somehow, this becomes an opportunity to deprecate women. It is quite common to find that men who work everyday side by side with non-Muslim women, and who maintain with these women the most congenial and respectful relationships, adopt a very exclusionary frame of mind vis-à-vis Muslim women in the mosque. Perhaps one of the most peculiar examples is a Muslim gynecologist who became upset when I suggested that women do not have to sit behind a curtain when listening to a lecture.[6]

The SAS *responsum* invoked this popular dynamic in that it artificially injected a side bar deprecating to women in a context that did not relate to women. What caught my attention about the SAS *responsum* was its representative and quite common quality—while living in the United States I have seen hundreds like it. Yet, this is the secret of its effectiveness. It is simple, straightforward, accessible, short, and in English. In the absence of any serious institutions of scholarship among Muslims in the West, it is bound to influence the standard for Muslim juristic discourses. In fact, ironically, *responsa* such as the one issued by SAS have defined the standard and lowered the bar so much so that more sophisticated approaches do not find a receptive audience. For instance, observe the relative marginality of the discourses of Muhammad Asad and Fazlur Rahman among Muslims in the West. The pedantic rhetoric of organizations such as SAS has squeezed out more responsible and learned scholarship. Of course, I fully realize that popular works tend to affect popular culture far more than serious works of

[6] I documented this incident and much of my experience in Abou El Fadl, *Conference of the Books*.

scholarship, but *The Authoritative and Authoritarian* was written with the express purpose of raising the bar for popular discourses. In many ways, *The Authoritative and Authoritarian* is part of a contest among Muslims in the West for defining their relationship to the Islamic intellectual legacy, and it is also a part of the struggle over standards. The Islamic Civilization eventually developed a class of specialists who generated a remarkably rich and sophisticated intellectual tradition. Contemporary Muslims, particularly those in the West, are plagued with a rampant, puritan, anti-intellectualism. Intellectuals are often seen as needlessly complicating matters and are often accused of corrupting the simplicity, clarity, and pristine nature of the Islamic message. In my view, this anti-intellectualism, while being more egalitarian and inclusive in opening the doors of discourse to minimally qualified individuals, is also prone to a greater degree of abusive despotism. Clear dichotomies that divide the world into heroes and villains tend to simplify and essentialize a complex world. By ignoring the subtleties and nuances, all generalizations tend to treat their subjects unfairly, and in doing so, these generalizations serve despotic structures well. It is this puritan anti-intellectualism that I find threatening to the richness and beauty of the Islamic tradition. Colonialism and the trauma of modernity have essentialized many Muslim discourses into anti-Westernism and pro-Westernism. In this process, the Islamic intellectual heritage has been reinvented to fit within this simplistic and unhelpful dichotomous view of the world. What is Islamic is now defined largely as the antithesis of what is Western, and as such, Islamic thinking in this century has remained largely apologetic, dependent, and reactive. The recent phenomenon of Muslims living in the West offered Muslims the real opportunity to overcome the legacy of Colonialism and the burdens of reactive thinking. Unfortunately, for a variety of reasons, Muslims in the West imported the ailments of their homelands, and thus remained an intellectually ineffective force. Even native converts to Islam reflect these ailments in a particularly aggravated and distilled form. A large number of the individuals who staff American-Muslim organizations are college dropouts who receive a superficial two-year education in Egypt, Jordan, Syria, or Saudi Arabia, and return to the United States posing as the beacons of the Islamic tradition. Others are medical doctors or engineers with no formal training whatsoever or recent converts who, after attaining a superficial knowledge of Arabic, become the guardians of a fantasized ideal called Islam. In all cases, what is invariably true is that such individuals are, to say the least, intellectually unaccomplished and dull. Organizations such as SAS find their sense of intellectual fulfillment in the indulgences of puritan dreams and not in the exertions of intellectual rigor. One cannot exaggerate the role that puritan fantasies play in these dynamics. These fantasies are a product of a sense of social alienation, and have much more to do with constructing a counter-culture of protest than anything genuinely related to the Islamic tradition. The dynamics of organizations such as SAS are far more rooted in modern social ailments and frustrations of disempowerment than in a genuine attempt to absorb, analyze, and develop the Islamic tradition. Fundamentally, these puritan dreams serve as a religious opiate that replaces the need for critical insight or diligent thought.

This points to another aspect of the SAS *responsum*. As noted above, several individuals advised me that: "I should have picked a fight with someone my own size." Although unwittingly flattering, their point is that I set up a straw man and then gallantly demolished it. Acting upon this advice, I analyzed a group of *responsa* issued by prominent jurists employed by an influential institution in a Muslim country.[7] Not surprisingly, I found that the methodology, style, and approach employed by these prominent jurists did not differ in any material respect from the SAS *responsum*. The only notable difference is that while SAS made some pedestrian mistakes, the prominent jurists were better informed.[8] This lends support to my argument that the SAS

[7] See Abou El Fadl, *Speaking in God's Name*.

[8] In a group of *responsa* issued by prominent Saudi Wahhābī jurists on the matter of standing up out of respect for someone, there is no qualitative difference between the SAS methodology and evidence, and that of the more prominent Saudi jurists. Ironically, in certain respects SAS's citation and discussion of the evidence is more thorough than their prominent colleagues in Saudi Arabia. The Wahhābī Saudi jurists conclude that a student should honor his or her teacher by standing up out of respect, while saying a soldier should not salute his commander or the flag, and should not stand up to an officer of higher rank. Ibn Bāz, *Majmūʿ Fatāwā*, 1:286; *idem, Majmūʿ Fatāwā wa Maqālāt Mutanawwiʿah*, 5:349; *Fatāwā al-Lajna al-Dāʾima*, 1:144-147, 148-150.

responsum is representative of a pervasive phenomenon in contemporary Islam, and that the lowering of the bar for discoursing about the Divine Will has become widespread. The problem, however, is not limited to lowering the bar for the individuals issuing the *responsa* but also the consumers of this material. As explained earlier, the SAS *responsum* was issued in the context of a general debate about a highly visible incident. The debate was conducted primarily by university students or graduates who also formed the main constituency for the SAS *responsum*. Importantly, my book was not directed to SAS itself as much as it was directed to this educated constituency. Assuming that the *responsum* found a receptive audience among this educated constituency, this would point to a serious problem. In my view, the source of the *responsum* or the form of the medium that was chosen to transmit it is largely irrelevant. The issue is assessing the standard of admissibility among the Muslim *intelligentsia* in the West. What standards of argument and persuasion does this *intelligentsia* consider sufficient when searching for God's law? I am not simply attempting to raise the bar or standard for those who speak in God's name but also those who consume the discourse. Consequently, whether the *responsum* came from SAS or from some other, more prominent organization is beside the point if the *responsum* meets the quality standards of the audience. This is precisely why I find the SAS example particularly relevant—it points to a remarkable deterioration in the standards of discourse among the Muslim *intelligentsia* in the West. If the SAS *responsum* did not find a receptive audience among educated Muslims, then I readily confess that I have studied a marginal oddity, and I should have found a more demonstrative example than the one I did pick.

Raising the Bar: Are We Going to Need a Jurist to Go to the Toilet?

Several critics did not take issue with my chosen case study but were unhappy about my purported goals. It was argued that I am raising the bar for the discourses about the Divine law to an exclusionary extent. Arguably, the standard demanded by this book is sufficiently taxing to the point that the discourses about the *Sharīʿah*, the Way of and to God, are going to become inaccessible and will be restricted to an elite. As one speaker commenting on my book put it: "This approach will eventually get us to the point that we cannot go to the bathroom without consulting a jurist, and then arguing about what God wants." It could be argued that this book, although ostensibly radical, is really quite conservative, that it legitimates the role of traditional jurists who have a monopoly over speaking in God's name, and that it is demanding the insignia of qualifications before one is permitted to speak.

I am sympathetic to these criticisms although I believe they misrepresent the intent of this book and its likely impact. Far from caring about the insignia of qualifications, this book is interested in the quality of the argument. There is a significant difference between expressing an opinion, claiming authoritativeness, and acting on one's beliefs. A person could form a conviction regarding a particular issue, and this conviction could be based on textual evidence, empirical experience, emotional inclinations, intellectual intuitions, a rigorous rational process, social habit, an irrational belief that father always knows best, a belief that she received a bad omen, or anything else. After forming the conviction, such a person could act on it believing that his or her behavior is justified. *The Authoritative and Authoritarian* is not interested in this particular type of dynamic. From the religious point of view, I would say that the justifiability, or lack thereof, of the conviction and the ensuing action is between the individual and God. I might advise the person that her behavior is irrational, silly, wrong, or sinful, but I would not describe the conduct of this individual vis-à-vis herself as authoritarian. Furthermore, expressing an opinion cannot be described as authoritarian if it is qualified as an opinion. *The Authoritative and Authoritarian*, it seems to me, does not preclude any person from expressing their opinion about God's law or way. But as the recipient of the opinion expressed, I would be well advised to assess the evidence cited and research alternative points of view. If I, for instance, express the opinion that men are an irrational gender, any listener is well advised to think through this assertion for himself. If the listener becomes convinced that my opinion is correct because they like my eyeglasses, I would argue that the listener is being frivolous but not necessarily authoritarian. The above two situations, acting upon a personal conviction or expressing a personal opinion, involve a very different dynamic than that which is implicated by the claim of authoritativeness. If I claim to represent the authoritative voice of God, and if the circumstances are such that my representation is bound to earn the deference of other individuals, I owe these individuals the duties of honesty, restraint, diligence, comprehensiveness, and reasonableness. If I violate these duties, apart from the issue of whether I am sinning vis-à-vis God, and apart from the issue of whether I am betraying my own integrity, I am also betraying the confidence of those individuals. I am breaching my duty towards them. To the extent that demanding the above values and duties are bound to limit accessibility, I would say, "So be it!" Doesn't this play a conservative legitimating role for the traditional juristic role in Islam? I am not sure. I do know that I am no less deferential to juristic representations of authority than I am to the declarations of a gynecologist about God's laws. Regardless of the degrees held, training obtained, or insignia of piety, if someone asks for my deference, I will grant my deference on the assumption that he or she fulfilled his or her duties towards me. If that person violates his or her duties, I would tend to think that he or she has not sufficiently respected my autonomy and worth as a person, and I will reach a point when I would accuse him or her of arrogance and intellectual despotism. In its essence, the type of dynamic that *The Authoritative and Authoritarian* sought to resist is well described in a statement by the early jurist Wakīʿ. He is reported to have said: "The people of knowledge (the scholars) document all the evidence [on a matter], whether pro or con. The people of whim, however, document only the evidence that supports their position [and ignore the rest]."[9] To the extent that the act of "documenting the evidence" involves persuading others of the authoritativeness of one's positions, Wakīʿ's statement describes a dynamic that is at the very core of authoritarianism.

I should confess that I do find the Islamic juristic heritage intellectually, and even spiritually, the most satisfying. The epistemology,

[9] "*Ahl al-ʿilm yaktibūn mā lahum wa mā ʿalayhim wa ahl al-ahwāʾ lā yaktibūn illā mā lahum.*" ʿAlī b. ʿUmar al-Dāraquṭnī, *Sunan al-Dāraquṭnī*, ed. Majdī b. Sayyid al-Shūrī (Beirut: Dār al-Kutub al-ʿIlmiyyah, 1996), 1:19.

hermeneutic process, and methodologies of the pre-modern discourse appear rich, nuanced, and reflective when compared to contemporary discourses. As I noted above, contemporary discourses have remained locked into the historical paradigms of Colonialism and have not become liberated from reactive or dependent thinking. If Colonialism has been an aberration or a forced and artificial disconnection from the historical processes that produced the Islamic intellectual legacy, the contemporary discourses seem to be dispossessed and disinherited, as if disembodied and suspended in mid-air. These discourses are uprooted from any recognizable intellectual tradition—perhaps, rooted only in a mythical ideal past that is through and through an invention of the modern age. In short, the Islamic modern intellect is without a history.

The Modern Dynamics and the Islamic Legal Tradition

Contemporary Islamic debates often sound like a *ḥadīth*-hurling competition. Opponents search for Prophetic traditions, or other anecdotal reports, which are then disembodied from any historical context or dynamic. These reports are used to wage a form of rhetorical combat over a presumed Islamic authenticity. But this authenticity is no more than an idealized and puritanical vision of either resistance or emulation of Western mores. Of course, the vision of Western mores that informs this process, like the Islamic vision, is not based in history or social context. Both the adopted Western vision, whether pro or con, and the Islamic vision are equally ahistorical and acontextual.

Although this book attempts to anchor the contemporary juristic discourses in the pre-modern heuristic tradition, I fear that the epistemology and methodology of that tradition is now dead and cannot be recovered. The pre-modern juristic tradition, like the Common law system, was always "a work in progress." The search for God's law was an act of worship that could never come to an end. This, in part, is why Islamic law exhibited such a remarkable degree of diversity and continued to resist codification despite the existence of strong centralized states in different periods of Islamic history. Muslim jurists never ruled directly, and so the Divine law remained protected from the vagaries of political shifts and social currents. Rather, Muslim jurists played an influential mediating role between the masses and the state—for both the ruler and ruled they performed a negotiative function. They explained and legitimated the rulers to the ruled, but they also restrained the excesses of the government against the masses. At times, they even led rebellions against despotic rulers, not to overthrow them, but to impress upon them the necessity of moderation and balance.[10] As the guardians of God's law, the jurists maintained the *Sharīʿah* as an amorphous concept, an ideal construct, and a *grundnorm* that binds the ruler and ruled. But it does not do so simply through the institutions because it is too enormous and important to be encapsulated by a particular human institution. To essentialize or summarize the *Sharīʿah* in order to fit it within a human institution was considered a corruption—a degradation and spoilation of God's mercy that allows for diversity to exist. Consequently, the progress and implementation of Islamic law had an incremental and dialectical quality.

The pre-modern dynamic, and the normative values and understandings that informed the practice of Islamic law, do not exist today. Arguably, the state in Muslim countries has become too powerful and hegemonic to permit the autonomous existence of the *Sharīʿah*. Furthermore, the Civil law system and the culture of legal codification have become pervasive in Islamic cultures. This has led to obsessive attempts to codify Islamic law, and to a compulsive tendency to focus all efforts on the implementation rather than the elucidation of the Divine law. Perhaps, considering the current circumstances, there is no real possibility of rekindling the Islamic juristic heritage.

---

[10] See Afaf Lutfi al-Sayyid Marsot, "The Ulama of Cairo in the Eighteenth and Nineteenth Century," in *Scholars, Saints, and Sufis*, ed. Nikki Keddi (Berkeley: University of California Press, 1972), 149-165,162-3. For an exhaustive study on the role of the *ʿulamāʾ* in legitimating rulers and rebellions through the use of their moral weight, see Abou El Fadl, *Rebellion.* On the social and political roles played by the *ʿulamāʾ*, see, Edward Mortimer, *Faith and Power: The Politics of Islam* (New York: Vintage Books, 1982), 299-307; Malcolm H. Kerr, *Islamic Reform: The Political and Legal Theories of Muḥammad ʿAbduh and Rashīd Riḍā* (Berkeley and Los Angeles: University of California Press, 1966), 196; Louis J. Cantori, "Religion and Politics in Egypt," in *Religion and Politics in the Middle East,* ed. Michael Curtis (Boulder, Colo.: Westview Press, 1981), 77-90.

The modern practice of Islamic law is, in a word, "suffocating"—a person with any respectable degree of intellectual curiosity or creativity will find very limited accommodations in the current intellectual climate. There are many complex reasons for this, but among the primary reasons is that Islamic discourses remain locked in the apologetic paradigms of the 1940s and 1950s or the pietistic regurgitations of the *ḥadīth* hurlers. Classical Muslim jurists used to describe their own role as akin to the role of doctors, and the role of the *ḥadīth* specialists as akin to the role of pharmacists.[11] In their view, pharmacy is a science while doctoring is an art, and an art without resourcefulness and creativeness is not worthy of the name. In the contemporary setting, it is clear that the pharmacists of Islam have become the doctors, and have substantially dispensed with the need for any form of art, resourcefulness, or creativity. Part of the problem is the currently prevailing conception of Islamic law.

What is Islamic law? Is it an amalgamation of positive rules or commandments (pl. *aḥkām*, sing. *ḥukm*)? If Islamic law consists of a group of positive commandments saying "do this" and "do not do that," then one must conclude that Islamic law in the contemporary age is thriving. The mass production of *aḥkām* (rules) goes on unhampered in the contemporary age.[12] Nevertheless, the *aḥkām* are only the external manifestations of the law, but they are not the law. The law, which is the *Sharīʿah*, consists of objectives (*maqāṣid*), principles (*qawāʿid*), methodologies of analysis and understanding (*uṣūl al-fiqh*), and positive commandments (*aḥkām*). In a sense, the *aḥkām* are the completed sentences of the language of *Sharīʿah*, and the remainder is the vocabulary and grammar. In a sense, the contemporary writers are prolific in

[11] A-Makkī, *Manāqib Abī Ḥanīfah,* 350. The jurist al-Baṣrī notes that there are many individuals who memorize and study the *ḥadīth* but who are not qualified to be jurists. Abū al-Ḥusayn al-Baṣrī, *al-Muʿtamad,* 2:362.

[12] Among the absurd manifestations of this tendency are two books produced by American Muslims who seem to have no sense of even the basics of Islamic law. In these two books, a long list of food products are casually declared *ḥarām* (forbidden), *makrūh* (reprehensible), or *mashbūh* (suspect). See Ahmad H. Sakr, *Understanding Halal Foods: Fallacies and Facts* (Lombard, Ill.: Foundation For Islamic Knowledge, 1996); Zaheer Uddin, *A Handbook of Halaal and Haraam Products* (New York: Center for American Muslim Research and Information, 1994).

producing sentences, but because they lack proficiency in vocabulary and grammar, their discourse is incoherent. Seen differently, the pharmacists are writing the prescriptions. Yet, this, by itself, is not the cause of the suffocating atmosphere. It is not only that the *aḥkām* have become the focal point in *Sharīʿah* discourses, and that there is a lack of competency in the usage of legal objectives and methodologies, but also that the objectives and methodologies of *Sharīʿah* have not been developed to meet contemporary advances in epistemology, hermeneutics, or social theory. In the contemporary age, Muslims end up with a rather ironic and painfully non-sensical paradigm. Modern inquiries in epistemology and hermeneutics are declared as contrary to the authentic classical methodologies and systems of knowledge, and therefore, are rejected out of hand. At the same time, the authentic classical methodologies are treated as too obscure, obsolete, or simply difficult and are, therefore, ignored or awarded the most cursory and superficial treatment. Having ignored the systems of juristic knowledge that prevailed in the past, and rejected those that exist in the modern age, what remains? What remains is a slavish and frantic adherence to the positive commandments as the vehicle for the salvation and perseverance of the Islamic identity.

I do think that it is not possible, nor even advisable, to try to regenerate or reproduce the dynamics of the pre-modern juristic tradition. However, this does not mean that the current juristic practice should be disjointed from its past. There is a difference between a slavish imitation of the past, and a creative developing of the past. One of the reviewers of *The Authoritative and Authoritarian* described the work as "a creative vision" of Islamic law in the modern age. I am satisfied with this description. I do not seek to resuscitate the body of traditional Islamic law so that it may live as a historical oddity in the modern age. Instead, I seek to derive inspiration and guidance from the pre-modern juristic heritage, and then to articulate a normative framework that would be more fitting for the modern age. For instance, I am well aware that the classical jurists did not speak in terms of self-restraint or proportionality, but there is no doubt that these concepts have their antecedents in the pre-modern tradition. Self-restraint was inspired by the numerous pre-modern discourses demanding that a jurist must base all judgments on the evidence and condemning the reliance on whim or self-interest in investigating the law. Similarly, the idea of proportionality was inspired by the concept of *ʿumūm al-balwā*, which was employed in a variety of usages all relating to an assessment of extent and impact.

Furthermore, at times it is necessary to completely abandon a pre-modern juristic position. As some critics of this book have noted, Muslim juristic sources often state that a jurist issuing a *responsum* is under no obligation to disclose the evidence on which his opinion is based to the petitioner. In fact, some sources suggest that a jurist should select the most appropriate juristic point of view and convey it to the petitioner without necessarily informing him of competing perspectives. Of course, this assertion is only partially correct. There is little doubt that pre-modern jurists distrusted the laity's ability to understand or evaluate legal evidence. However, these jurists did not deny the right of the laity to know the evidence; they were far more concerned about the mechanics of the interaction between the jurist and the layperson posing the question. Pre-modern jurists were worried about preserving the dignity and aura of the jurist, and about over-burdening the jurist with repetitive questioning. Therefore, several jurists argued that if the layperson wishes to understand the evidentiary basis for a legal opinion, such a person should arrange for a private meeting with the jurist who issued the *responsum*, and in that meeting, the layperson can ask for a thorough explanation of the evidence. Furthermore, most pre-modern authorities argued that if a jurist is dealing with a novel legal issue or a contentious interpretation, or if the jurist is claiming that another jurist's interpretation is erroneous, and if the *responsum* is in writing, then a full explanation of the evidence is necessary.[13] If one

[13] There is a vast debate in the pre-modern literature on these issues. For example, al-Khaṭīb al-Baghdādī (d. 463/1072) suggests that the *muftī* must be conscious of the laity's limited ability to comprehend his *fatwā* (*siflat al-nās*), and therefore must make every effort to present simple and concise, but thorough, responses, see Abū Bakr Aḥmad b. ʿAlī b. Thābit al-Khaṭīb al-Baghdādī, *Kitāb al-Faqīh wa al-Mutfaqqih* (n.p.: Maṭbaʿat al-Imtiyāz, 1977), 319, 320. Furthermore, al-Baghdādī cautions the laity not to burden the *muftī* with questions about his proofs (*ḥujja*) or to ask why or how he arrives at his answer (*wa lā yaqūl limā wa lā kayf*). However, if the lay questioner wishes to learn the evidence the *muftī* relies upon, he should

examines the *responsa* of Ibn Taymiyyah (d. 728/1328), Taqī al-Dīn al-Subkī (d. 756/1355), Ibn ʿĀbidīn (d. 1252/1836-1837), Ibn Rushd (d. 520/1122), and al-Wansharīsī (d. 914/1508), one will find that these jurists do, in fact, engage in lengthy justifications of their preferred legal positions. Most of these lengthy justifications occur when the issue raised is novel, complex, or contentious, and a simple and straightforward response would be inappropriate. Notably, there is also a difference between the issuance of a written legal *responsum* to be used as an authority in a variety of formal and informal contexts, and the issuance of a verbal response to a specific problem raised by a particular individual. Muslim jurists did provide extensive documentation for their opinions when the *responsum* was in writing, instead of oral,

---

arrange for a separate opportunity after receiving the *fatwā* to sit with the *muftī* and ask him for the evidence. Ibid., 313. Ibn al-Ṣalāḥ (d. 643/1245) does not oppose the idea of the *muftī* presenting the evidence for his *fatwā* where such evidence is a clear, concise textual proof (*naṣṣ wāḍiḥ mukhtaṣar*). Where the evidence is based on a rational proof, though, the *muftī* is not subject to any disclosure requirements. However, Ibn al-Ṣalāḥ does suggest that where the issue is vague or ambiguous (*ghumūḍ*), it is better (*ḥasan*) if the *muftī* indicates his evidence. Abū ʿAmr ʿUthmān b. ʿAbd al-Raḥmān b. al-Ṣalāḥ al-Shahrazūrī, *Adab al-Muftī wa al-Mustaftī*, ed. Muwaffaq b. ʿAbd Allāh b. ʿAbd al-Qādir (n.p.: Maktabat al-ʿUlūm wa al-Ḥikam, 1986), 134, 151-152. On the other hand, if the lay questioner, after having received a *fatwā*, wishes to learn the evidence used by the *muftī*, Ibn al-Ṣalāḥ states that he should ask the *muftī* in a different sitting or in the same sitting without expressing defiance. Ibn al-Ṣalāḥ also reports that other jurists have argued that nothing ought to prevent the lay questioner, out of concern for his well-being, from asking the *muftī* for his evidence. In this case, the *muftī* is required to elucidate his evidence if the evidence is clear and unambiguious (*in kāna maqṭūʿan bih*). If the evidence is ambiguous, the jurist ought not elucidate upon such evidence because the laity does not have the ability to properly evaluate the matter. Ibid., 171. Shihāb al-Dīn al-Qarāfī (d. 684/1285-1286) argues that where the lay questioner asks about a grave matter (*wāqiʿa ʿaẓīma*) involving important matters of faith or the welfare of Muslims, it is better if the *muftī* explains his position in great detail (*al-ishāb fī al-qawl*), provides increased elucidation (*kathrat al-bayānāt*), and mentions the evidence that invokes the significant interests raised by the question (*al-adillah al-ḥāththah ʿalā tilka al-maṣāliḥ al-sharīfah*). However, where the question is not so grave, such measures need not be taken. Shihāb al-Dīn Abū al-ʿAbbās al-Qarāfī, *al-Iḥkām fī Tamyīz al-Fatāwā ʿan al-Aḥkām wa Taṣarrufāt al-Qāḍī wa al-Imām*, ed. Abū Bakr ʿAbd al-Rāziq (Cairo: al-Maktab al-Thaqāfī lī al-Nashr wa al-Tawzīʿ, 1989), 124. Abū al-Ḥusayn al-Baṣrī (d. 436/1044), addressing this issue in the context of *taqlīd*, indicates that the Muʿtazila of Baghdād prohibited the laity from simply following the views of jurists in legal particulars (*furūʿ*) before the latter had

and when it was expected to carry normative weight. In addition, in the pre-modern context, the qualifications, rank, and school of thought to which any particular jurist belonged were easily identifiable. Today, the context is very different, particularly in the West. As noted earlier, there are no reliable insignia of competence or qualification, and the standard for authoritativeness is shamefully low. But more importantly, I have no hesitation in stating that the pre-modern scholars, who argued that a jurist owes no duty to the petitioner—not even the duty of an explanation—and only owes a duty to God, are clearly wrong.[14] As explained

---

fully disclosed the evidentiary basis for their rulings. However, the majority of theologians and jurists, al-Baṣrī argues, permitted *taqlīd* in *furūʿ* without requiring a full presentation of the evidence. Nevertheless, the jurist must exert his best efforts in reaching a determination, and if he does, then by definition, the result reached is correct. Abū al-Ḥusayn al-Baṣrī, *al-Muʿtamad,* 2:360-363. Al-Kalūzānī (d. 510/1116), *al-Tamhīd,* 4:397-399, argues that the laity can understand the fundamentals, and the broader issues, but not the technicalities of law. Abū Ḥāmid al-Ghazālī (d. 505/1111) asserts that the very definition of *taqlīd* is to adopt another's view without assessing his evidence (*qubūl qawl bi lā ḥujja*). Al-Ghazālī contends that this type of imitation is reprehensible because an individual remains responsible for his decisions. In legal matters, while the layperson cannot dedicate himself to the evaluation and weighing of the legal evidence, the layperson must diligently select a knowledgeable jurist to follow. This is not considered a form of reprehensible imitation because legal opinions must be based on the evidence, otherwise they should not be followed. Abū Ḥāmid Muḥammad b. Muḥammad al-Ghazālī, *al-Mustaṣfā min ʿIlm al-Uṣūl* (Baghdad: Maktabat al-Mathannā, n.d.), 2:387-389. Al-Shīrāzī (d. 476/1083), *Sharḥ al-Lumʿa,* 2:1035, argues that the jurist should explain and clarify his opinions (*yajibu an yubayyina al-jawāb*). He adds that if the matter is complex, the jurist should exhaustively address the possibilities and details. Contemporary writers often include the discussion on the *muftī-mustaftī* relationship within a general discussion of *taqlīd*, and assert that *taqlīd* is simply following the opinion of another without knowing the evidences upon which he relied. Ibn Qayyim al-Jawziyyah, *Iʿlām al-Muwaqqiʿīn ʿan Rabb al-ʿĀlamīn,* ed. ʿAbd al-Raḥmān al-Wakīl (Cairo: Maktabat Ibn Taymiyyah, n.d.) 4:161-4, argues that a *muftī* should mention the evidence supporting his ruling. Especially if the *muftī's* opinion is unprecedented or unusual (*ḥukm mustaghrab*), he must fully explain the basis for his ruling. Wahbah al-Zuḥaylī, *al-Wasīṭ fī Uṣūl al-Fiqh al-Islāmī,* 2nd ed. (Beirut: Dār al-Fikr, 1969), 666; al-Dībānī, *al-Minhāj fī ʿIlm Uṣūl al-Fiqh,* 2:363.

14 Some jurists have argued that a jurist can be held financially liable for negligence in discharging his or her duties in the issuance of *responsa*. Ibn Qayyim al-Jawziyyah, *Iʿlām al-Muwaqqiʿīn,* 4:225-7. This means that a muftī owes a fiduciary duty to the person posing a question. If the jurist negligently discharges such duty and misleads the questioner, the jurist must compensate those who relied on his opinion to their detriment and, as a result, suffered some form of injury or loss.

earlier, Islamic theology insists that each Muslim is individually and directly liable to God, and that blind imitation of any person is reprehensible. Furthermore, Islamic theology demands that a person not defer to any particular institution or individual and that a person only defer to God and His Prophet. But the reality today is such that God and His Prophet speak only through the agency of the human being (and perhaps nature and history). It is logical to conclude that before deferring to any determination, a Muslim is entitled to a reasonable assurance that the determination is, in fact, based on legitimate evidence. Non-deference or freedom from obligation is an individual right that is compromised only on a conditional basis. Deference is granted to an individual only on the condition that the authoritative individual will honor the duties of authority. There is little doubt that the very idea of a set of rights or entitlements that are retained by individuals, and that are delegated only on a conditional basis is the product of contemporary notions of personal autonomy and personal responsibility, but it is also thoroughly grounded in Islamic theology and tradition. In short, a careful and reflective synthesis must be worked out between modernity and tradition. But reactive or defensive clinging to either modernity or tradition is not coherent.

On the matter of tradition, a rather rambunctious critic once accused me of being unfair to the Wahhābīs and SAS. According to this fellow, the Wahhābīs care little for the juristic tradition, and advocate two complementary steps: One, a return to the original sources of the Qur'ān and *Sunnah* unburdened and unfettered by inherited modes of thinking; and two, a reasonable assessment of what is useful in the tradition, and selecting the best elements (this is sometimes referred to as *talfīq*). Yet, this fellow claimed that I blame SAS for ignoring, or not discussing, the juristic tradition, which according to their own terms is not binding anyway. Put differently, SAS, and by extension, Wahhābism, and Salafism, does not care if such and such a jurist said such and such, and yet, this is what I fault them for not doing.

This criticism misses the point at several levels. First and foremost, the so-called two steps outlined by this fellow are unremarkable. Most contemporary Islamist approaches would agree with the sensibility of these two steps, but this is hardly the issue. The issue is: What normative values is one applying to the process of determination? To say that one ought not care which jurist said what is intellectually arrogant and unwise. Any text has the potential of creating cumulative determinations of meaning, and such cumulative determinations could develop into communities of meaning. When we speak about the text of the Qur'ān, or the various texts that comprise the *Sunnah*, we are necessarily speaking of texts that acquired meaning within contexts of cumulative interpretations and determinations. A word, any word, sentence, phrase, or passage does not exist in a vacuum; we have a sense of these symbols of meaning because of the cumulative efforts at the acquiring and transmission of meaning through a long expanse of time. A text comes packaged in a set of symbolic significations and usages, and this package, in turn, produces interpretive efforts, which in turn, generate further packaging for subsequent generations of texts. When the Qur'ān, for instance, says, "Don't fornicate!" we have a sense of what that means because of a process of acculturation into the meaning of fornicate. Perhaps a specialist will have a different acculturation so that for him or her, fornicating might have a more technical meaning, but in the case of the layperson and the specialist, both have gone through a process of acquiring meaning. This acquired meaning is the product of a long, incremental dynamic of building communities of meaning. Therefore, when we refer to the Qur'ān and *Sunnah*, we are not simply referring to the verses of the Qur'ān and the reports of the *Sunnah*. We are also referring to the institutions of meaning that formed around both—we are referring to the transmissions of Ibn ʿAbbās (d. 68/686), Ibn Masʿūd (d. 32/653), and ʿUthmān b. ʿAffān (d. 35/656); to the readings and usages of ʿUmar (d. 23/644) and ʿAlī (d. 40/661); to the creative and selective activity that preserved the collective memories of these individuals; to the later constructions of Ibn Muqātil (d. 248/862-863), al-Thaʿālibī (d. 429/1037-1038), and al-Ṭabarī (d. 310/923); to the critical and selective work of al-Bukhārī and Muslim, and many, many others. Therefore, first and foremost, we need to acknowledge that our efforts at understanding are not possible without the efforts of those who preceded us. In short, by invoking the Qur'ān and *Sunnah*, we are also invoking the whole package that comes with the Qur'ān and *Sunnah*. The Qur'ān and *Sunnah, qua* Qur'ān and *Sunnah*, that speak by themselves without the context of numerous determinations by many historical individuals, do not exist.

The question at this point becomes: Can one construct meaning by picking and choosing from the package that accompanies the invocation of the Qur'ān and *Sunnah*? Unless one is willing to venerate the tradition to the point of mindless idolization, the answer would have to be, yes. Nevertheless, unless one is willing to argue that one should pick and choose according to whim,[15] one would need to have a reason for relying on a part of the package and not another. One can argue that a particular part of the package is more moral, more reasonable, more sensible, more authentic, more reliable, more meaningful, more coherent, more consistent with other parts of the package, and so on. Whichever set of values is relied upon as a basis for the selection, a conscientious person will select conscientiously. In other words, the individual must be conscious of the values that inform his or her selections. Furthermore, if the individual is claiming authoritativeness, the basis for the selection must be disclosed so that others may freely decide whether to defer to his or her judgment or not. Put simply, a person claiming authoritativeness must disclose the basis upon which he or she relied on some evidence to the exclusion of the other.

What if a person claims to represent the rule of *Sharīʿah* or Islamic law? What is the relevant community (or package) in this situation? The very concept of Islamic law is fairly incoherent without the cumulative determinations of generations of jurists from a wide variety of schools and perspectives. There is hardly a field of Islamic law that has not been formed and shaped by the jurists. Whether one is talking about prayer, fasting, marriage, inheritance, investments, sales, or international relations, the normative values, the categories, the conditions, and the remedies that are known collectively as Islamic law, have been constructed by jurists. So, for instance, every observant Muslim knows that there are five basic values to *Sharīʿah* (religion, life, intellect, honor or lineage, and property), and that acts are divided into mandated, permissible,

[15] Whim is descibed as *hawā* in the Quran and is treated as a form of sinful self-indulgence. Qur'ān, 2:120, 2:145, 4:135, 5:48-49, 5:77, 6:56, 6:119, 6:150, 7:175-176, 13:37, 23:71, 18:28, 20:16, 25:43, 28:50, 30:29, 38:26, 42:15, 45:18, 45:23, 47:14, 47:16, 53:1-4, 54:3.

forbidden, recommended, and reprehensible. But these categories, so fundamental for the understanding of Islamic law, are the product of juristic determinations. Similarly, what a person must refrain from consuming during the fast of Ramadan or what Qur'ānic verses must be recited in prayer are all determined by the conscientious work of jurists. It is practically impossible to invoke the label of Islamic law without invoking the juristic tradition. To speak of Islamic law as if it is an institution that is not bounded by a historical context is not sensible. Every single concept in Islamic law, and every single rule, is founded on a thick bed of juristic determinations that empower it with meaning and legitimacy. In fact, if the juristic tradition is discarded altogether, nothing would remain of Islam other than the theology—and a highly partial and deformed theology at that. Even what we think we know about the legacy of the Prophet is due, to a large extent, to the interpretive efforts of the jurists. For example, contrary to popular belief, someone like al-Bukhārī, the master of traditions, did not simply narrate reports without a view to their coherence or message. As Ibn Ḥajar al-ʿAsqalānī (d. 852/1449) noted, al-Bukhārī selected and organized the traditions of the Prophet according to normative legal categories.[16] Consequently, if one would proclaim the exclusion of the juristic tradition, most of Islam as we know it would vanish. Not surprisingly, those who make such proclamations are often forced into contradictions—they will inevitably find themselves citing particular jurists in support of their opinions. For example, the Wahhābīs cannot but rely on the determinations of al-Bukhārī, Ibn Ḥajar al-ʿAsqalānī, Ibn Taymiyyah, Ibn Qayyim al-Jawziyyah, and others. This takes us back full circle to the justification of selectivity—if some opinions are relied upon to the exclusion of others, the selectivity has to be justified.

One can anticipate that Muslim critics will respond by contending that my argument effectively negates the role of the Prophet. Arguably, Islamic theology and practice were founded by the Prophet, speaking for God, and not by the jurists. Arguably, the jurists did no more than

---

16 See Muhammad Fadel, "Ibn Ḥajar's Hady al-Sārī: A Medieval Interpretation of the Structure of Al-Bukhārī's al-Jāmiʿ al-Ṣaḥīḥ: Introduction and Translation," *Journal of Near Eastern Studies* 54:3 (1995): 161-197.

fill in a few gaps here and there as the circumstances might have required. In response, I would say that this is certainly true only to the extent that one has experienced the Prophet directly and without mediation. The closest Companions of the Prophet might have had the opportunity to model their behavior on the basis of direct and unmitigated experiences of the Prophet. However, upon the death of the Prophet, the direct and corrective role of revelation came to an end. The role of revelation was replaced by the efforts of memory. But memory is a part of retrieving, re-living, and continuing the experience. Nevertheless, through memory, the experience is continued and developed without the direct participation of revelation—the Prophet, as a symbol and power, is lived, experienced, and developed, but without the actual physical existence of the Prophet. This means that through memory, the Prophet is lived and experienced vibrantly and creatively. This is exactly why, despite the fact that there was only one Prophet, a scholar can easily identify a character or personality to the memories of those who experienced the Prophet first hand. The memories of some Companions can be categorized as conservative, and others as more liberal. Put differently, the reports coming by the way of particular Companions tend to be more conservative or liberal than others. This is because memory is imprinted with the subjectivities of the person doing the remembering. Notably, the story only gets more complex from thereon—each Companion, in turn, is experienced subjectively and creatively within his or her own context. Importantly, it is the Companions and the generations that followed them who constructed the Islamic theological and juristic tradition. It is significant that, for the most part, we know about the memories and interpretations of the Companions and the early generations only through the juristic texts in the 3rd/9th century and onwards. Hence, if we discard the texts of the early jurists, such al-Shāfiʿī, Mālik, and al-Shaybānī, our knowledge of the Islamic orthodoxy and orthoproxy would become quite flimsy. Indeed, the Qurʾān and *Sunnah* would stand disembodied and disjointed without the accompanying packaging of the juristic tradition.

Aside from the issue of the dependence of the Islamic orthodoxy and orthoproxy on the juristic tradition, there is also a point of simple humility and logic. Assume that I look at a report attributed to the Prophet designated as X. Assume further that I read X and decide that it means Y. However, other more prominent jurists, such as al-Shāfiʿī, Abū Zakariyyā al-Anṣārī (d. 926/1520), al-Ramlī (d. 1004/1595), and Tāj al-Dīn al-Subkī (d. 771/1370), who read X as well had concluded that it means Z and not Y. I, however, remain firmly convinced that X means Y and not Z. I would argue that I have a right to remain firm to my belief in the correctness of my position, but only if I satisfy two conditions. One, I must be aware of the competing determinations; and two, I must give the competing determinations due consideration. If I am unaware of the competing determinations, I do not have the right to dismiss what I do not know. Furthermore, I must give alternative determinations due consideration, otherwise I cannot make the moral claim that my determinations deserve consideration by others. In other words, considering that the authorities that preceded me were not inconsequential intellects, I am morally bound to give these intellects a full hearing. But in order to avoid the arrogance of intellectual dismissiveness, and in order to give alternative points of view a fair opportunity to persuade me, I must first know about their existence. Practically, this means that I must take the trouble to read what others had to say about the meaning of X before I make up my mind. This dynamic becomes more compelling if I am claiming to be an authority vis-à-vis others. A reasonable Muslim who wants to discharge his or her obligations towards God would be concerned with why other authorities said that X means Z, and why I, on the other hand, say that X means Y. Even if such Muslim will defer to my judgment, a reasonable Muslim would want the assurance of knowing that I am aware of the Z determination, that I considered it, and that I have a conscientious reason for excluding it. To put it more straightforwardly, even SAS, the Wahhābīs, or the Salafīs are duty-bound to examine the opinions of the jurists on any given matter, are duty-bound to give these views due consideration, and, if they want to claim authoritativeness, they must be able to explain the reasons that convince them to choose an alternative point of view. Being a Wahhābī or Salafī ought not be a license for intellectual arrogance.

Lecherous Suspicions: Do You Dare Question the Ḥijāb?

Strangely enough, most of the hostility generated by *The Authoritative and Authoritarian in Islamic Discourses* had little to do with either standing up for the national anthem or even the prostrating tradition. Most of the hostility seemed to center around the suspicion that my work was surreptitiously intending to deconstruct and undermine the institution of *hijāb* in Islam. As proof, those critics cited footnote seventy-three of *The Authoritative and Authoritarian* in which I argued that, regardless of whether the *ḥijāb* is claimed to be a part of the *uṣūl* or *furūʿ*, it is appropriate to discuss the whole issue of veiling in Islam.[17] *Ḥijāb*, and its necessity, has become one of those sacred territories in Islamic discourses that measure the Islamicity of individuals.[18] If a person questions the imperative of veiling, that is often an indication that such a person is secularized, Westernized, Americanized, an Uncle Tom, or a sell-out. I remember a speaker from overseas who stated in a lecture that the *ḥijāb* is a *wājib* (duty) in Islam. Several men were enraged because he suggested that veiling is not a *farīḍah* (one of the basic requirements of Islam, the denial of which leads to the charge of apostasy).[19] Another speaker alleged that *ḥijāb* is the sixth pillar of Islam (*rukn*), which is an unprecedented claim in Islamic juristic history. Particularly among Muslims of the Wahhābī or puritan orientation and Muslims in the West, it is fair to say that no single topic is so heavily stressed and emphasized as that of the requirement of veiling for women.

The practice of *ḥijāb* is part of a complex social and political dynamic particularly in Muslim societies. It is, at times, adopted as a form of affirmation of identity or as a form of social protest against the

---

[17] Footnote 76 on page 79.

[18] By veiling, I mean the practice of covering the full body including the hair and exposing only the face and hands, or the practice of covering the whole body including the hands and face except for one or two eyes.

[19] The Ḥanafī school and some jurists from other schools distinguish between a *farīḍah* and *wājib*. Most jurists from the other schools did not. Kamali, *Principles of Islamic Jurisprudence*, 321, 324-325.

dilution of Islamic culture and against the Westernized secular dictatorships that rule most Muslim countries.[20] This, however, is not the issue that concerned me in *The Authoritative and Authoritarian*. The issue I was dealing with was whether declaring that the *ḥijāb* is part of the *uṣūl* of religion should foreclose all debates on the matter, and whether anyone who questions the imperative of the *ḥijāb* should be considered an apostate. At a personal level, I am not interested in being for or against the *ḥijāb*. Not having to worry about wearing it, my interest is purely juristic and not sufficiently vested. What does concern me is the extent to which this discourse is utilized as a means of beating Muslim women into submission to patriarchical institutions. This does not mean that every woman who wears the *ḥijāb* is submitting to patriarchy—far from it. But every time men, or women, force a woman to wear the *ḥijāb*, this does raise a concern about the promulgation of the oppressive institutions of patriarchy.[21] The most worrisome aspect about this debate, particularly in the West, is that *ḥijāb* is virulently espoused by men, and that these espousals seem to affirm the stereotype about women as a seething source of *fitnah* (seduction).

Fitnah might very well be an empirical issue and not a legal determination. What is unduly sexually arousing and how, when, and where, might pose difficult socially based empirical questions. For instance, if we assume that there is a community that endures on a fetish according to which veiling women are considered particularly seductive, should

[20] Many studies on the veil address it in the larger context of women's rights and social status in Islamic history and the modern Middle East. See, Murtaza Mutahhari, *Mas'ala-i Hijāb* (Tehran: Anjuman-i Islām-yi Pizhishkan, 1969); Juliette Minces, *Veiled Women in Islam*, trans. S.M. Berrett (Watertown, Massachusetts: Blue Crane Books, 1994); Ahmed, *Women and Gender*; Ziba Mir-Hosseini, *Islam and Gender: The Religious Debate in Contemporary Iran* (Princeton: Princeton University Press, 1999); Fadwa El Guindi, *Veil: Modesty, Privacy and Resistance* (Oxford: Berg, 1999); Mernissi, *Veil and the Male Elite*; Arlene Elowe Macleod, *Accommodating Protest: Working Women, The New Veiling, and Change in Cairo* (New York: Columbia University Press, 1991). Also see Kathleen Moore, "The Hijab and Religious Liberty: Anti-Discrimination Law and Muslim Women in the United States," in *Muslims on the Americanization Path?* eds. Yvonne Haddad and John Esposito (Oxford: Oxford University Press, 2000), 105-127.

[21] Women or men could effectively enforce the institutions of patriarchy; the gender of enforcer is irrelevant.

that mean that women ought to discard their veils, or should we ignore the empirical reality in favor of a juristically-constructed reality? Alternatively, assume that in a particular society, young, blond men are considered particularly desirable by women and men. Should these blond men cover their hair or faces so as not to be a source of *fitnah*? If the focal issue in *ḥijāb* determinations is the issue of *fitnah*, arguably in the first hypothetical, the solution should be to uncover, and in the second hypothetical, it ought to be to cover.

Alternatively, one could argue that the *ḥijāb* is not about *fitnah*, but about *ʿawrah* (the private parts that a person must cover). If the *ḥijāb* is about covering the *ʿawrah* of a woman, and not necessarily about *fitnah*, then the empirical issue of what causes or does not cause sexual enticement becomes largely immaterial. In other words, the empirical question of whether, for example, the hair or arms of a woman cause sexual enticement becomes largely irrelevant. These body parts must be covered because they are private, not because they sexually arouse. Most classical sources state that the issue of covering is a matter of *ʿawrah*, but most modern discourses deal with it as a matter of *fitnah*. This leaves the position of empirical inquiries into the realities of seduction quite ambiguous. Interestingly, what becomes known in modern discourses as the *ḥijāb* is discussed in classical juristic sources in the chapter on prayer. In that chapter, among other things, the jurists discuss what needs to covered by men and women in prayer, and from that, the issue of *ʿawrah* (private parts that ought to be covered by clothing) is discussed as well. In prayer, a Muslim man or woman must cover their full *ʿawrah*, or what the law considers to be the private parts of a human being. Presumably, what is considered to be the *ʿawrah* while in prayer is also the *ʿawrah* outside of prayer—i.e., what needs to be covered in prayer also needs to be covered outside of prayer. This is at the heart of the debates on *ḥijāb*—the *ḥijāb*, in that sense, is whatever covers the private parts (*mā yastur al-ʿawrah*).[22]

---

[22] The term *ʿawrah* is defined by referring to those parts of the body that must be covered during prayer and that are prohibited from being seen. Ibn Mufliḥ, *al-Mubdiʿ*, 1:359. Linguistically, it refers to something faulty (*nuqṣān* or *ʿayb*) or repulsive (*mustaqbaḥ* or *qubḥ*). Al-Bahūtī, *Kashshāf al-Qināʿ*, 1:312; Ibn Nujaym, *al-Baḥr al-Rāʾiq*, 1:467. Generally, jurists provide a definition of the *ʿawrah* when

The Qur'ān commands Muslim men and women to lower their gaze, be modest, and not to flash their adornments (*zīnah*) except when

---

addressing how a Muslim should dress when making obligatory prayers (*ṣalāt*). Interestingly, the earliest traditions on the subject do not reflect a specific discussion on *'awrah.* Rather, they address different dress styles and, at least in the case of women, draw distinctions between certain classes of women. For instance, early works relate traditions of the Prophet praying while wrapped in a single *thawb* or garment that draped over his shoulders and covered his front and back (*layukhālifu bayna ṭarafayhi 'alā 'ātiqihi*). Abū Bakr 'Abd al-Razzāq b. Hammām al-Ṣan'ānī, *al-Muṣannaf,* ed. Ḥabīb al-Raḥmān al-A'ẓamī, 2nd ed. (Beirut: al-Maktab al-Islāmī, 1983), 1:350, 353. See also, Abū Bakr 'Abd Allāh b. Muḥammad Ibn Abī Shaybah, *al-Kitāb al-Muṣannaf fī al-Aḥādīth wa al-Āthār,* ed. Muḥammad 'Abd al-Salām Shāhīn (Beirut: Dār al-Kutub al-'Ilmiyyah, 1995), 1:275-277. Others suggest that it is better to pray with two garments, namely one wrapped around the waist (*izār*) and another draped around the shoulders (*ridā'*). Al-Ṣan'ānī, *al-Muṣannaf,* 1:349, 353-354, 356; Ibn Abī Shaybah, *al-Kitāb al-Muṣannaf,* 1:275-276. See also al-Ramlī, *Nihāyat al-Muḥtāj*(1992), 2:13; al-Bahūtī, *Kashshāf al-Qinā',* 1:316-317. However, the conflict over men's proper attire arises when one's garment is too small. One set of traditions hold that if a man's garment is large enough, he should drape it over himself (*mutawashshiḥ*), but if it is small, he should pray with the garment wrapped around his waist (*muttazir* or *yukhālifu bayna ṭarafayhi*). Al-Ṣan'ānī, *al-Muṣannaf,* 1:352, 353; Ibn Abī Shaybah, *Kitāb al-Muṣannaf,* 1:275, 276, 277. See also Shihāb al-Dīn Abū al-'Abbās Aḥmad b. Idrīs al-Qarāfī, *al-Dhakhīrah,* ed. Sa'īd A'rāb (Beirut: Dār al-Gharb al-Islāmī, 1994), 2:112; Ibn Mufliḥ, *al-Mubdi,'* 1:64. Others argued that he can pray with a single garment as long as part of it can be draped over his shoulder. Al-Ṣan'ānī, *al-Muṣannaf,* 1:353; Ibn Abī Shaybah, *Kitāb al-Muṣannaf,* 1:278. See also al-Bahūtī, *Kashshāf al-Qinā',* 1:318; Muḥammad Amīn Ibn 'Ābidīn, *Ḥāshiyat Radd al-Muḥtār,* 2nd ed. (Cairo: Muṣṭafā al-Bābī al-Ḥalabī, 1966), 1:404. According to the Companion Ibn Mas'ūd, if one cannot find sufficient material, then it is permissible to pray with only one garment. However, if sufficient material is available, then he should pray with two. However, others such as 'Umar b. al-Khaṭṭāb disagreed, and held that only one garment wrapped around the waist was sufficient for prayers. Al-Ṣan'ānī, *al-Muṣannaf,* 1:356; Ibn Abī Shaybah, *Kitāb al-Muṣannaf,* 1:278-279. See also, Ibn Rushd, *Bidāyat al-Mujtahid.* 1:159. Incidentally, one report suggests that wearing a garment around the waist was endorsed partly to distinguish the Muslims from the Jews. Al-Ṣan'ānī, *al-Muṣannaf,* 1:352; Ibn Abī Shaybah, *Kitāb al-Muṣannaf,* 1:278. Notably, the term *'awrah* does not appear in this discussion. Likewise, it is not used in the early discussion on women's attire in prayer. The traditions instead address the kinds of clothing a woman must wear in prayer, and distinguishes between the appropriate attire for free and slave women. Specifically, al-Ṣan'ānī relates traditions on two issues. The first issue concerns what a free woman must wear when praying. Generally, the items for consideration are a *khimār, jilbāb, dir' sābigh,* and *milḥaf.* Al-Ṣan'ānī, *al-Muṣannaf,* 3:128-129, 131, 135; Ibn Abī Shaybah, *al-Muṣannaf,* 2:36-37. See also al-Māwardī, *al-Ḥāwī al-Kabīr,* 2:169; Ibn Mufliḥ, *al-Mubdi',* 1:366; al-Ramlī,

appropriate, such as with husbands or wives.[23] Early Islamic reports do not tie the issue of what eventually becomes known as the *ḥijāb* to the problem of *fitnah*, but they do tie it to social status and the physical safety of women. Because of these reports, Muslim jurists distinguished between the *ʿawrah* of free women and of slave girls—according to most jurists, free women are to cover all of their body except for the hands and face, and slave girls do not have to cover their hair, arms, and calves.

The issue of *ʿawrah* is complex partly because it is extremely difficult to retrace and reclaim the historical process that produced the

---

Nihāyat al-Muḥtāj (1992), 2:13-14; al-Bahūtī, *Kashshāf al-Qināʿ*, 1:318; Ibn Ḥazm, *al-Muḥallā*, 2: 2:249-250. The second issues concerns whether a slave woman must also wear a *khimār* for prayer. The *khimār* is generally a garment that covers a woman's head. Abū al-Faḍl Jamāl al-Dīn Muḥammad b. Makram Ibn Manẓūr, *Lisān al-ʿArab* (Beirut: Dār Ṣādr, n.d.),4:257; Ibn Mufliḥ, *al-Mubdiʿ*, 1:366; al-Bahūtī, *Kashshāf al-Qināʿ*, 1:318. The meaning of *dirʿ sābigh* generally suggests some type of loose-fitting garment that extends to one's feet. The relevant distinction is that a *dirʿ* does not necessarily cover a woman's head. Ibn Manẓūr, *Lisān al-ʿArab*, 8:81-82; Ibn Mufliḥ, *al-Mubdiʿ*, 1:366; E.W. Lane, *Arabic-English Lexicon* (Cambridge, England: Islamic Texts Society, 1984), 1:871-872. *Jilbāb* refers to a garment that is larger than a *khimār* and generally covers a woman's head and chest area, but may also cover her entire body. In some cases, it is used as a synonym for *khimār*, and in others for an *izār*. Ibn Manẓūr, *Lisān al-ʿArab*, 1:272-273. And a *milḥaf* is a blanket (*dithār*) or cover which is wrapped over other clothes. Ibn Manẓūr, *Lisān al-ʿArab*, 9:314. Al-Ṣanʿānī reports that the Prophet said that menstruating free women must wear a *khimār*, otherwise their prayer will not be accepted. Al-Ṣanʿānī, *al-Muṣannaf*, 3:130, 131; Ibn Abī Shaybah, *Kitāb al-Muṣannaf*, 2:39-40. The reference to menstruation is generally regarded as a reference to adulthood or the age of majority. Al-Marghīnānī, *al-Hidāyah*, 1:43. Women who are not adults are not necessarily subject to this requirement. Al-Ṣanʿānī, *al-Muṣannaf*, 3:132. In another tradition, a woman is supposed to wear a *khimār*, a *dirʿ*, and an *izār*, although there are some countervailing traditions against this position. Ibn Mufliḥ, *al-Mubdiʿ*, 1:366. Some traditions suggest that an acceptable *dirʿ* must be long and loose enough to cover the appearance of a woman's feet, although without a *khimār*, it is insufficient. Al-Ṣanʿānī, *al-Muṣannaf*, 3:128; Ibn Abī Shaybah, *Kitāb al-Muṣannaf*, 2:36. One tradition relates that ʿĀʾishah was seen wearing during prayer a garment around her waist (*muʾtazirah*), a *dirʿ*, and a thick *khimār*. Al-Ṣanʿānī, *al-Muṣannaf*, 129. On the other hand, Umm Ḥabībah, a wife of the Prophet, is reported to have worn a *dirʿ*, and an *izār* that was large enough to drape around her and reach the ground. Notably, she did not wear a *khimār*. Ibid. Yet another tradition relates that the Prophet's wives Maymūna and Umm Salmah would wear a *khimār* and a *dirʿ sābigh*. Ibn Abī Shaybah, *Kitāb al-Muṣannaf*, 2:36.

[23] Qurʾān, 24:30-1; 24:60.

determinations as to *'awrah*. The dominant juristic schools of thought argued that the *'awrah* of men is what is between the knee and navel. A man ought to cover what is between the knee and navel inside and outside of prayer. A minority view, however, argued that the *'awrah* of men is limited to the groin and buttocks only; the thighs are not *'awrah*. The *'awrah* of women was a more complex matter. As noted, the majority argued that all of a woman's body except the hands and face is *'awrah*. Abū Ḥanifa held that the feet are not *'awrah*, and some argued that half the arm up to the elbow, or the full arm, is not an *'awrah*. A minority view held that even the face and hands are *'awrah* and, therefore, must be covered as well. An early minority view held that the hair and calves are not *'awrah*. In addition, some argued that women must cover their hair at prayer, but not outside of prayer. Importantly, the jurists disagreed on whether the covering of the *'awrah* is a condition precedent for the validity of prayer. The majority held that covering the *'awrah* is a *farḍ* (basic and necessary requirement), so that the failure to cover the *'awrah* would invalidate a person's prayers. The minority view (mostly, but not exclusively, Mālikī jurists) held that covering the *'awrah* is not a condition precedent for prayer—accordingly, this school argued that covering the *'awrah* is among the *sunan* of prayer (the recommended acts in prayer), and that the failure to cover the *'awrah* would not void a person's prayers. A large number of Ḥanafī jurists argued that as long as three-fourths of the body is covered, the prayer is valid. Furthermore, the vast majority of jurists held that the *'awrah* of a slave girl, or even a female servant girl, is different. Some jurists argued that the *'awrah* of such a woman is between the knee and navel—the same as a man. The other jurists held that the *'awrah* of such a woman is from the beginning of the chest area to the knees and down to the elbows. Therefore, the majority agreed that a slave girl or servant girl may pray with her hair exposed. A minority view argued that slave girls should cover their hair in prayer, but do not have to do so outside of prayer.[24]

[24] See, on the law of *'awrah*: Abū Bakr 'Abd al-Razzāq al-Ṣan'ānī, *al-Muṣannaf*, ed. Ḥabīb al-Raḥmān al-A'ẓamī (Beirut: al-Maktab al-Islāmī, 1983), 3:128-136 (documents some of the early opinions). *For Mālikī school,* see Ibn Rushd (II), *Bidāyat al-Mujtahid,* 1:156-158; Abū al-Walīd Muḥammad b. Aḥmad Ibn Rushd (I), *al-Muqaddimāt al-Mumahhidāt*, ed. Muḥammad Ḥajjī (Beirut: Dār al-Gharb

Reportedly, the early jurists Dāwūd b. ʿAlī and Jarīr al-Ṭabarī, the founder of a now extinct school of jurisprudence, held that the *ʿawrah* of men and women, slave or otherwise, is the same.[25] In addition, the Ẓahirī jurist Ibn Ḥazm unequivocally rejected the authenticity of the traditions that asserted that the *ḥijāb* Qurʾānic verses were revealed to distinguish between free and slave women. According to Ibn Ḥazm, these traditions are outright lies. His proffered reasons for rejecting the authenticity of the reports are morally based. He argued that it is entirely unbelievable that God would seek to protect the Muslim free women of Medina from molestation while leaving slave girls to suffer. Simply, this would be wrong. Consequently, Ibn Ḥazm denies that there could be any distinction between the *ʿawrah* of slave girls and of free women. All women, slaves or not, have the same *ʿawrah*.[26]

---

al-Islāmī, 1988), 1:183-185; Saḥnūn b. Saʿīd, *al-Mudawwana al-Kubrā* (Beirut: Dār Ṣādir, n.d.), 1:94; Abū ʿAbd Allāh Muḥammad b. Muḥammad b. ʿAbd al-Raḥmān al-Maghribī al-Raʿīnī al-Ḥaṭṭāb , *Mawāhib al-Jalīl li Sharḥ Mukhtaṣar Khalīl* (Beirut: Dār al-Kutub al-ʿIlmiyyah, 1995), 2:177-187; Shihāb al-Dīn Abū al-ʿAbbās al-Qarāfī, *al-Dhakhīrah*, ed. Saʿīd Aʿrāb (Beirut: Dār al-Gharb al-Islāmī, 1994), 2:101-105. *For Shāfiʿī school,* see Abū ʿAbd Allāh Muḥammad b. Idrīs al-Shāfiʿī, *al-Umm* (Beirut: Dār al-Fikr, n.d.), 1:109; Shams al-Dīn Muḥammad al-Ramlī, *Nihāyat al-Muḥtāj ilā Sharḥ al-Minhāj fī Fiqh ʿalā Madhhab al-Imām al-Shāfiʿī* (Beirut: Dār Iḥyāʾ al-Turāth al-ʿArabī, 1992), 2:7-8, 13; Abū al-Ḥasan ʿAlī b. Muḥammad b. Ḥabīb al-Māwardī, *al-Ḥāwī al-Kabīr fī Fiqh Madhhab al-Imām al-Shāfiʿī*, eds. ʿAlī Muḥammad Muʿawwaḍ and ʿĀdil Aḥmad ʿAbd al-Mawjūd (Beirut: Dār al-Kutub al-ʿIlmiyyah, 1994), 2:165-171. *For the Ḥanafī school,* see Zayn al-ʿĀbidīn b. Ibrāhīm Ibn Nujaym, *al-Baḥr al-Rāʾiq Sharḥ Kanz al-Daqāʾiq*, ed. Zakariyyā ʿUmayrāt (Beirut: Dār al-Kutub al-ʿIlmiyyah, 1997), 1:467, 469-476; Ibn ʿĀbidīn, *Ḥāshiyat Radd al-Muḥtār,* 1:405; Abū Bakr b. Masʿūd al-Kāsānī, *Badāʾiʿ al-Ṣanāʾiʿ fī Tartīb al-Sharāʾiʿ*, eds. ʿAlī Muḥammad Muʿawwaḍ and ʿĀdil ʿAbd al-Mawjūd (Beirut: Dār al-Kutub al-ʿIlmiyyah, 1997), 543-546. *For the Ḥanbalī school,* see Ibn Qudāmah, *al-Mughnī,* 1:601; Abū Isḥāq Burhān al-Dīn Ibn Mufliḥ, *al-Mubdiʿ fī Sharḥ al-Muqniʿ*, ed. ʿAlī ʿAbd Allāh Āl Thānī (Beirut: al-Maktab al-Islāmī, 1974), 1:361-367; Manṣūr b. Yūnus al-Bahūtī, *Kashshāf al-Qināʿ ʿan Matn al-Iqnāʿ*, ed. Abū ʿAbd Allāh Ismāʿīl (Beirut: Dār al-Kutub al-ʿIlmiyyah, 1997), 1:315-317. *For the Jaʿfarī school,* see Abū Jaʿfar Muḥammad b. al-Ḥasan b. ʿAlī al-Ṭūsī, *al-Mabsūṭ fī Fiqh al-Imāmiyyah* (Tehran: al-Maṭbaʿah al-Ḥaydariyyah, 1387 AH), 1:87-88.

[25] See al-Māwardī, *al-Ḥāwī al-Kabīr,* 2:167. Also see Ibn al-Athīr al-Jazrī, *al-Nihāyah fī Gharīb al-Ḥadīth wa al-Athar,* 3:288.

[26] Abū Muḥammad ʿAlī b. Aḥmad b. Saʿīd b. Ḥazm, *al-Muḥallā bi al-Āthār,* ed. ʿAbd al-Ghaffār al-Bandārī (Beirut: al-Kutub al-ʿIlmiyyah, n.d.), 2:239.

An additional difficulty with *'awrah* reports and determinations is that a portion of them is virulently hostile, even hateful, towards women as a gender. For instance, it is transmitted that 'Abd Allāh b. 'Umar narrated that the Prophet said, "[The whole of] a woman is an *'awrah* and so if she goes out, the devil makes her the source of seduction."[27]. Other reports take this a step further by drawing a connection between women and the devil. For example, a tradition attributed to the Prophet, proclaims, "A woman comes in the image of a devil, and leaves in the image of a devil." The rest of the tradition goes on to say that if a man is aroused by a foreign woman, he should satisfy his desire lawfully with his wife.[28] In yet another tradition, the Prophet reportedly says, "Women are the snares of the devil."[29] Perhaps not surprisingly, this uncharitable view of women, and their role, extends to their fate in the Hereafter. Therefore, we find a number of traditions stating that women will comprise the majority of the population of Hellfire.[30] This

[27] Al-Mubārakfūrī, *Tuḥfat al-Aḥwadhī*, 4:283.

[28] Shams al-Dīn Abī 'Abd Allāh Muḥammad b. Abī Bakr Ibn Qayyim al-Jawziyyah, *'Awn al-Ma'būd Sharḥ Sunan Abī Dāwūd*, ed. 'Abd al-Raḥmān Muḥammad 'Uthmān. 2nd ed. (Medina: al-Maktabah al-Salafiyyah, 1968/1969)., 6:187-188; al-Mubārakfūrī, *Tuḥfat al-Aḥwadhī*, 4:280-281.

[29] Al-Jirāḥī, *Kashf al-Khafā'* (1968), 315-316; 'Abd al-Raḥmān b. 'Alī b. Muḥammad b. 'Umar al-Shaybānī, *Kitāb Tamyīz al-Ṭayyib min al-Khabīth fī mā yadūr 'alā Alsinat al-Nās min al-Ḥadīth* (Beirut: Dār al-Kitāb al-'Arabī, n.d.), 183. Another tradition asserts: " If not for women, God would have been [faithfully] served on this earth." Although this version has been declared unauthentic by many jurists, it is proof of an atmosphere in which anti-women circulations were common. See al-Jurjānī, *al-Kāmil fī al-Ḍu'afā'*, 6:495; Ibn al-Jawzī, *al-Mawḍū'āt*, 2:162. In another often quoted tradition, the Prophet reportedly said, "I have not left in my people a *fitnah* more harmful to men than women." Ibn Ḥajar al-'Asqalānī, *Fatḥ al-Bārī* (n.d.), 9:137; al-Mubārakfūrī, *Tuḥfat al-Aḥwadhī*, 8:53; al-Nawawī, *Sharḥ Ṣaḥīḥ Muslim* (1996), 17/18:57; Muḥammad b. Aḥmad b. Jār Allāh al-Ṣa'adī al-Yamānī, *al-Nawāfiḥ al-'Aṭirah fī al-Aḥādīth al-Mushtahirah*, ed. Muḥammad 'Abd al-Qādir 'Aṭā (Beirut: Mu'assasat al-Kutub al-Thaqāfiyyah, 1992), 306; al-Jirāḥī, *Kashf al-Khafā'* (1968), 183; Muḥammad 'Abd al-Raḥmān al-Sakhāwī, *al-Maqāṣid al-Ḥasanah fī Bayān Kathīr min al-Aḥādīth al-Mushtahirah 'alā al-Alsinah*, ed. Muḥammad 'Uthmān al-Khasht. 2nd ed. (Beirut: Dār al-Kitāb al-'Arabī, 1994) 428; al-Shaybānī, *Kitāb Taymīz al-Ṭayyib*, 144.

[30] Ibn Ḥajar al-'Asqalānī, *Fatḥ al-Bārī* (n.d.), 1:483; Abū Zakariyyā al-Nawawī, *Sharḥ Ṣaḥīḥ Muslim al-Musammā al-Minhāj Sharḥ Ṣaḥīḥ Muslim b.´ajjāj* (Beirut: Dār al-Ma'rifah, 1996), 1/2: 253-256; al-Mubārakfūrī, *Tuḥfat al-Aḥwadhī*, 7:300-

trend of hostility towards the role that women play in society culminates in traditions that relate the *'awrah* to the grave. In these traditions, women are portrayed as an *'awrah* that must, in one way or another, be concealed. However, clothing is insufficient to cover a woman's *'awrah*; rather, a whole institution is needed. The institutions that can perform that role are marriage and death. In a tradition transmitted through Ibn 'Abbās, the Prophet reportedly says, "A woman has ten *'awras*; when she marries, her husband covers one of her *'awras*, and when she dies, the grave covers the rest." A different version, also transmitted through Ibn 'Abbās, states that a woman has two covers of modesty (*sitrān*), marriage and the grave.[31] The logical conclusion to be drawn from this tradition is that for a woman to be thoroughly modest, she ought to be married, or dead and buried. Not surprisingly, Abū Ḥāmid al-Ghazālī relies on these traditions in arguing that a married woman ought to remain in the depths of her home, not leave her house

301; Ibn Qayyim al-Jawziyyah, *'Awn al-Ma'būd*, 12:438-439; al-Bayhaqī, *Kitāb al-Sunan al-Kubrā*, 7:294; Abū Ḥāmid al-Ghazālī, *Iḥyā'*, 2:56. In a version of this report, the Prophet was praying with his congregation when the Sun eclipsed. Shortly afterwards, the Prophet was overtaken by tremors and nearly collapsed. The Prophet then informs the congregation that he just saw Hell and that women formed most of its population. When asked about the reason for this, the Prophet responds that it is because women are ungrateful to their husbands. Ibn Ḥajar al-'Asqalānī, *Fatḥ al-Bārī* (n.d.), 9:298. In a version transmitted by Abū Hurayrah states that the Prophet passed by a group of women when he addressed them. The Prophet proclaimed, 'O' women! Increase your prayers, and the give more alms for I have seen that women are the majority of the inhabitants of Hell.' A wise woman asked, 'Why are we [women] the majority of the inhabitants of Hell, O' Prophet of God?' The Prophet responded, 'Because you frequently slander and curse, and you are ungrateful to your companions. I have not seen anyone more deficient in intellect and religion, who is able to prevail (mislead) the wise, than you.' So, they (the women) asked, 'And, what is [our] deficiency in intellect and religion?' The Prophet said, '[Your] deficiency in intellect is in the fact that the testimony of a man is worth [the testimony] of two women, and your deficiency in religion is that you spend days without fasting or praying (because of the menstrual cycle). In a version of this genre of traditions, Aḥmad b. Ḥanbal transmitted through Abū Umāmah that the Prophet said, "I have seen Heaven, and a few of its inhabitants are women." The Prophet was asked, "And, where are the women?" The Prophet said, "They have become pre-occupied with gold and cloth (i.e. material things)." This tradition is reported through a weak chain of transmission.

[31] These traditions are considered to be of weak transmission. See Abū Ḥāmid al-Ghazālī, *Iḥyā'*, 2:58.

without permission, and avoid talking to the neighbors. If she goes out, she should walk in the least crowded places and avoid speaking to anyone; she should busy herself with pleasing her husband, and little else; and she should refrain from playing any public role.[32] Effectively, al-Ghazālī projects the grave unto life—a woman lives in this life as if existing in a grave. This existence is mandated by the dictates of modesty, and when she dies, the grave will continue guarding this modesty. A woman's *ʿawrah* is properly guarded either by a grave-like existence on this earth, or an actual grave in the earth. These traditions mandate death for women inside and outside the grave. The issue here is not whether these traditions are represented by strong chains of transmission—I have little doubt that they are fabrications. Rather, the issue is that they are informative as to the historical milieu and negotiative dynamics that surrounded the early debates on *ʿawrah*. *ʿAwrah* debates and determinations were not the product of a value-neutral or objective social process. They were the product of a vibrant and contentious debate in early Islam about the role and nature of women. *ʿAwrah* determinations were the product of a historical context that must be carefully, and bravely, investigated. In short, traditions, debates, and determinations regarding the *ʿawrah* are not simply expressions of the Divine Will, but are articulations of social beliefs, contentions, and anxieties about the definition of womanhood in early Muslim society.

These various arguments and determinations indicate that the story of the *ʿawrah* in Islamic law is not simple and straightforward.[33] There is a complex historical process and a nuanced story that entirely

[32] Abū Ḥāmid al-Ghazālī, *Iḥyāʾ*, 2:59.

[33] Some of the late jurists argued that if a slave girl will cause a *fitnah*, she must cover her breasts or hair. Al-Ḥaṭṭāb relates that although a slave woman's *ʿawrah* is the same as a man's, some have said that it is reprehensible for someone who is not her owner to view what is under her garments, or to view her breasts, chest, or whatever else "leads to *fitnah*" (*wa mā yadʿū al-fitnah minhā*). Consequently, despite having the same *ʿawrah* as men, it is preferred that she bare her head but cover her body. Al-Ḥattāb, *Mawāhib al-Jalīl*, 2:180, 184. See also al-Qarāfī, *al-Dhakhīrah*, 2:103-104. Al-Bahūtī relates views suggesting that as a matter of caution (*iḥtiyāṭ*), it is preferrable that the slave girl cover herself in the same fashion as an adult free woman, including covering her head during prayer. Al-Bahūtī, *Kashshāf al-Qināʿ*, 1:316. Ibn ʿĀbidīn also argues that most of the scholars of the Ḥanafī school do not permit a slave woman to have her breasts, chest, or back exposed; however, it is said

escapes us today. Notably, some of the early sources such as the *Muwaṭṭa'* of Mālik, the *Muṣannaf* of ʿAbd al-Razzāq, and the *Muṣannaf* of Ibn Abī Shaybah express views that a few centuries later seem to have completely vanished or to have lost their significance or urgency.[34] Being mindful of these various ambiguities and complexities leads me to articulate six material points that, I believe, warrant careful examination in trying to analyze the laws of *ʿawrah*, and that largely have been ignored in contemporary discussions on the *ḥijāb*. These points also invite us to re-examine the relationship between *ʿawrah* and *fitnah*, and to question the notion that the *ʿawrah* is covered primarily to fend off sexual seduction. These six points partly summarize the determinations discussed above, but they also identify new elements that might contribute to a more meaningful discourse on the law of *ʿawrah* in Islam. The six points are the following:

> One, early jurists disagreed on the meaning of *zīnah* (adornments) that women are commanded to cover. Some jurists argued that it is all of the body including the hair and face except for one eye. The majority argued that women must cover their full body except for the face and hands. Some jurists held that women may expose their feet and their arms up to the elbow. Importantly, someone such as Saʿīd b. Jubayr asserted that revealing the hair is reprehensible, but also stated that the Qur'ānic verses did not explicitly say anything about women's hair.[35]
>
> Two, the jurists frequently repeat that the veiling verse was revealed in response to a very specific situation. As explained above, corrupt young men would harass and, at times, assault

---

that a slave woman's chest is part of her *ʿawrah* only in prayer but not otherwise. Nevertheless, Ibn ʿĀbidīn finds this latter view unconvincing. Ibn ʿĀbidīn, *Hāshiyat Radd* (1966), 1:405. See also Ibn Nujaym, *al-Baḥr al-Rā'iq*, 1:474; al-Marghīnānī, *al-Hidāyah*, 1:44.

34 Most of these reports related to the covering of the hair being a *Sunnah* in prayer, or dealt with the insufficiency of clothing in general. There are numerous early reports indicating that finding sufficient amount of fabric to cover the body was a serious problem in early Islam. Therefore, there are reports about men not finding enough clothing to cover the lower half of their bodies, or of women not finding more than a single garment that is tied to their bodies with a rope, or of men and women wearing garments with large rips or holes.

35 Abū Bakr Aḥmad b. ʿAlī al-Razī al-Jaṣṣāṣ, *Aḥkām al-Qur'ān* (Beirut: Dār al-Kutub al-ʿIlmiyyah, 1994), 3:410.

women at night as these women headed to the wild to relieve themselves. Apparently, when confronted, these men would claim that they did not realize that these women were Muslim women. Rather, they claimed that they thought that these were non-Muslim slave girls, and, therefore, not under the protection of the Muslim community. In Medinan society, any individual was under the protection of either a clan or, if the individual was Muslim, he or she would be under the protection of Muslims. Therefore, these verses seem to address a very specific, and even peculiar, historical social dynamic. The interaction between the text and the text's social context is not easily transferable or projectable to other contexts.

Three, as noted above, Muslim jurists consistently argued that the laws mandating the covering of the full body did not apply to slave girls. In fact, it is reported that ʿUmar b. al-Khaṭṭāb prohibited slave girls from imitating free women by covering their hair. Apparently, Muslim jurists channelled the historical context of the verses into legal determinations that promulgated a particular social stratification. However, it is not clear whether the social stratification addressed by the Qur'ān are the same as the stratification endorsed by the jurists.

Four, the jurists often argued that what could be lawfully exposed in a woman's body was what would ordinarily appear, according to custom (*ʿādah*), nature (*jibillah*), and necessity (*ḍarūrah*). Relying on this, they argued that slave girls do not need to cover their hair, face, or arms because they live an active economic life that requires mobility, and because by nature and custom, slave girls do not ordinarily cover these parts of their bodies. This makes the focal point of the law custom and functionality. Arguably, however, women in the modern age live an economically active life that requires mobility and, arguably, custom varies with time and place.[36] In other words, if the rules prescribing veiling were mandated to deal with a specific type of harm, and slave girls were exempted because of the nature of their social role and function, arguably, this means that the rules of veiling are contingent and contextual in nature.

Five, several reports state that women in Medina, Muslim or non-Muslim, normally would wear long head-covers—the cloth

[36] For instance, Khamīs b. Saʿīd al-Shaqaṣī al-Rustāqī, *Manhaj al-Ṭālibīn wa Balāgh al-Rāghibīn* (Oman: Wizārat al-Turāth al-Qawmī wa Thaqāfī, n.d.), 8:21, 26, argues that every place and time has its own laws. He states that in some places it is acceptable for women to reveal their hair, while in Oman it is considered ugly (*qabīḥ*). He concludes by stating that whatever Muslims see as ugly is, in fact, ugly.

usually would be thrown behind ears and shoulders. Women would also wear vests open in the front, leaving their chests exposed. Reportedly, the practice of exposing the breasts was common until late into Islam. Several early authorities state that the Qur'ānic verse primarily sought to have women cover their chests up to the beginning of the cleavage area.

Six, there is a sharp disjunction between the veiling verses and the notion of seduction. Seduction could be caused by slave girls, or could be between woman and man, woman and woman, or man and man.[37] A man could be seduced by a slave girl, and a woman could be seduced by a good looking man, yet neither slave girls nor men are required to cover their hair or faces. Does the fact that a man might be sexually enticing to women affect the obligations of concealment as to this man?[38]

These six points are neither exhaustive nor thorough, and they are not intended to be a full discussion of the issue of *'awrah* or *ḥijāb*. Furthermore, these six points do not lead to any firm conclusions about the juristic place of the *ḥijāb* in Islam. Considering the historical

[37] Ibn Taymiyyah is one of the few jurists who addressed the issue of homosexual attractions in the context of veiling. See the discussion in Taqī al-Dīn Ibn Taymiyyah, *al-Tafsīr al-Kabīr*, ed. 'Abd al-Raḥmān 'Umīrah (Beirut: Dār al-Kutub al-'Ilmiyyah, n.d.), 5:346-353.

[38] For the six points above, see Abū Ja'far Muḥammad b. Jarīr al-Ṭabarī, *Jāmi' al-Bayān fī Tafsīr al-Qur'ān* (Beirut: Dār al-Ma'rifah, 1989), 18:93-95, 22:33-34 (mentions a variety of early opinions including the up-to-the-elbow and the beginning-of-cleavage-area determinations; also mentions the distinction between free and slave girls; mentions the historical practice); Abū al-Barakāt 'Abd Allāh b. Maḥmūd al-Nasafī (d. 710/1310-1311), *Tafsīr al-Nasafī* (Cairo: Dār Iḥyā' al-Kutub al-'Arabiyyah, n.d.), 3:140, 313, (mentions *'ādah, jibillah*, and *ḥājah*; women need to reveal their faces, hands, and feet by custom, nature, and need; mentions the distinction applicable to slave girls; mentions the historical practice); al-Jaṣṣāṣ, *Aḥkām*, 3:409-410, 486, mentions that slave girls do not have to cover their hair; mentions the historical practice); 'Imād al-Dīn b. Muḥammad al-Kiyyā al-Harrāsī (d. 504/1110), *Aḥkām al-Qur'ān*, ed. Mūsā Muḥammad 'Alī and 'Izzat 'Alī 'Īd 'Aṭiyyah (Cairo: Dār al-Kutub al-Ḥadītha, 1974), 4:288, 354 (notes that slave girls do not have to cover their faces or hair); Abū Bakr Muḥammad b. 'Abd Allāh Ibn al-'Arabī (d. 543/1148), *Aḥkām al-Qur'ān*, ed. 'Alī Muḥammad al-Bijāwī (Beirut: Dār al-Ma'rifah, n.d.), 3:1368-78, 1586-87 (mentions a variety of details to adornments; discusses the rule as to slave girls); al-Qurṭubī (d. 671/1273), *al-Jāmi'*, 12:152-153, 157; 14:156-157 (mentions that the verse was revealed to address the harassment of women, and to differentiate slave girls from Muslim women; notes the opinion that held that the verse called for the covering of the bosom area); 'Imād al-Dīn Abī

context of the *ʿawrah* and *fitnah* determinations in pre-modern Islam, the six points do suggest, however, that the contemporary debates on these issues are somewhat anachronistic. Most importantly, the historical setting and the complexity of the early context do suggest that the inquiries into the juristic basis of the *ḥijāb* cannot be considered heretical. In this sense, labelling the *ḥijāb* as a part of the *uṣūl*, and using that label as an excuse to end the discussion on this matter, is obscenely despotic. It might very well be that this is yet another legal issue where the law of God is pursuant to the convictions of the pious adherent.

In order to properly evaluate the interpretive enterprise that generated the juristic determinations relevant to women and their role in society, it is essential to evaluate the history of gender dynamics in various episodes of Islam. Focusing on gender dynamics in history will permit

---

al-Fidāʾ Ismāʿīl b. Kathīr (d. 774/1372-1373), *Mukhtaṣar Tafsīr Ibn Kathīr*, ed. Muḥammad ʿAlī al-Ṣābūnī (Beirut: Dār al-Qurʿān al-Karīm, 1981), 2:600; 3:114-115, (mentions determinations as to the bosom; also notes that free Muslim women must cover their faces); Muḥammad b. Yūsuf Abū Ḥayyān al-Andalusī, *Tafsīr al-Baḥr al-Muḥīṭ*, eds. ʿĀdil ʿAbd al-Mawjūd and ʿAlī Muḥammad Muʿawwaḍ (Beirut: Dār al-Kutub al-ʿIlmiyyah, 1993), 6:412; 7:240-241 (mentions custom, nature, necessity; mentions the historical practice as to revealing the bosom; mentions the distinction as to slave girls); Abū al-Qāsim Jārr Allāh Maḥmūd b. ʿUmar al-Zamakhsharī (d. 538/1144), *al-Kashshāf ʿan Ḥaqāʾiq al-Tanzīl wa ʿUyūn al-Aqāwīl fī Wujūh al-Taʾwīl* (Beirut: Dār al-Fikr, n.d.), 3:60-62, 274 (mentions the historical practice, distinction as to slave girls, the rules as to functionality and custom, mentions that covering ought not cause hardship); Abū al-Faraj Jamāl al-Dīn b. al-Jawzī, *Zād al-Masīr fī ʿIlm al-Tafsīr*, ed. Aḥmad Shams al-Dīn (Beirut: Dār al-Kutub al-ʿIlmiyyah, 1994), 5:377-378; 6:224 (mentions *mashaqqah*—hardship); Abū al-Ḥasan ʿAlī b. Muḥammad b. Ḥabīb al-Māwardī (d. 450/1058), *al-Nukat wa al-ʿUyūn*, ed. al-Sayyid b. ʿAbd al-Maqṣūd b. ʿAbd al-Raḥīm (Beirut: Dār al-Kutub al-ʿIlmiyyah, 1992), 4:90-93, 424-425, (notes the opinion that the purpose of revelation was to instruct women to cover their bosoms; mentions the differentiation as to slave girls); Muḥammad al-Amīn b. Muḥammad al-Mukhtār al-Jakanī al-Shinqīṭī (d. 1363/1944), *Aḍwāʾ al-Bayān fī Īḍāḥ al-Qurʾān bi al-Qurʾān* (Beirut: ʿĀlam al-Kutub, n.d.), 6:192-203, 586-600 (mentions a variety of positions; mentions determinations as to revealing the arm up to the elbow and the view that the point is to cover the bosom; mentions the historical practice and differentiation as to slave girls; author supports covering the face); Ibn Taymiyyah, *al-Tafsīr*, 6:23, (notes that the law of veiling does not apply to slave girls); Fakhr al-Dīn Muḥammad al-Tamīmī al-Bakrī al-Rāzī, *al-Tafsīr al-Kabīr (a.k.a Mafātīḥ al-Ghayb)* (Beirut: Dār al-Kutub al-ʿIlmiyyah, 1990), 23:176-179; 25:198-199, (mentions *al-ʿādah al-jāriyah* [the habitual custom] and functionality as the focal issues in determining what women ought to cover; mentions the historical practice and the distinction as to slave girls);

us to understand the motivations behind determinations related to gender roles, and the way these determinations were understood and practiced. For instance, there is evidence that as late as the 3rd/9th century, the meaning and role of the veil was still contested in Islam. In wonderfully eloquent epistles, the Muʿtazilī scholar al-Jāḥiẓ (d. 255/869) launches an attack against men who he accuses of attempting to seclude and repress women. Al-Jāḥiẓ claims that pre-Islamic Arabia did not seclude women from men, and that the practice of seclusion, in general, was unknown until the Qur'ān commanded the wives of the Prophet, in particular, to adopt the *ḥijāb*.[39] Al-Jāḥiẓ criticizes the zealots who forbid what God has permitted, therefore implying that the rule of seclusion should have been applied only to the wives of the Prophet. Al-Jāḥiẓ makes this point explicit by arguing that early Islamic authorities such as

Abū Muḥammad ʿAbd al-Ḥaqq b. Ghālib b. ʿAṭiyyah al-Andalusī (d. 542/1148), *al-Muḥarrar al-Wajīz fī Tafsīr al-Kitāb al-ʿAzīz*, ed. ʿAbd al-Salām ʿAbd al-Shāfī (Beirut: Dār al-Kutub al-ʿIlmiyyah, 1993), 4:178, 399 (mentions the determinations as to the bosom and arm up to the elbow; mentions the rule of functionality and custom; mentions the historical practice and the distinction as to slave girls); Jalāl al-Dīn al-Suyūṭī (d. 911/1505), *al-Durr al-Manthūr fī al-Tafsīr bi al-Ma'thūr* (Cairo: Maṭbaʿat al-Anwār al-Muḥammadiyyah, n.d.), 5:45-46, 239-241 (mentions the determinations as to the arm up to the elbow and the bosom; notes the discussion regarding the beginning of the cleavage area; mentions the historical practice and the distinction as to slave girls); Ismāʿīl Ḥaqqī al-Burūsī, *Tanwīr al-Adhhān min Tafsīr Rūḥ al-Bayān*, ed. Muḥammad ʿAlī al-Ṣābūnī (Damascus: Dār al-Qalam, 1989), 3:57-59, 254-255, (mentions the determinations as to the arm up to the elbow and the bosom; mentions the historical practice and distinction as to slave girls); Abū Ḥafṣ ʿUmar b. ʿAlī Ibn ʿĀdil al-Dimashqī, *al-Lubāb fī ʿUlūm al-Kitāb*, eds. ʿĀdil Aḥmad ʿAbd al-Mawjūd and ʿAlī Muḥammad Muʿawwaḍ (Beirut: Dār al-Kutub al-ʿIlmiyyah, 1998), 14:355-358; 15:588-590 (mentions that according to some reports, the verse was revealed to vindicate ʿAlī's family. Also mentions that other reports contend that hypocrites of Medina would solicit women at night. Girls who practiced prostitution would respond to their solicitation. The verse was revealed partly to end this practice. Mentions the rule of practice and custom (mā uʿtīda kashfuh), and functionality and rule of necessity; mentions the distinction as to slave girls); Abū al-Faḍl Shihāb al-Dīn Maḥmūd al-Alūsī, *Rūḥ al-Maʿānī fī Tafsīr al-Qur'ān al-ʿAẓīm wa al-Sabʿ al-Mathānī* (Beirut: Dār Iḥyā' al-Turāth al-ʿArabī, 1985), 18:140-142; 22:89, (mentions the issue of functionality and that slave girls lead an active economic life; mentions custom, habit, and nature; mentions the historical practice); Aḥmad al-Ṣāwī, *Ḥāshiyat al-ʿAllāmah al-Ṣāwī ʿalā Tafsīr al-Jalālayn* (Beirut: Dār Iḥyā' al-Turāth al-ʿArabī, n.d.), 3:136-137, 288-289 (mentions various positions).

[39] *Ḥijāb*, in this context, refers to the seclusion of women from men.

al-Ḥusayn b. ʿAlī, al-Shuʿbī, ʿUmar b. al-Khaṭṭāb, and Muʿāwiya, did not forbid speaking or mixing with women.[40] To this point, Al-Jāḥiẓ's discussion is rather unremarkable; there are many jurists who made this same argument in Islamic history. Al-Jāḥiẓ's polemic becomes interesting when he starts talking about the attitude of some men towards women. Al-Jāḥiẓ strongly criticizes the attitude of the Ḥashawiyyah towards women, accusing them of espousing unduly oppressive laws.[41] In an explicitly critical passage, al-Jāḥiẓ states the following: "We do not say, and any reasonable person cannot say, that women are above men or lower than men by a degree or two or more. But we have seen people who revile [women] the worst of revilements and disdain them and deny them most of their rights. Most certainly, it is true impotence for a man to be incapable of fulfilling the rights of fathers or uncles unless he disparages the rights of mothers and aunts."[42] Al-Jāḥiz contends that it is a misguided sense of male jealousy over pride and honor that accounts for the tendency to oppress women. Zeal in the protection of honor, he argues, is admirable unless it forbids what God has allowed. Some have

---

[40] ʿAmr b. Baḥr b. Maḥbūb al-Jāḥiz, "Kitāb al-Qiyān" in *Rasāʾil al-Jāḥiẓ: al-Rasāʿil al-Kalāmiyyah*, ed. ʿAlī Abū Milḥim (Beirut: Dār al-Hilāl, 1987), 66-71.

[41] al-Jāḥiz, "Kitāb al-Qiyān," 69. Al-Ḥashawiyyah (also known as *ahl al-Ḥashw*) was a deprecatory term used to describe the literalist traditionists who accepted anthropomorphicism. The Muʿtazilah contemptuously described the whole of *aṣḥāb al-ḥadīth* (people of tradition) as Hashawiyyah because of their anti-rational positions, and their espousal of the doctrine of *bilā kayf* (without asking how or why). The expression *bilā kayf* became associated with conservative literalists who rejected rational inquiries into the metaphorical meanings of text or the objectives and purposes of law. Text, according to this trend, ought to be read and understood literally without asking why or how. In the modern age, this expression once again has been made popular by the Wahhābīs. On the Ḥashawiyyah see W. Montgomery Watt, *The Formative Period of Islamic Thought* (Oxford: Oneworld Publications, 1998), 270.

[42] al-Jāḥiz, "Kitāb al-Nisāʾ" in *Rasāʾil al-Jāḥiẓ: al-Rasāʿil al-Kalāmiyyah*, ed. ʿAlī Abū Milḥim (Beirut: Dār al-Hilāl, 1987), 99-100. A bit later in the text, al-Jāḥiz inconsistently states, "And, although we believe that, as to the affairs of men and women in general, the virtue of men is superior and more apparent, we must not deny women their rights. It is not proper for someone who wants to honor fathers to deny mothers their rights. The same applies to brothers and sisters, and sons and daughters. Although I could believe that one is entitled to a greater set of rights, granting [equal rights] is more merciful." Al-Jāḥiz also argues that as to certain matters, women are superior to men. See pp. 97 and 101.

used modesty as an excuse to prohibit women from speaking or dealing with men. Al-Jāḥiz sums up the attitude and practice of who he calls the transgressors with the following statement, "This is a matter where they have transgressed beyond the zeal for honor to the realm of bad manners and the lack of probity."[43]

At a minimum, al-Jāḥiz's discourse indicates that gender relations were contested and that the implications of the *ḥijāb* continued to be the subject of debate in the 3rd/9th century. Furthermore, evidence from later Islamic centuries demonstrates that the role played by women in Islamic history was complex and multi-faceted. We find, for instance, that late jurists such as al-Sakhāwī (d. 902/1497), Ibn Ḥajar al-ʿAsqalānī (d. 852/1449), and al-Suyūṭī (d. 911/1505) had studied with a large number of women. Among the prominent Muslim jurists, Ibn Ḥajar studied with 53 women, al-Sakhāwī studied with 46, and al-Suyūṭī studied with 33.[44] In addition, there are a considerable number of women scholars and jurists who are listed in biographical dictionaries. For example, al-Sakhāwī lists 1075 notable women, 405 of whom are scholars of traditions or jurists.[45] Of the 191 women who Ibn Ḥajar lists, 168 were teachers of traditions or law.[46] According to Ruth Roded, 88 percent of the women in Ibn Ḥajar's biographical dictionary studied only with male teachers, 6 percent studied under male and female teachers, and 6 percent studied only under women. Of the women that al-Sakhāwī lists, 70 percent studied only with male teachers, 25 percent studied with male and female teachers, and 5 percent studied with women only.[47]

---

[43] al-Jāḥiz, "Kitāb al-Qiyān," 71. Also see Abou El Fadl, *The Conference of the Books*, 11-15.

[44] Ruth Roded, *Women in Islamic Biographical Collections: From Ibn Saʿd's to Who's Who* (Boulder, Colo.: Lynne Rienner Publishers, 1994), 68.

[45] Roded, *Women in Islamic Biographical Collections*, 68; see Shams al-Dīn Muḥammad b. ʿAbd al-Raḥmān al-Sakhāwī, *al-Ḍawʾ al-Lāmiʿ li-Ahl al-Qarn al-Tāsiʿ* (Beirut: Maktabat al-Ḥayāh, n.d.), vol. 12.

[46] Roded, *Women in Islamic Biographical Collections*, 68; see Aḥmad b. ʿAlī Ibn Ḥajar al-ʿAsqalānī, *al-Durar al-Kāminah fī Aʿyān al-Miʾah al-Thāminah*, ed. ʿAbd al-Wārith Muḥammad ʿAlī (Beirut: Dār al-Kutub al-ʿIlmiyyah, 1997). Unlike al-Sakhāwī, Ibn Ḥajar integrates the entries of women with the entries of men. Al-Sakhāwī collects all the women entries in the final volume of his work.

[47] Roded, *Women in Islamic Biographical Collections*, 73.

The public role and function of women in various Islamic periods have not been adequately studied. But it is unlikely that there would have been such a large number of licensed women teachers if the *ḥijāb* was interpreted to mean the seclusion of women. As noted above, women were educated by men and, in turn, educated men. At the very least, this points to the fact that the dynamics and practices of the *ḥijāb* continued to be complex late into Islamic history. Importantly, this evidence also indicates that the practice behind the idea of *fitnah* was not as dogmatic and puritanical as many contemporary Muslims seem to assume.

Is Morality a Bad Word?

My final comment is about the invocation of morality in Islamic discourses. In the debates that followed the publication of this book, there was a bit of controversy over what was at times referred to as the "footnote sixty issue."[48] What was designated as footnote sixty in the previous edition of this book suggested that certain discourses or legal results could be immoral regardless of the evidence presented. As I noted in the beginning of this book, the very idea of a morality that can exist independent of the law is considered, at best, an oddity in contemporary puritan thinking. Puritanism appears to follow an extreme form of positivism that recognizes the positive law as the ultimate moral value that must take priority over any other normative consideration. In a pseudo-intellectual engagement in which I was foolishly defending myself against accusations of insignificance, a fellow calmly said, "You seem to rely on an idea of morality—assertions of morality are arrogant and authoritarian!" By this statement, I presume he meant that, unlike textually-based law, morality is without foundation, and therefore, it is capricious, arrogant, and despotic. I am not a philosopher and cannot present a coherent vision of morality even if I tried. My comments on morality are mere reflections on the Islamic tradition.[49]

---

[48] See note 50 on page 66.

[49] I ought to note, however, that my conception of morality tends to be deontological more than teleological. In other words, I tend to think that the right precedes the good, and that what is right is good rather than the other way around. Furthermore, I

Unfortunately, my calm and self-confident critic is not an oddity in contemporary Islamic discourses. In fact, there has been a rising trend among modern Muslims that claims that there is no concept of *akhlāq* (proper manners or morality) in Islam. According to this trend, to speak of *akhlāq* is to create a category separate and apart from the law. Proper manners or morality are defined and encompassed by the law of *Sharīʿah*, and therefore, the only relevant category for an Islamic discourse is the law, and nothing beyond the law. *Akhlāq* is simply a term that describes the prescriptions of the law, but it neither informs the law nor carries any independent normative weight for Muslims. To my knowledge, this attempt to negate the role of *akhlāq* is unprecedented in Islamic history.

Of course, the Qurʾān itself refers to that very concept when it describes the Prophet as a man of great moral character (*wa innaka la ʿalā kuluqin ʿaẓīm*).[50] Furthermore, the Prophet reportedly described his role, as a messenger of God, as one who was sent to perfect the moral character of human beings (*innama buʿithtu li utammima makārim al-akhlāq*).[51] But quite apart from whether the word was used in a Qurʾānic verse or Prophetic tradition, one ought to wonder: Does a human being

doubt that a teleological theory of morality is not possible without a prior deontological commitment. Consequentialist and utilitarian theories of morality strike me as unprincipled and even opportunistic. Nonetheless, I do not believe that all moral constraints are equally absolute. I would argue that seen in an institutional framework, there are gradations of moral constraints. The priority of a particular moral constraint depends on the extent it is essential or at the core of other moral constraints. All moral constraints are asserted as *prima facie* normative values, but whether these normative values become absolute imperatives depends on whether such an absoluteness would denigrate or promote other contingent moral constraints. All moral constraints are derived from our understanding of the responsibilities that God has charged us with as human beings. What I think of as absolute moral constraints are those that the violation of which would deny another human being the ability to attain a higher level of moral fulfillment. Of course, this issue requires a separate study, but the important point is that unless Muslims are prepared to acknowledge the existence of a morality that is not solely derived from the law, explorations into the idea of moral constraints, as opposed to legal constraints, will remain an oddity in contemporary Muslim discourses.

50 Qurʾān 68:4.

51 Abū Bakr ʿAbd Allāh b. Muḥammad Ibn Abī Shaybah, *al-Kitāb al-Muṣannaf fī al-Aḥādīth wa al-Āthār*, ed. Muḥammad ʿAbd al-Salām Shāhīn (Beirut: Dār al-Kutub al-ʿIlmiyyah, 1995), 6:328; Mālik b. Anas, *al-Muwaṭṭaʾ*, ed. Bashshār ʿAwād Maʿrūf, 2nd ed. (Beirut: Dār al-Gharb al-Islāmī, 1997), 2:490; Ibn Ḥajar al-ʿAsqalānī, *Fatḥ al-Bārī*

need a textual authorization in order to think about or try to adopt proper manners and moral conduct? It is strange to expect the law to legislate all notions of decency and goodness. Do human beings need laws to tell them when or how to greet someone, thank someone, smile in someone's face, or empathize with someone? Do human beings need laws to tell them what is a lie, what is hypocrisy, what is hate, what is love, or what is beauty? I suspect that if a person needs a law to tell him or her to be good or decent, then that person is neither good nor decent. The law can define the limits for proper conduct, but it cannot define the quality of such conduct. If I smile in someone's face or greet someone because the law commands me to do so, then in reality, I have neither smiled nor greeted. Furthermore, this negation of the position of *akhlāq* seems to have a remarkably unrealistic expectation of the role of religious law. A religious law can provide that one ought to be sensitive to the feelings of others or that one ought to be respectful of others, but it cannot define the quality of this sensitivity or respectfulness. This is the ambiguity that is addressed by *akhlāq*. Moreover, the reliance on law to mandate and define moral conduct is often no more than an indication of moral lethargy. This moral lethargy effectively means that one is shifting the burden of moral responsibility and probity upon a set of mechanical rules. For instance, a man could examine some of the proper conduct regulations in Islamic law and conclude that the following applies: initiate *al-salāmu ʿalaykum* (the greeting of peace) with male Muslims, but not with female Muslims or non-Muslims, male or female; clean your teeth with a *miswāk*; drink liquids in three gulps while in a sitting posture; eat from the plate in front of you and eat with your right hand; bathe before congregational prayers on Friday; do not face the *qiblah* when going to the bathroom and do not urinate while standing up; smile

(n.d.), 7:173, 10:455; Abū Zakariyyā Muḥyī al-Dīn b. Sharaf al-Nawawī, *al-Minhāj Sharḥ Ṣaḥīḥ Muslim al-Ḥajjāj,* ed. Khalīl Maʾmūn Shīḥā (Beirut: Dār al-Maʿrifah, 1996), 15/16:250-251; in one tradition reported by Bukhārī, Muslim, Aḥmad and al-Ṭabarānī the Prophet reportedly said, "The best of you are those who have the best manners (*khiyārukum aḥāsinakum akhlāqā*)." Al-Nawawī, *al-Minhāj,* 15/16:77-78; Ibn Ḥajar al-ʿAsqalānī, *Fatḥ al-Bārī* (n.d.), 10:456; Ibn Ḥanbal, *Musnad,* 2:216. Also see al-Jurjānī, *al-Kāmil fī Ḍuʿafāʾ al-Rijāl,* 4:367. In another version, the Prophet is reported as saying, "The best of [the believers] are those who treat their women best (*khiyāruhum khiyāruhum li nisāʾihim*)." Ibn Ḥanbal, *Musnad,* 2:329.

with dignity but do not laugh out aloud; do not laugh without a reason and do not jest all the time; allow your beard to grow and shave or shorten your mustache; do not wear gold and so on. What do these rules yield? A moral character? The risk is that a person will comply with all of these pedantic rules and righteously feel comforted by a sense of moral compliance.[52] The risk is that a person will consider that abiding by these rules will constitute complete and sufficient compliance with the imperatives of morality. Therefore, one ends up with the ironic paradox that, in compliance with the appearance of modesty, a man may shorten his garment up to the ankle but treat everyone who does not do so with an arrogant air of self-righteous superiority.[53]

The Qur'ān persistently refers to values such as justice, fairness, mercy, kindness, and truthfulness as if they have an innate meaning to human beings. Some scholars have noted that the Qur'ān gives expression to a coherent ethical order or, at least, considers a particular set of ethical values to be at the core of what it means to be human.[54] Premodern scholars debated at length whether good and evil are defined by scripture or text alone, or by text and reason.[55] The juristic tradition focused the debate on the issue of *ḥusn* (goodness, beauty, or what is

---

[52] Muḥammad al-Ghazālī used to call compliance with these rules, compliance with the superficial surface of Islam (*iltizām al-qushūr*).

[53] See, on this precise phenomenon, Muḥammad al-Ghazālī, *Khuluq al-Muslim* (Cairo: Dār al-Kutub al-Islāmiyyah, 1983); *idem, Dustūr al-Wiḥdah*; *idem, Humūm Dā'iyah* (Cairo: Dār al-Bashīr, 1984).

[54] Rahman, *Major Themes;* Toshihiko Izutsu, *Ethico-Religious Concepts in the Qur'ān* (Montreal: McGill University Press, 1966); *idem, God and Man in the Koran* (1964; reprint, North Stratford, N.H.: Ayer Company Publishers, 1995).

[55] The rationalist Mu'tazilīs adhered to the view that through the use of reason, one can arrive at an understanding of good and evil. On the other hand, their opponents, such as the Ash'arīs and traditionist Ḥanbalīs, argued that good and evil are determined by revelation. God alone determines good and evil, and to hold otherwise would deny God's authority. The implications of this theological dispute extend to conceptions of law and justice. For instance, the Mu'tazilīs, who called themselves the Partisans of Justice and Oneness (*ahl al-'adl wa al-tawḥīd*), argued that God only upholds that which is just. Further, they argued that justice on earth is known through reason. Therefore, if one asserts that performing a particular act is just as a matter of reason, it thereby becomes the law of God, albeit an approximation of Divine justice. The Ash'arīs and traditionists, however, would argue that the law of God is established by revelation. The fact that a particular act is commanded or

beautiful) and *qubḥ* (the condemnable, ugliness, or what is ugly).[56] This debate revolved around the idea of whether there is an objective reality to beauty or ugliness, or whether beauty and ugliness are necessarily subjective. The Muʿtazilah contended that whatever is good has an intelligible moral essence that is recognizable through reason (*al-ḥusn wa al-qubḥ ʿaqlīyān*). The Ashʿarīs, however, opposed the idea of intelligible moral essences, and argued that unless good and evil are derived from scripture, they are constructed and conceived by the subjective self (*ṭabāʾiʿ al-nufūs*).[57] Hence, if good and evil are not based on scripture, they are invariably the product of human whim or desire. In essence, the Ashʿarīs rejected the possibility that reason, unaided by scripture, is capable of discerning the nature of good or evil. Scripture is the only reliable identifier of morality.[58] Although this debate has

---

prohibited by revelation is what makes the legal outcome just. See Majid Khadduri, *The Islamic Conception of Justice* (Baltimore, Md.: Johns Hopkins University Press, 1984), 39-77; Oliver Leaman, *An Introduction to Medieval Islamic Philosophy* (London: Cambridge University Press, 1985), 123-165; George F. Hourani, "Divine Justice and Human Reason in Muʿtazilite Ethical Theology," in *Ethics in Islam*, ed. Richard G. Hovannisian (Malibu, Calif.: Undena Publications, 1985), 73-83. See also A. Kevin Reinhart, *Before Revelation: The Boundaries of Muslim Moral Thought* (Albany, N.Y.: State University of New York Press, 1995).

56 See, for example, Abū al-Thanāʾ Maḥmūd b. Zayd al-Lāmishī, *Kitāb fī Uṣūl al-Fiqh*, ed. ʿAbd al-Majīd Turkī (Beirut: Dār al-Gharb al-Islāmī, 1995), 66-68; al-Juwaynī, *al-Burhān*, 8-14; Abū Ḥāmid al-Ghazālī, *al-Mustaṣfā*, 1:55-61; Fakhr al-Dīn al-Rāzī, *al-Maḥṣūl* (1997), 1:105-109; al-Bukhārī, *Kashf al-Asrār*, 1:389-446; Abū al-Ḥusayn Muḥammad b. ʿAlī b. al-Ṭayyib al-Baṣrī, *Kitāb al-Muʿtamad fī Uṣūl al-Fiqh*, ed. Muḥammad Ḥamīd Allāh, Muḥammad Bakr, and Ḥasan Ḥanafī (Damascus: Institut Français, 1964), 1:177-180; Badrān Abū al-ʿAynayn Badrān, *Uṣūl al-Fiqh* (Cairo: Dār al-Maʿārif, 1965), 15-16; Muḥammad Maʿrūf al-Dawālībī, *Madkhal ilā ʿIlm Uṣūl al-Fiqh*, 5th ed. (n.p.: Dār al-ʿIlm li al-Malāyīn, 1965), 166-173.

57 *Ṭabāʾiʿ al-nufūs* was used in a variety of contexts with different nuances of meaning. At times, it referred to whim or desire, but it is also used to mean human nature or the natural intimations and intuitions of human beings. Muslim theorists used the expression both in a positive and negative sense. In its negative sense, it referred to the whimsical subjectivity of moral values. In its positive sense, it referred to the ability of people with sound dispositions to recognize and accept moral values (*mā yulāʾim aṣḥāb al-Ṭabāʾiʿ al-salīmah* or *mā yunāsib aṣḥāb al-nufūs al-sawiyyah*).

58 For a helpful introduction to the thought of al-Ghazālī, al-Rāzī, and al-Qarāfī on the issue of *ḥusn* and *qubḥ*, see Sherman A. Jackson, "The Alchemy of Domination? Some Ashʿarite Responses to Muʿtazilite Ethics," *International Journal of Middle Eastern Studies* 31 (1999): 185-201.

serious implications for the role of scripture and text in Islamic law, neither the rationalist nor the scripturalist approach necessarily defines the relationship between morality and law. The role of morality is not determined by conceding hegemony to either scripture or reason.

As to the issue of the origin of beauty and ugliness, most jurists conceded that God creates both categories.[59] But more important than the origin of these values is the matter of how God creates them in the first place. It is not the case that every piece of scripture defines good and evil or beauty and ugliness. Rather, God creates the laws of the universe and nature that, in turn, make the categories of beauty and ugliness necessary and compelling. Beauty and ugliness are produced and defined according to the laws of creation and nature that God had set in place. Muslim jurists, however, did not seem to treat this particular issue as legally material. More pertinent to their purposes was the nature of beauty and ugliness. Most jurists differentiated between what is intrinsically beautiful (*ḥasan bi-dhātih*) or ugly, and what is derivatively so (*ḥasan li-ghayrih*). Certain values and acts are beautiful by their very nature—their beauty is derived from the laws of creation but nothing else. Other values and acts are derivative but in a very different sense. The beauty of these derivative values and acts are the product of their circumstance or context, or are contingent on their consequences. For example, a large number of jurists argued that justice is intrinsically good and beautiful. Justice is beautiful regardless of the circumstances or results. Similarly, love of God is intrinsically beautiful and does not depend on circumstance or context. By contrast, the love of a woman was a subject of disagreement. Some argued it is intrinsically beautiful while others argued that it is beautiful if it does not lead to fornication or adultery. According to the former view, if love results in fornication or adultery, then love remains beautiful, but the acts of fornication or adultery are ugly. In other words, the ugliness of fornication or adultery ought not affect the value of love. The jurists also disagreed on whether drinking alcohol is intrinsically or derivatively ugly. Some argued that the drinking of fermented foodstuffs is intrinsically ugly while others

59 Several jurists argued that God creates only beauty. Ugliness is simply the absence of beauty. This is often discussed under the heading of causality.

argued that drinking alcohol is ugly because it leads to intoxication. One last example: Some jurists argued that whether war is beautiful or ugly depends entirely on its causes (circumstances) and results. Other jurists argued that war is never beautiful; it is an ugliness that must be endured at times for collateral reasons.

These discourses get far more complex and tend to produce rather elaborate conceptual categories.[60] Considering the richness of these discourses, I do hope that in the future I will be able to devote a full study to this matter. Nevertheless, at this point, we might ask: What is the significance of debate on the beautiful and the ugly as it relates to Islamic law? First, the existence of this discourse demonstrates that God-fearing Muslims can talk about normative moral values without necessarily being heretical. To the extent that the practices of the generations that preceded us carry persuasive weight, these practices chart out possible approaches to the issue of morality and Islamic law. Second, these discourses are material for understanding and evaluating the purpose or object of Islamic law. Muslim jurists started out with the assumption that God desires for human beings to maximize what is beautiful in life.[61] For instance, we know that mercy, compassion, and justice are good because they are beautiful. These values are good and beautiful either because God made them so or because they are inherently so. In either case, God created laws, or sanctioned the laws, that define beauty in the created existence. These laws of beauty are not created by the *Sharīʿah—Sharīʿah*, for instance, does not define whether a flower is beautiful or ugly. Rather, the laws of beauty are respected, accessed, and sustained by *Sharīʿah*. Since the *Sharīʿah* is the Way to God, and God is the epitome of beauty, *Sharīʿah* must, by necessity, preserve and protect beauty. Therefore, studying and analyzing beauty (or the laws of beauty)

[60] Ibn Taymiyyah argues that the intellect can discern the good and bad. Good is everything that seeks out God or is intended and directed towards God (*yurād bi-hā wajh Allāh*). Rational proof and the revealed truth collaborate in identifying the acts, deeds and things that are directed towards God. See Taqī al-Dīn Ibn Taymiyyah, *Majmūʿat al-Rasāʾil wa al-Masāʾil*, ed. Muḥammad Rashīd Riḍā (Mecca: Dār al-Bāz, 1976), 5:25-28; Binyamin Abrahamov, "Ibn Taymiyya on the Agreement of Reason with Tradition," *Muslim World* 82 (1992): 256-272.

[61] Muslim jurists relied, in part, on a tradition attributed to the Prophet that states: "God is beautiful and loves beauty."

is part and parcel of studying *Sharīʿah.* Put differently, figuring out the laws of beauty is a fundamental part of discovering the *Sharīʿah* itself. The purpose of *Sharīʿah,* according to most jurists, is to achieve the welfare of the people (*taḥqīq maṣāliḥ* or *manāfiʿ al-ʿibād*), because the well-being and happiness of the people are part of what is good and beautiful.[62] As I mentioned earlier, Muslim jurists differentiated between *Sharīʿah,* which is goodness in the abstract or ideal sense, and *fiqh,* which interprets and implements the *Sharīʿah.*[63] Put simply, *Sharīʿah* is the ideal and *fiqh* is the concrete approximation of the ideal, and therefore, *Sharīʿah* is perfect and immutable, but *fiqh* is not. So, for example, Ibn al-Qayyim (d. 751/1350) argues that it is impossible for the *Sharīʿah* to result in an injustice, and if it does then that only means that the interpretation or positive regulations giving effect to the *Sharīʿah* were flawed.[64] What Ibn al-Qayyim means is that if there is a flaw, this is not because the beautiful is deficient, but because the attempt to comprehend or implement the beautiful has failed.

This paradigm becomes meaningful when we consider the purpose of the law and the logic of legal change. If the law mandates the abstention or performance of a certain act, we must ask, is compliance demanded for its own sake or for the sake of attaining certain results? If the law mandates compliance for its own sake, then the purpose of the law must be intrinsically beautiful or beautiful by its nature (*ḥasan bi dhātih*), otherwise we must suspect that we misunderstood the law or its purposes. If, on the other hand, the law mandates compliance in

---

62 Maḥmaṣānī, *Falsafat al-Tashrīʿ,* 199-200; Abū Zahrah, *Uṣūl al-Fiqh,* 291; Muṣṭafā Zayd, *al-Maṣlaḥah fī al-Tashrīʿ al-Islāmī wa Najm al-Dīn al-Ṭūfī,* 2nd ed. (Cairo: Dār al-Fikr al-ʿArabī, 1964), 22; Yūsuf Ḥāmid al-ʿĀlim, *al-Maqāṣid al-ʿĀmmah li al-Sharīʿah al-Islāmiyyah* (Herndon, Va.: International Institute of Islamic Thought, 1991), 80; Muḥammad b. ʿAlī b. Muḥammad al-Shawkānī, *Ṭalab al-ʿIlm wa Ṭabaqāt al-Mutaʿallimīn: Adab al-Ṭalab wa Muntahā al-ʿArab* (n.p.: Dār al-Arqam, 1981), 145-151. The Qurʾān supports this contention. See Qurʾān, 2:173, 6:145, 16:115. See also Ibn Ḥajar al-ʿAsqalānī, *Fatḥ al-Bārī* (n.d.), 1:196; 8:60; 10:524.

63 Maḥmaṣānī, *Falsafat al-Tashrīʿ,* 199-200; Abū Zahrah, *Uṣūl al-Fiqh,* 291; Zayd, *al-Maṣlaḥah,* 22; al-ʿĀlim, *al-Maqāṣid al-ʿĀmmah,* 80; al-Shawkānī, *Ṭalab al-ʿIlm,* 145-151.

64 Shams al-Dīn Abū Bakr b. Qayyim al-Jawziyyah, *Iʿlām al-Muwaqqiʿīn ʿan Rabb al-ʿĀlamīn,* ed. ʿAbd al-Raḥmān al-Wakīl (Cairo: Maktabat Ibn Taymiyyah, n.d.), 3:5.

order to attain certain results, then the law, in this situation, is a means to an end and not an end in itself. The end must be beautiful—whether the means are beautiful or not depends on whether it is able to achieve its ends or not. This is called *ḥasan li ghayr dhātih*. Therefore, in every evaluative step, we must ask, is the law the law for its own sake or for the sake of a higher end? If it is the law for its own sake, the law cannot reflect the attributes of ugliness. If the law is the law for the sake of a higher end, then we must make sure that the law is serving its purpose.

Muslim jurists noticed that most laws pertaining to worship (*ʿibādah*) are good for their own sake, and most affairs pertaining to interaction between human beings are only a means to a higher end. Furthermore, the more general and abstract the legal injunction, the more likely it connotes an intrinsic good. Therefore, Muslim jurists reasoned that principles of law and commands pertaining to worship (*ʿibādāt*) are not susceptible to much change, while specific laws and laws pertaining to human interaction (*muʿāmalāt*) are susceptible to much change (*al-aṣl fī al-ʿibādāt al-ittibāʿ wa al-aṣl fī al-muʿāmalāt al-ibtidāʿ*).[65] From a different perspective, one could argue that laws that regulate the relationship between human beings and God *tend* to be stable while laws that regulate the interaction of human beings *tend* to change. When we speak of tendencies in this context, we are speaking of presumptions that are not conclusive. This analysis does not create irreproachable determinancies. Rather, the purpose of the analysis is to force the jurist to engage in the analytical exercise of evaluating the morality (beauty) of the law and its ultimate impact. For example, modesty is arguably an intrinsic value—as a value, it expresses a sense of humility, responsibility, diffidence, restraint, chastity, and dignity. If there is a law that says, "Be modest!" this law is vague but constant. If another law says, "Do X so that you can be modest," X, as a law, is neither beautiful nor ugly. X's beauty or ugliness depends on whether it is serving the intrinsic value of modesty. Evaluating X's performance vis-à-vis modesty is partly an empirical issue, but it also depends on how we understand the meaning of modesty.

---

65 Muḥammad al-Ghazālī, *Kayf Nafham al-Islām* (Cairo: Dār al-Kutub al-Islāmiyyah, 1983), 162-163.

My argument is that the ultimate overriding values or the *grundnorms* of *Sharīʿah* are most certainly based in scripture. But scripture recognizes the values that are part of the law or logic of creation—balance, justice, fairness, mercy, compassion, beauty, dignity, and humility are part of Godliness, and are reflected by the Creator upon creation. In my view, Godliness and the attributes of Godliness are intrinsically beautiful. Positive legal prescriptions are derivatively beautiful—their beauty, or lack thereof, depends on their ability to fulfill these higher values, within a specific set of circumstances or context. As such, any legal prescription could potentially become the source of ugliness or evil depending on whether it fulfills its normative purposes. Assessing whether, in fact, a law fulfills its objects is a matter of rational and empirical assessment, and not a matter of scriptural truth.

The challenge to this argument is that it makes the specific subject to negation by the general and not the other way around. In other words, if the law says, "be modest," and then says, "do X in order to be modest," most jurists argued that the prescription of X clarifies and specifies the general principle of modesty. Therefore, doing X would make one modest, and even further, perhaps, doing X and only X would make one modest. Of course, this argument is illogical—just because doing X is a way to modesty does not necessarily mean that doing X is the only way one can be modest. But other than matters of logical flow, this issue is related to a classical debate about the dynamics between the general and specific in legal analysis. Most jurists tended to argue that in case of a conflict between general legal indicants and specific legal indicants, the specific prevails over the general. This means that the specific defines and limits the general.[66] Other jurists such as Shāṭibī argued that the general indicants ought to prevail over the specific, and that all juristic determinations ought to be guided by the purposes of *Sharīʿah* (*maqāṣid al-Sharīʿah*).[67] The generalities or universals of the law should guide, limit, and if necessary, negate the specifics.

66 For instance see Aḥmad b. Idrīs al-Qarāfī, *Sharḥ Tanqīḥ al-Fuṣūl fī Ishtiṣār al-Maḥṣūl fī al-Uṣūl* (Cairo: Dār al-Fikr, 1973), 394.

67 Al-Shāṭibī argued that general indicants or legal universals are certain while the specific indicants are probable and, therefore, the generals or universals ought to prevail. A jurist figures out the universals by considering the objectives or purposes

Furthermore, general legal indicants should be given greater weight in analysis to specific legal indicants.

In principle, I agree with al-Shāṭibī's methodology although I would argue that moral inquiries ought to occupy a more aggressive role in formulating the law. Moral values should be derived from the generalities of scripture. For instance, justice, dignity, or beauty are known to be moral values because the Qur'ān emphasizes them as normative imperatives. The meaning and connotations of these moral values should be explored through the use of reason, intuition, and observations of the social laws of nature. Intuition and reason will yield a fuller and more in depth awareness of the meaning and implications of these values. Specific legal injunctions, even if based on text, must be evaluated in light of the general Islamic normativities. Therefore, whether women, in some circumstances, ought to inherit half of what a man inherits, or whether the testimony of women counts as half of a man's testimony, should be evaluated in light of the overriding Islamic normative values such as justice, dignity, or beauty.[68] If these specific legal injunctions lead to results that are contrary to the Islamic moral values, then, depending on the circumstances, they should be re-interpreted, suspended, or negated. One might object to this argument by asserting that the specific legal injunctions, such as those pertaining to the inheritance or testimony of women, effectively define the meaning of Islamic moral values. Therefore, justice, dignity, or beauty is defined and given shape by the scriptural legal injunctions, and it is just, dignified, and beautiful for women to inherit half that of men, or for their testimony to count as half of that of men. Although this objection represents the current orthodox Muslim position, I believe it is unpersuasive. As noted above, just because the scripture details one way of fulfilling the Islamic moral values this does not mean that this becomes the only way of

---

of the law, and the cumulative evidence identifying the general precepts of the law. Specific precepts do not limit or specify the general precepts but may constitute a circumstancial exception to the legal universals. See al-Shāṭibī, *al-Muwāfaqāt*, 3:261-271.

68 These laws are based on Qur'ānic injunctions found in Qur'ān 4:11 and 2:282. There is no indication that these specific Qur'ānic injunctions were intended to articulate a moral principle. Rather, they seem to have been functional and convenient for the time. This means that their construction and implementation is subject to the overriding moral imperatives of *Sharī'ah*.

doing so. More importantly, the real issue is whether the Divine charge to Muslims is to implement specific laws or to realize ultimate moral values? When the Qur'ān commands that justice or safety and security be established, and then sets out particular laws, does this mean that these particular laws are the absolute embodiment of the moral values that God commands Muslims to observe?

In my view, the laws of *'ibādāt* (laws pertaining to worship) quite frequently connote an ultimate moral value in themselves—the value of worshipping God as God wishes to be worshipped.[69] In *mu'āmalāt* (laws pertaining to civil interaction), the laws, for the most part, do not have an inherent moral value. Rather, their morality is derivative and contingent on their ability to uphold and fulfill higher moral purposes. The specific legal injunctions contained in scriptural sources, depending on the authenticity of the particular source, could be presumptively moral—they are presumed to be moral because, arguably, they were the preferred Divine solution to a particular problem under a specific set of circumstances. This, however, should not mean that the presumption of morality is irrefutable. With the change of circumstances, the specific legal injunctions could fail to fulfill their moral purposes, and must be re-considered.

Similar types of issues plague the debates on *maṣlaḥah* (public interest) in Islamic law. There have been extensive juristic discourses on the relationship between Islamic law and public interest or what might be called empirical social welfare. Many jurists have debated the ways in which considerations of public interest might lead to the re-interpretation or modification of Islamic legal injunctions.[70] My point, however, is that moral considerations are more rooted in Islamic scripture than purely

---

[69] If, under exceptional circumstances, the laws pertaining to worship lead to immoral results (often physical hardship), it is possible to entertain exceptions and modifications to these laws. However, often the hardship exceptions are explicitly set out in scriptural sources.

[70] See Muṣṭafā Zayd, *al-Maṣlaḥah fī al-Tashrī' al-Islāmī* (Cairo: Dār al-Fikr al-'Arabī, 1964), 206-240; Najm al-Dīn al-Ṭūfī, *al-Bulbul fī Uṣūl al-Fiqh* (Cairo: Maktabat al-Shāfi'ī, 1989), 144; Badrān Abū al-'Aynayn Ibn Badrān, *Nuzhat al-Khāṭir al-'Āṭir* (Beirut: Dār al-Kutub al-'Ilmiyyah, 1922) 1:416; Ihsan Abdul-Wajid Bagby, *Utility in Classical Islamic Law: The Concept of Maṣlaḥah in Uṣūl al-Fiqh*, Ph.D. thesis, University of Michigan, 1986; Felicitas Meta Maria Opwis, "Maṣlaḥa: An Intellectual History of A Core Concept in Islamic Legal History" (Ph.D. diss., Yale University, 2001).

functional or opportunistic considerations. It makes little sense to admit appraisals of public interest in deducting the operative causes (*ʿilal*) of laws, or in considering whether a law ought to be implemented or modified, and yet exclude considerations of morality. I will discuss two examples to differentiate between a morality-based approach and a public interest-based approach. Consider, for instance, the highly problematic case of sexual intercourse with a non-consenting wife or slave girl. Islamic jurists have tended to believe that the husband or the male owner of a slave girl has a right to sexually enjoy his wife or his slave girl. Therefore, they argued, coercing either a wife or slave girl into sexual intercourse is not considered a criminal offense, and the vast majority did not even consider it a sin. Some jurists, however, considered it to be contrary to proper manners (*makārim al-akhlāq*). In terms of scriptural sources, there are traditions that emphasize the duty of a wife to submit sexually to her husband, and the Qurʿān mentions that it is not blameworthy for a man to have a sexual relationship with his spouse or slave girl.[71] Nevertheless, the Qurʿān systematically seems to disfavor all forms of compulsion and coercion, and considers coercive acts, in general, to be unacceptable or reprehensible.[72] Consequently, the Qurʿān establishes voluntarism as a normative value and, as a general matter, condemns oppression and compulsion. Through the use of reason and an analysis of scripture, we will conclude that, at times, coercion is morally justifiable as, for instance, when one is forced to compensate a victim for an injury or when one is forced to suffer a punishment for a crime. I believe that if one analyzes the Qurʿānic moral commands on justice, dignity, compassion, and beauty, one will quickly reach the conclusion that forcing a criminal to pay for an offense is not similar to forcing a wife or slave girl to submit sexually. The coercion legitimated in criminal punishment is not comparable to the coercion used in a claim of right.[73]

---

71 Qurʿān 23:6.

72 Qurʿān 2:256; 24:33; 10:99.

73 For one, arguably, marriage does not vest either the husband or wife with a right to the other's body. Rather, it creates a permission or license to engage in a sexual relationship. Neither husband nor wife has the right to injure or damage the body of the other. Marriage does not permit one to abuse the body of the other. Meanwhile, there can be little doubt that rape is a physical and moral injury.

There ought to be little doubt that rape or sexual coercion is not consistent with human dignity or any sense of moral beauty. Therefore, one can make a compelling argument that marital rape or the rape of a slave girl should be considered unlawful in Islamic jurisprudence, and that all scriptural sources should be re-interpreted in a fashion that is consistent with Islamic morality. Importantly, a public interest analysis will not necessarily lead to the same re-evaluations. Public interest could opportunistically conclude that wives ought not to be empowered against their husbands, and that slave girls ought not to have any grounds to object to sexual exploitation.

Slavery, in itself, provides us with our second example. On the one hand, there are scriptural sources that assume the existence of slavery in society, and on the basis of this assumption, jurists have proceeded to legislate a variety of injunctions concerning manumission and the use of slaves as property. On the other hand, the Qurʿān exhibits a clear distaste for slavery by consistently emphasizing that the manumission of slaves will earn God's pleasure or is a way to expatiate for one's sins.[74] Although the Qurʿān does not explicitly outlaw slavery, it clearly encourages the manumission of slaves under a broad set of circumstances. Because of the heavy emphasis on the desirability of freeing human beings from bondage, it is reasonable to conclude that the manumission of slaves is a scriptural moral value. If that is so, then it is proper for Islamic jurisprudence to strive to fulfill this moral value in every way possible. It is appropriate to examine the Qurʿānic moral trajectory and strive to fulfill it in every conceivable way. Any textual or scriptural specific injunctions regulating the treatment of slaves must be read in light of the overriding moral value of manumission. The most effective way to achieve the moral value of manumission is to simply outlaw slavery. In contrast, an approach that does not consider the normative values of *Sharīʿah* is bound to consider the specific injunctions relating to the treatment and handling of slaves as somehow legitimating and legalizing the practice of slavery. Considerations of *maṣlaḥah* will opportunistically look to whether the practice of slavery

[74] See Qurʿān 4:92; 5:89; 58:3. At one point, the Qurʿān likens the act of freeing a slave to the challenge of overcoming a hurdle to Heaven, see Qurʿān 90:13.

is in the public interest or not, rather than adopting a principled stand based on scriptural moral universals.

The approach advocated here mandates that the specifics of the law be governed and navigated according to the universals, and not the other way around. The main objection to this approach will be that it tends to use morality to overrule specific scriptural injunctions, and therefore, it places morality above the Divine law. My response to this is that it all depends on how one defines the Divine law; is the Divine law about specific laws (*aḥkām*) or about moral injunctions that are pursued through a methodology that produces specific laws? The approach I am advocating is not a license for the casual overturning of scriptural injunctions under the guise of morality. Rather, it is an invitation to take the scriptural moral commands as seriously as the positive legislations. When the Qur'ān commands that human beings break the bonds of oppression or establish justice, either these scriptural commands are to be taken seriously or not. If they are to be taken seriously, then they must be explored, analyzed, understood, and implemented. The overwhelming majority of the Qur'ān consists of these moral universals, and if these universals are not adequately explored, effectively most of the Qur'ān is rendered a nullity or pure dictum while the few specific injunctions are given disproportionate weight.[75] My argument is that there is a presumption of morality that applies to all specific injunctions. Nevertheless, taking the Qur'ānic morality seriously means that the greater the impact of the specific injunction, the more one confronts a duty of heightened scrutiny. After carefully evaluating the impact of a particular specific injunction, and after scrutinizing its authenticity, its operative cause, and purpose, one might need to conclude that it can no longer be observed without violating the moral universals of *Sharī'ah*. This demands that the researcher in God's law have a solid understanding of the normative priorities of *Sharī'ah*, and that he or she exercise diligence, honesty, and self-restraint in investigating the Divine command. As noted earlier, most morally problematic issues will be resolved under the proportionality test discussed above. The more widespread the

[75] It is this tendency to focus on the specifics over the universals that led many jurists to declare the general verses of the Qur'ān are abrogated by the more specific verses. Often, this led to the complete negation of Qur'ānic moral injunctions.

impact of a textual source, the higher the level of scrutiny, and the higher the level of authenticity that this source must enjoy. But beyond the issue of authenticity, if a specific injunction frustrates the moral purposes of the *Sharīʿah*, it might become necessary to give priority to the moral purposes, and not the specific injunctions. This, however, must be a last resort; one should not discount the specific injunctions of *Sharīʿah* without first exploring the limits of interpretation. Perhaps through interpretation, the moral discrepancy might be resolved. But in the end, most laws that regulate social interactions are as moral as the objectives they serve and the results they achieve, and it might be necessary to void a law that is no longer serving its purpose.

Now, returning to the issue of footnote sixty, when I wrote that footnote, I was suggesting that we should inquire into the purpose and impact of legal determinations that reinforce the dominion of men over women. Are those legal determinations consistent with the morality and universals of *Sharīʿah*? Are these legal determinations consistent with the Qurʿānic vision of justice, compassion, dignity, and honor? Is the degradation of women a beautiful value? Even if the law does not intend to demean women, if the impact of the law is to eviscerate the dignity of women, doesn't that obligate us to pause and reflect on the purpose of the law, and to inquire whether the law is achieving its moral purposes? If the law invokes a variety of competing moral values, shouldn't we evaluate how we can achieve a balance between these moral values? If one argues that a particular law is designed to guard the modesty of women, we need to also ask what is the impact of the law on the dignity or sense of self-worth for women, and why is modesty, as a value, more important or compelling than dignity? It is my belief that we cannot coherently speak of God's law without asking these challenging and difficult questions. In short, before repeating the rhetoric about how Islam liberated women, we must investigate the universals of *Sharīʿah* and the scriptural moral foundations as they pertain to women, and evaluate the evidence in light of those moral imperatives.

• • •

Perhaps the true challenge put forth by God to human beings is the test of morality and intelligence. Ultimately, I fear that it is rather easy to "dump" the refuse of human self-indulgence upon God's law—it is easy to throw the effect of the lethargy of human conscience and the impotence of intellect upon the Divine Will. It is easy to commit ugliness and say, "God wants it so." It is even easier to flatter and empower oneself with puritan fantasies, and to befuddle the senses so as not to notice the ugliness that exists within. In fact, the very idea of "The Law" can effectively numb the senses to any pursuit of beauty. All of this is easy for those who claim to know the law of God with certitude and precision. But again, it has always been easy to claim authority, legitimate it through God, and then impose an ugly authoritarianism. Representing God's law to other human beings is truly an onerous burden. The burden is not simply to represent the evidence of God's particular injunctions, but to also internalize God's goodness and morality within oneself. The burden is one of diligence and honesty, not just with the textual sources, but with oneself—to bring the intellect and conscience to bear upon how we evaluate and understand the evidence. The burden is to internalize the morality of the Divine message, and to sift through the evidence in order to identify the indicants that have become tainted with human ugliness or that were initially articulated as concessions to human weaknesses, and then to rise above this ugliness and weakness so as to articulate a vision of the law that reflects the beauty of Godliness. In all of this, the most challenging burden is to consistently be mindful of the fact that despite all the efforts and investigations, no person can rest with the assurance of being forever right.

The Qurʿān persistently affirms the notion that there are soldiers of God who are dedicated to the upholding what is good, beautiful, and just, as there are soldiers of Satan who spread injustice and oppression. In Qurʿānic symbolism, there is an enduring battle between the forces of evil and the forces of God. Ultimately, however, it is the party of God (*ḥizbu Allāh*) that will invariably prevail over the forces of evil and corruption.[76] The Qurʿān states that "God has the soldiers (legions) of the Heavens and the Earth; God is the All-Wise and All-Knowing,"[77] and in a decisive first-person voice it pronounces: "And, Our soldiers will be victorious."[78]

---

[76] See Qurʿān 5:56; 58:19; 58:22.

[77] Qurʿān 47:4.

[78] Qurʿān 37:173.

Among the issues raised by this Qur'ānic discourse is the nature of the victory of which it speaks. Victory could take a quantifiable and mundane form, but it could also be non-quantifiable, ethereal, and moral. It would be pedantic to think that victory is simply a matter of controlling a plot of land, attaining greater financial power, or maintaining a higher score in some form of numerical competition. Victory could consist of the ability to wage the battle against evil without gradually slipping into the ranks of the Devil. Put differently, being on God's side ought to be a stance on the side of the beauty and morality that God embodies. Often, victory is the ability to continue representing God's beauty and morality despite the provocations of ugliness. Hence, at times, migration, patience, perseverance, and even martyrdom could be the ultimate victory. In the end, a Divine victory cannot be reduced to who gets to plant a flag on contested territory or how high one gets to raise the banner of pride and power.

It appears that the line dividing the ranks of God's soldiers and Satan's soldiers is diffuse and permeable. What divides one from the other is not territory, a recognizable insignia, an ethnicity, or some formalistic structure of authority. What separates one from the other is the intangible and imperceptible morality of Godliness. One can raise the banner of God, but in conduct and demeanor end up representing the very antithesis of Godliness. One can raise the banner of God, and end up a member of a banished, mutinous, and vigilante army. It is possible for one to declare an intent to join the ranks of God's soldiers, but end up in the service of an ungodly authority.

In this dynamic, even the law or adherence to the law is an insufficient guarantee of the authenticity and quality of the soldiering. If God's beauty and morality is immutable and infinite, the law is not. No law, even a law that claims divinity, is capable of being co-extensive or proportionate to God's beauty and majesty. The law is not the co-equal of God. This means that while the law is sought as part of the means to the Divine, God is the ultimate objective, and the values that God represents cannot be bounded or limited by the law, even God's law. The formulation, application of the law, and the very status of being God's devout soldier is an aspiration of Godliness, but the certainty of its fulfillment is privileged knowledge, knowable only to God.

Perhaps all of this is all too obvious. Islamic theology has long resisted the idea that there are infallible temporal representatives of the Divine. Perfect knowledge has long been assumed to belong only to God. Nevertheless, I think that there can be little doubt that the idea that there are soldiers who are empowered, supported, and legitimated by God, is a powerful symbolic construct that could easily fuel the fantasies and delusions of many authoritarians. I think that the real challenge to a soldier of God is to be painfully aware of the limitations of his or her commission, and to internalize the realization that the Commander of the legion is above and beyond an allegiance to a flag or some blind rank and file association. The challenge is to realize that the commission is to submit to God and to personify the beauty that is God, but not to dominate in the name of God.

APPENDIX

The SAS Fatwā

[Note: The following *fatwā* appeared as presented here on electronic mail. When distributed, it was replete with transliteration and grammar mistakes. In order to preserve the integrity of the SAS text, I have made no corrections.]

From: *Sunnah*@aol.com
Date: Sun, 17 Mar 1996 04:34:20 -0500
Subject: Abdul Rauf's case: The Islamic Ruling

During the past week, a number of postings have appeared from both individuals and organizations, expressing their opinions about Mahmoud Abdul Rauf's decision to not stand for the singing of the national anthem. Some have even claimed that standing for the anthem "does not violate Islam."

Irrespective of the differing views, few of them have succeeded in clarifying (a) whether this act, i.e., standing for the anthem, is an act which is permissible in Islam, and (b) what are the Shariah proofs to determine the act's permissability or impermissability. Thus to clarify and settle this issue, let us review this matter based on Allah's book, and the *Sunnah* of His Messenger (sallallahu alaihi wa salam).

We can deduce the Islamic ruling by first understanding the meaning of the word "worship." Worship or "ʿibadah" could be reduced to the secular understanding of the word, but ʿibadah means, according to the shariah, "all that Allah is pleased with from actions of the heart, tongue and limbs." (al-Ubudiyah). Therefore, the matter of standing for the anthem can be shown to be impermissable based on four counts.

1. The Shariah has prohibited specific body movements, as a sign of respect, let alone worship, to other than Allah. This can be seen clearly from four incidents in the Prophet's *Sunnah*.

I. Standing out of respect:
(a) Anas said, that no one was dearer to (the companions) than Allah's messenger (sallallahu alaihi wa salam), but when they saw

him they did not stand up because they knew his dislike of that. (At-Tirmidhi)

(b) Muawiyah reported that Allah's Messenger (sallallahu alahi wa salam) said, "Let he who likes people to stand up before him, let him recieve his place in Hell." Abu Dawud í At-Tirmidhi

II. Bowing out of respect:
It is narrated in at-Tirmidhi that the Prophet (sallallahu alahi wa salam) forbade bowing to anyone out of respect.

III. Prostrating out of respect:
Abu Hurayrah reports that when Muadh ibn Jabal returned from Sham, he came to the Prophet (sallallahu alahi wa salam) and prostrated before him, saying that he had seen the people of Sham prostrating in respect to their monks, and that the Messenger (sallallahu alahi wa salam) deserved greater respect than than what Muadh had seen the people of Sham give to their monks. The Prophet (sallallahu alahi wa salam) replied, "Were I to have commanded anyone to prostrate to anyone, I would have commanded the wife to prostrate to her husband. At-Tirmidhi

Even though no worship was intended in each case, whether by standing, bowing or prostrating, the Prophet (sallallahu alaihi wa salam) forbade the action. Thus it is understood from the Shariah, that the act of standing in respect is, at the very best, makroo' (disliked) and at worst, haram (absolutely forbidden).

2. Among the greatest principles of Islam is that a person must not show wala' to the unbelievers and their objects of worship. Wala' is rooted in the heart and manifested by the tongue and limbs. When one stands in allegiance or wala' to the flag of a nation, he is expressing his wala to all of what that system represents. None can argue that the American flag symbolizes Islam, on the contrary, it symbolizes disbelief in Allah and His Prophet.

A. Idris Palmer
Executive Director
The Society for Adherence to the Sunnah (SAS)
Washington, DC

Sunnah@aol.com

Glossary of Terms

بسم الله الرحمن الرحيم

ʿAbbāsid

The second ruling dynasty of the Muslim empire after the Umayyads. Flourished in Baghdad from 132/750 to 656/1258. Thereafter, it survived as a shadow Caliphate until 923/1517. See *Umayyad.*

adab

Good manners, propriety, good character, decency, social etiquette, proper human conduct.

adab al-ʿIbādah

Proper etiquette or manners concerning acts of worship.

adab al-Muʿāmalāt

Proper etiquette and manners concerning transactions and human dealings.

ʿādah

Physical rules of nature; regular or habitual practice. See also *ʿādat al-nās.*

ʿādat al-nās

Habitual practice of people. See also *ʿādah.*

afʿāl jibilliyyah

As distinguished from *afʿāl tashrīʿiyyah,* actions of the Prophet that were not intended to be of legal import. Examples of this are his personal preferences, the attire he wore, and even his strategies in war. Also relates to specialized or technical knowledge in fields like medicine, commerce, agriculture, etc., or to matters that are peculiar to the person of the Prophet, such as the obligation of praying large portions of the night. See also *tashrīʿiyyah.*

āḥādī

Ḥadīth reported by a singular transmission whose legal effect is debated by the various schools of Islamic jurisprudence. Such reports tend to create probabilities of belief. See also *mutawātir.*

aḥadīth (sing. *ḥadīth*)
See *ḥadīth.*

aḥkām (sing. *ḥukm*)
Rules of law, positive commandments. See also *ḥukm.*

ahl al-ʿadl wa al-tawḥīd
See Muʿtazila.

ahl al-ḥadīth
As distinguished from *ahl al-raʾy,* scholars who favor a literalist approach and de-emphasize the role of reason in the analysis of source texts or *nuṣūṣ.* See also *ahl al-raʾy* and *naṣṣ.*

ahl al-ra'y
As distinguished from *ahl al-ḥadīth,* rationalist scholars who employed reason in legal analysis in contradistinction to literalists. The role of reason was often limited to the use of analogy. However, the parameters and methodology of analogy was widely debated. Also used to refer to Kufan or Ḥanafī jurists. See also *ahl al-ḥadīth.*

Ahl al-Sunnah wa al-Jamāʿah
Adherents to the *Sunnah* of Prophet Muḥammad and the greater community of Muslims. Often used to refer to the orthodox group or the group representing the true Islam.

akhlāq (sing. *khuluq*)
Propriety, proper conduct, good manners. The Prophet described his function as one who was sent to perfect the moral standards of people.

ʿaqā'id (sing. *aqīdah*)
Lit., derives from the triliteral ʿ-qa-da, "to tie a knot" or "to enter into a contract." Islamic theology: belief system or articles of faith to which one is tied, as in a contract.

ʿaql
Mind, intellect, reason, rationality. The Qurʾān consistently calls upon men and women to apply their intellects in reflection and analysis.

Ashʿarī (Ashʿariyyah)
Adherent of the theological school named after its eponym Abū Ḥasan al-Ashʿarī (d. 324/936). One of two main Sunnī theological schools, it spread widely during the ʿAbbāsid Caliphate. The school argued that the anthropomorphic expressions about God in the Qurʾān are to be interpreted to disallow for any likeness between the Creator and His creatures. The school was attacked by the Ḥanbalīs for using rational arguments and by the Māturīdiyyah for being too conservative. See also Ḥanbalī.

awlawiyyāt al-Sharīʿah
The priorities of Islamic Law.

al-awlawiyyāt al-Sharʿiyyah
The field of jurisprudence concerned with legal priorities.

ʿawrah
Private areas of the human body to be covered in prayer or in the presence of others in order to preserve modesty. Whether cultural norms may be considered in defining modesty is subject to debate. The areas that should be covered are different for men and women.

Azharī
A graduate of al-Azhar University in Cairo, Egypt, which was founded by the Fāṭimid dynasty in 360/970.

badhl al-naẓar
Expending every possible effort in conscientiously and diligently searching and evaluating the evidence of God's law.

Banū Qurayẓah
A Jewish tribe that was nestled just southeast of Medina during the era of the Prophet. They were punished for violating a treaty with the Muslims by coordinating an assault with the Makkan tribe of Quraysh during the Battle of the Trench (5/627).

Battle of Ṣiffīn
Took place in the year 37/657 between ʿAlī b. Abī Ṭālib, the fourth of the Rightly Guided Caliphs, and Muʿāwiyah, then the governor of Syria. Ultimately, this political conflict led to an arbitration attempt between the forces of ʿAlī and Muʿāwiyah, which was generally unsuccessful. The assassination of ʿAlī by one of the Khawārij (Seceders) eventually led to the recognition of Muʿāwiyah as the first Umayyad Caliph.

bidaʿ (sing. *bidʿah*)
See *bidʿah.*

bidʿah (pl. *bidaʿ*)
Lit., innovation, often refers to a heretical or illegal innovation in religion. *Bidʿah ḥasanah* is a good or desirable innovation while *bidʿah sayyiʾah* is a bad or undesirable innovation.

ḍaʿīf (ḥadīth)
Refers to reports attributed to the Prophet that are considered weak or suspect.

dalālah ʿaqlīyyah wāḍiḥah
Rational proof, an element in the legal analysis dictated by rational proof or evidence; also known as *dalīl ʿaqlī.*

dalālah samʿiyyah wāḍiḥah

Textual evidence or proof, evidence from a textual source; also known as *dalīl samʿī* or *dalīl naṣṣī*.

faqīh (pl. fuqahāʾ):

Jurist; a specialist in Islamic law.

farḍ (pl. furūḍ)

Syn. of *wājib*. Islamic law: one of the five categories or values of *Sharīʿah*, connoting that which is obligatory or mandatory. Some schools of law, such as the Ḥanafī school, distinguish *farḍ* from *wājib*. See also *wājib* and *Sharīʿah*.

fatwā (pl. *fatāwā*)

Responsum. Non-binding legal opinion issued in response to a legal problem.

fiqh

Lit., the understanding or comprehension. Islamic law: the process of jurisprudence by which the rules of Islamic law are derived. The word is also used to refer generally to law.

fitan (sing. *fitnah*)

See *fitnah*.

fitnah (pl. *fitan*)

Calamity, corruption, civil discord. Enticement or seduction.

furūʿ (sing. *farʿ*)

Branch, sub-division, as distinguished from *aṣl*. Islamic law: a branch or sub-division in which disagreement is permitted; a new and original problem or case. See also *uṣūl*.

gharīb

A type of *aḥādī* tradition that is narrated from only one narrator to another, and so forth, throughout the entire transmission, or throughout a portion thereof. See also *aḥādī*.

ḥadīth (pl. *aḥādīth*)

Lit., report, account or statement. Islamic law: a Prophetic tradition transmitted through a chain of narrators by which the Prophet or his *Sunnah* is known. The term may also be used to refer to a statement by one of the Companions. See also *Sunnah* and *ahl al-ḥadīth*.

ḥājah

Need or necessity.

ḥajj

The fifth of five pillars of Islam in which the devotee travels to Mecca to perform the rites of pilgrimage.

ḥalāl

Syn. of *mubāḥ*. Islamic law: one of the five categories or values of *Sharīʿah*, connoting that which is permitted or allowed. Most schools hold that everything is permitted unless there is evidence declaring it to be prohibited. Most schools adhere to a presumption of permissibility, and so the burden of proof is against the person arguing for a prohibition. See also *Sharīʿah*.

ḥālat tazāḥum

Conflicting obligations of the *Sharīʿah* in which a jurist must perform a priorities analysis (*baḥth fī awlawiyyāt al-Sharīʿah*) in order to determine which obligation must supersede the others.

Ḥanafī (Ḥanafiyyah)

Adherent of the Sunnī juristic school of thought named after its eponym Abū Ḥanīfah al-Nuʿmān (d. 150/767). One of the four main Sunnī jurisprudential schools, it originated in Kufa and Basra, but spread in the Middle East and Indian subcontinent.

Ḥanīfiyyah

An early monotheistic faith in the Arabian Peninsula prior to the revelation of the Qurʾān in Mecca. Not much is known about them or their rituals.

Ḥanbalī (Ḥanābilah)

Adherent of the Sunnī juristic school of thought named after its eponym Aḥmad b. Ḥanbal (d. 241/855). One of the four main Sunnī jurisprudential schools, its adherents are found primarily in Saudi Arabia.

ḥarām

Islamic law: one of the five categories or values of *Sharīʿah*, connoting that which is forbidden or sinful. See also *Sharīʿah*.

ḥasan bi dhātih

That which has an inherent moral quality.

ḥasan (ḥadīth)

Ḥadīth attributed to the Prophet whose authenticity is considered good.

hawā

Whim, caprice, or fancy.

ḥijāb

Lit., obstruction, shield, shelter, protection, cover, screen, seclusion, obscure and hide. The veil with which a Muslim woman usually covers her head, except her face.

ḥikmat al-ḥukm

Purpose or ultimate wisdom behind a ruling or law. See also *qiyās ʿalā al-maqṣad*.

ḥukm (pl. *aḥkām*)
Decree of God. Islamic law: a legally binding judgment, ruling, rule of law. See also *aḥkām*.

ḥukm qiyāsī
Ruling arrived at through the use of analogy (*qiyās*); a rule derived from a prior precedent.

ḥukm shar'ī
Legal ruling on an issue; the rule of *Sharī'ah*. See also *Sharī'ah*.

ḥusn
Lit., the beautiful or good. Islamic law: that which is moral and good. See also *qubḥ*.

'ibādah
Lit., servitude and submission. Islamic law: an act of worship arising out of the relationship between Creator and created.

'ibādāt
As distinguished from *mu'āmalāt*, laws of worship regulating the relationship between humans and God, concerning the rights of God over people (*ḥuqūq Allāh*).

Ibāḍī
A follower of the Ibāḍiyyah, a sect descended from the early Khawārij. However, the Ibāḍiyyah has modified much of the original doctrines of the Khawārij, and they now resemble Sunnī Muslims.

ijmā'
Lit., consensus, agreement. Islamic law: consensus of legal opinion. Jurists differed, however, about the binding nature of *ijmā'*, requirements of eligibility, conditions for its nullification, whether or not it is limited by time and place, etc.

ijtihād
Lit., exertion. The process of exerting one's utmost in an effort to deduce laws from sources in unprecedented cases. Novel or original legal solutions, the effort of a jurist in searching for and deducing the correct law. See also *taqlīd*.

ikhtilāf
Juristic disagreement and diversity of opinion.

'ilal
Field within the science of *ḥadīth* (*'ilm al-ḥadīth*) related to the defects of Prophetic reports, as part of the process of substantive *matn* analysis. See also *'ilal qādiḥa fī al-matn*.

ʿilal qādiḥah fī al-matn

Category within the field of *ʿilal* (defects) in the science of *ḥadīth* (*ʿilm al-ḥadīth*) that is utilized when the authenticity of a report is suspect or rejected because it contains grammatical or historical errors, contradicts the Qur'ān, or is contrary to the laws of nature, common human experience, or the dictates of reason, regardless of how sound the chain of transmission. See also *ʿilal* and *ʿilm al-ḥadīth.*

ʿillah (pl. *ʿilal*)

Lit., the cause. Islamic law: the operative or effective cause of a ruling, the *ratio legis*. In the language of jurists, "*al-ʿillah tadūr maʿa al-maʿlūl wujūdan wa ʿadaman*" [The rule exists if the operative cause exists and the rule does not exist if the operative cause does not exist].

ʿilm al-dirāyah

Branch of *ʿilm al-ḥadīth*, also known as *ʿilm al-ḥadīth al-khāṣṣ bi-al-dirāyah*, which evaluates the historical plausibility, social implications, and categories of *ḥadīth* as factors to be considered in a legal decision or in formulating the law. See also *ʿilm al-riwāyah.*

ʿilm al-ḥadīth

Science of *ḥadīth* methodology, comprising the authentication of *ḥadīth* based on chains of transmission and contextual analysis. See also *ḥadīth.*

ʿilm al-kalām

Science of theology and dogmatics, scholastic theology, theological disputations. Considered reprehensible in contemporary Wahhābī thought.

ʿilm al-riwāyah

Science of transmission that focuses on the evaluation of the transmitters of *ḥadīth*, and an assessment of their trustworthiness, and the soundness of reports. See also *ʿilm al-ḥadīth* and *ʿilm al-dirāyah.*

imām

Lit., one who stands out in front. Islamic law: leader of prayer or of a congregation. Commonly used to refer to a religious leader.

Ismāʿīlī (Ismāʿīliyyah)

An adherent to a sect that branched off from the Shīʿah. Ismāʿīlīs trace the imāmate through Jaʿfar al-Ṣādiq's son Ismāʿīl, after whom the sect is named. After the death of Jaʿfar al-Ṣādiq in 148/765, a group of his followers held fast to the imāmate of his son Ismāʿīl, who had been named by Jaʿfar as successor but who had predeceased his father. Some of Ismāʿīl's followers maintained that Ismāʿīl had not died and would reappear as the qā'im or mahdī (rightly guided leader from the family of the Prophet). See also Jaʿfarī, and Zaydī.

isnād

Chain of transmission for a report or tradition traced back to Prophet Muhammad. One of two prongs tested to establish the authenticity of a *ḥadīth*, the other being contextual analysis of meaning, i.e., *matn* analysis. See also *matn* and *ḥadīth*.

al-istibdād bi al-ra'y

Authoritarianism, intellectual despotism.

isti'dhān (or isti'dhāniyyāt)

See *adab*.

ittiḥād al-ʿillah

Unity of operative causes (*ʿillah*) between two or more cases, which must be established in order to extend the ruling of a precedent to the unprecedented case. See also *ittiḥād al-qaṣd* and *ʿillah*.

ittīḥād al-qaṣd

Unity of objectives or purposes (*qaṣd*) between two or more cases, which most jurists would not accept as a valid determination for the use of analogy (*qiyās*) unless rigorously justified and defended. The scope of laws that are derived according to this method is much broader than that derived from determining a unity of operative causes (*ittiḥād al-ʿillah*). See also *ittiḥād al-ʿillah* and *qiyās*.

Jaʿfarī (Jaʿfariyyah)

Adherent of the Shīʿī juristic school of thought named after its eponym Jaʿfar al-Ṣādiq, the sixth Imām in Shīʿī theology. One of the main jurisprudential schools founded in Medina. See also Ismāʿīlī, and Zaydī.

jibillah

Natural disposition, nature, temper.

jahd al-qarīḥah

See *badhl al-naẓar*.

kāfir (pl. *kuffār*)

Non-believer, someone who denies God or the prophethood of Muḥammad. Someone who is ungrateful towards God. See also *kufr*.

khafiyy

Subtle or not apparent.

kalām

See *ʿilm al-kalām*.

kharq al-ʿādah

Breach of the physical rules of nature.

khulʿ
A legal procedure by which a woman divorces herself from her husband provided that she returns her dowry or abandons all financial claims in exchange for a no-cause divorce

khuṭba
A religious sermon most often delivered during Friday prayers.

madhhab (pl. *madhāhib*)
School of thought, juristic school, legal guild, orientation, opinion or view. A juristic school of thought is distinguished by its jurisprudential methodology for deducing laws. Disagreements over methodology often distinguish one school from another. Legal school of thought such as Shāfiʿī, Mālikī, Ḥanafī and Ḥanbalī.

maḍmūn al-naṣṣ
See *mafhūm al-naṣṣ.*

mafhūm al-naṣṣ
The implied meaning in a text or that which is inferred by implication.

mafsada
Corruption or evil; that which leads to a corrupted state of affairs.

makrūh
Islamic law: one of the five categories or values of *Sharīʿah*, connoting that which is reprehensible, discouraged, not preferred. See also *Sharīʿah.*

Mālikī (Mālikiyyah)
Adherent of the Sunnī juristic school of thought named after its eponym Mālik b. Anas (d. 179/795) and distinguished for its emphasis on the practice of the inhabitants of Medina. One of the four main Sunnī jurisprudential schools that later predominated in Muslim Spain and North Africa. Today, it is widespread in North and sub-Saharan Africa.

mandūb
See *mustaḥabb* and *Sharīʿah.*

maqāṣid
Purpose or ultimate wisdom behind an endeavor, be it an idea, intent, or system, such as *maqāṣid al-Sharīʿah,* or the ultimate wisdom behind Islamic law. See also *qiyās ʿalā al-maqṣad* and *Sharīʿah.*

maqṣad (pl. *maqāṣid*)
See *maqāṣid.*

matn
Substance, text. Islamic law: generally refers to the textual content of a *ḥadīth.* A *matn* analysis of a *ḥadīth* is one of two prongs relied upon to establish the authenticity of a *ḥadīth*, the other being chain of transmission.

Accordingly, a *ḥadīth* may be rejected if it contains grammatical or historical errors, contradicts the Qur'ān, conflicts with the laws of nature, common experience, or the dictates of reason, regardless of the authenticity of its chain of transmission. See also *isnād* and *ḥadīth.*

mīthāq al-naṣṣ

See *mafhūm al-naṣṣ.*

mu'āmalāt

As distinguished from *'ibādāt*, laws that pertain to human intercourse and concern the rights of people over one another (*ḥuqūq al-'ibād*).

mubāḥ

See *ḥalāl.*

muftī

A jurist who issues legal *responsa.*

muḥaddith

Scholar who memorizes *ḥadīth* with their chains of transmission and transmits them. See also *ḥadīth.*

mujtahid

As distinguished from *muqallid*, a jurist who performs *ijtihād* or is qualified to perform *ijtihād.* See *ijtihād* and *taqlīd.*

Murji'īs

Adherent of the Murji'ah theological school, a branch in early Islam that played a significant political role. Their ideas were often described as politically quietist or passive. The basic tenet of their belief was that those who committed grave sins do not cease to be Muslims. They also believed in the suspension of judgment (*irjā'*) on political conflicts until God resolves all matters in the Hereafter.

musnad (pl. *masānīd*)

Islamic law: a *ḥadīth* with a continuous chain of transmitters; a compilation of reports and traditions from and about the Prophet and the Companions organized by the name of the transmitter. Often distinguished from *sunan*, which is arranged topically.

mustaḥabb

Islamic law: one of the five categories or values of *Sharī'ah*, connoting that which is recommended, commendable, preferred. See also *Sharī'ah.*

mutawātir

Ḥadīth reported by a large number of people; a report having cumulative authenticity because of the presumption that it could not have possibly been fabricated by such a large number of transmitters. *Mutawātir* reports are considered to be authentic beyond doubt. See also *aḥādī.*

Mu'tazilah
Rationalist school of Islamic theology that emphasized the role of reason and the belief in the absolute necessity of God's justice and human free will. The term came to connote a variety of theological and juristic orientations. The basic tenets of the school were the belief that the Qur'ān was created and that the physical attributes of God mentioned in the Qur'ān are allegorical.

Mu'tazilī
Adherent of the Mu'tazila theological school. See also *Mu'tazilah.*

naṣṣ (pl. *nuṣūṣ*)
Text from which the law is derived; an injunction or textual ruling.

Qadarīs
Early theological school in Islam that believed in free will. Considered the precursors to the Mu'tazila.

qawwāmūna
Those who provide support, protection maintenance, guardianship, sustenance. Refers to the duties of men towards women.

qiyās
Deduction by analogy. Islamic law: juristic methodology that relies on the use of analogy for unprecedented cases in which the source texts do not provide a conclusive legal decision. A methodology by which the ruling of a precedent is extended to a new case. The method of analogizing from a preexisting law to a new situation. See also *qiyās adnā* and *qiyās 'alā al-maqṣad.*

qiyās adnā
A subtle analogy whose second premise is less forceful than the first. For example, the statement of Mālik and Abū Ḥanīfah: "If amputation of a legally designated limb according to a given measure is obligatory in the case of theft, then taking back dowries while married carries the same [punishment]." The following of an indirect precedent or precedent that is not directly on point. See also *qiyās* and *qiyās 'alā al-maqṣad.*

qiyās 'alā al-maqṣad
An analogy based on a similarity of purposes or objectives. This type of *qiyās* does not focus on the operative cause (*'illah*) of the ruling (*ḥukm*), but on the purpose or reason (*maqṣad*) behind the ruling. The scope of such an analogy is far-reaching as opposed to an analogy based on a unity of operative causes. See also *qiyās*, *qiyās adnā*, *'illah*, *ḥukm*, and *maqāṣid.*

qiyās khafiyy
See *qiyās adnā.*

qubḥ
Ugliness. Islamic law: immorality. See also *ḥusn.*

Ramaḍān

Ninth month of the Islamic calendar year. Marks the fourth of five pillars of Islam during which Muslims abstain from food, drink, conjugal relations, and all sins and indecencies from dawn to sunset each day.

rāwī

Lit., one who orally transmits, a narrator, transmitter. Islamic law: transmitter of *ḥadīth*. See also *riwāyah* and *ḥadīth*.

riwāyah

Narration, usually referring to a *ḥadīth*. See also *ʿilm al-riwāyah*.

ṣaḥīḥ

Lit., authentic, valid, true, correct. Islamic law: report or tradition considered validly traced to the Prophet after analysis based on chain of transmission and contextual meaning. The six canonical collections (*ṣiḥāḥ*) of *ḥadīth* considered to be authoritative by Sunnī Muslims were compiled by al-Bukhārī, Muslim, al-Nasāʾī, Ibn Mājah, Abū Dāwūd and al-Tirmidhī.

Salafism

An ideology that advocates the return to the pristine origins of the rightly guided predecessors, which usually refers to the Prophet and his Companions. Also calls for the abandonment of: 1) the accumulations of the past, 2) superstitions, and 3) the blind adherence to legal precedent or the traditional legal schools of thought. Wahhābism, in its present form, is a particular orientation within Salafism. Wahhābism exhibits a greater hostility, than Salafism, to Sufism, the juristic heritage, and all forms of rationalistic orientations in the Islamic tradition. It is fair to say that all puritanical groups in the Muslim world are Salafī in orientation but not necessarily Wahhābī.

ṣawm al-wiṣāl

Perpetual fasting from dawn to sunset. Such an exercise was forbidden to Muslims as it stood contrary to the Islamic call for balance and moderation.

Shāfiʿī (Shāfiʿiyyah)

Adherent of the Sunnī juristic school of thought named after its eponym Muḥammad b. Idrīs al-Shāfiʿī (d. 204/820). One of the four main Sunnī jurisprudential schools, it is currently widespread in Egypt and South East Asia.

shakk

Suspicion, doubt.

sharʿ man qablanā

Precedent legislation of bygone generations; past course of conduct of people, which is considered in investigating the Divine Will.

sharʿī fatwā

Legal *responsum* that is issued in conformity with the rules and principles of Islamic law.

Sharīʿah

Lit., water source, the way, the path. Islamic theology and law: the path or way given by God to human beings, the path by which human beings search God's Will. Commonly translated as "Islamic law," or "Divine law," but *Sharīʿah* carries a much broader meaning as the sum total of categorizations of all human actions, namely: mandatory (*farḍ* or *wājib*), encouraged (*mustaḥabb* or *mandūb*), permissible (*ḥalāl* or *mubāḥ*), discouraged (*makrūh*), and forbidden (*ḥarām* or *maḥẓūr*). *Sharīʿah* is not restricted to positive law *per se* but includes moral and ethical values, and the jurisprudential process, itself.

sīrah

Lit., derives from *sāra*, he walked. Refers to the biography of the Prophet, i.e., how he walked and the path he tread throughout his life. Also means the conduct of those from the past.

Ṣūfī

Lit., one who wears a coat of wool. This term has been applied to Muslims who seek to achieve higher degrees of spiritual excellence or those who pursue Islamic mysticism or those who belong to a mystical order.

Ṣūfism

Theology and practice that emphasizes the attainment of higher stations of spiritual awareness and moral excellence. See also Ṣūfī.

sunnah

Lit., the way or course or conduct of life. Islamic law: the example of the Prophet embodied in his statements, actions, and those matters that he silently approved or disapproved of as reported in *ḥadīth* literature. Also refers to Sunnī Muslims as distinguished from the Shīʿah branch of Islam. See also *ḥadīth.*

sunnah tashrīʿiyyah

Sunnah of the Prophet that has normative legal value.

sunnat al-kawn

Laws through which God sustains the universe, which are considered in investigating the Divine Will. See also *sunnat al-khalq*.

sunnat al-khalq

Laws of nature, patterns of creation. See also *sunnat al-kawn.*

ṭabīʿat al-khalq

Human nature or the habits and intuitions of human beings which are considered in investigating the Divine Will.

taḥqīq maṣāliḥ al-ʿibād
To achieve the welfare or good of the people; purpose or object of Islamic law. See also *Sharīʿah.*

takhṣīṣ
Specification of a Qurʾānic verse or Prophetic tradition of general legal scope.

taklīf
Islamic law: legal charge or obligation. It often refers to duties imposed by God upon human beings.

ṭalab al-ʿilm
Seeking knowledge, which is a religious obligation upon every Muslim man and woman.

talfīq
Choosing between, and mixing the opinions of, various schools of jurisprudence in order to reach the most prudent and useful result.

taqlīd
Lit., imitation. Islamic law: the term signifies the imitation of more knowledgeable scholars, usually within a particular school of thought. *Taqlīd* is often considered the opposite of *ijtihād.* See also *ijtihād.*

tashrīʿiyyah
As distinguished from *afʿāl jibilliyyah,* actions of the Prophet that fall under one of the five categories of *Sharīʿah.* Covers matters relating to the Prophet's roles as messenger of God, as head of state, or as judge. Examples of this are his verdicts related to marriage and divorce, inheritance, and commercial dealings. Also included are matters related to the practice of Islam's five pillars. See also *afʿāl jibilliyyah* and *Sharīʿah.*

tawātur
See *mutawātir.*

Umayyad
First Muslim dynasty initiated after the death of the Rightly Guided Caliphs. Established by Muʿāwiyah b. Abī Sufyān (d. 60/680) upon the death of ʿAlī b. Abī Ṭālib (d. 40/661), it lasted from 41/661 to 132/750.

ummah
Community of Muslims; the Muslim nation.

ʿumūm al-balwā
Of widespread affect, impact, or connotation.

uṣūl (sing. *aṣl*)
Lit., origins, foundations, fundamentals. The foundations of faith or fundamentals of religion upon which disagreement is not tolerated. See also *furūʿ* and *uṣūl al-fiqh.*

uṣūl al-fiqh
The principles upon which Islamic jurisprudence is based; the jurisprudential methods of Islamic law.

Uṣūlīs
As distinguished from *Furūʿīs,* a jurist qualified in the science of jurisprudential theory and trained to formulate law from the hermeneutic principles of jurisprudence. See also *uṣūl* and *furūʿ*. In practice, the Uṣūlīs came to connote jurisprudential orientation or discipline that emphasized reliance on the totality of the evidence in deducing the law. Often connotes an orientation opposed to Ahl al-Ḥadīth or, in the Shiʿī context, the Akhbārīs. See also *uṣūl al-fiqh.*

Wahhābīs (Wahhābiyyah)
Follower of the strict puritanical teachings of Muḥammad b. ʿAbd al-Wahhāb (d. 1207/1792). Wahhābīs are hostile to the intercession of saints, visiting the tombs of saints, Sufism, Shīʿism, and rational methods of deducing laws. The Wahhābī creed is markedly restrictive of women and dominates in Saudi Arabia and many other parts of the Muslim world.

wājib (pl. *wājibāt*)
Syn. of *farḍ*. Islamic law: one of the five categories or values of *Sharīʿah,* connoting that which is obligatory, mandatory. In the Ḥanafī school, an essential obligation or duty drawn from a clear, precise, and definitive source is termed *fare,* whereas a lesser obligation drawn from a source whose proof value is not necessarily clear and certain, but rather probable is termed *wājib*. See also *wājibāt, farḍ* and *Sharīʿah.*

wājibāt (sing. *wājib*)
Islamic legal obligations or duties. See also *wājib.*

walāʾ
Loyalty or fidelity.

yaqīn qaṭʿī
Certainty, certitude, or solid conviction; definitive, certain, and non-speculative legal proof. The opposite of *ẓann*. See also *ẓann.*

Ẓāhirīs (Ẓāhiriyyah)
Adherent of the Sunnī juristic school of thought named after its dominant heuristic method of relying on the literal meaning (*ẓāhir*) of texts. The founder of the school was Dāwūd b. Khalaf (d. 270/884). Its most famous

proponent was the jurist Ibn Ḥazm of Muslim Spain. The school is now largely defunct, although the works of Ibn Ḥazm are still in circulation.

zakāh

Lit., to purify, bless, increase. Islamic law: the third of five pillars of Islam in which one purifies one's wealth or property by donating at least 2.5% of one's net income after expenses. This amount is collected annually at the end of Ramaḍān and distributed to any of eight categories of people, as the Qur'ān details in {9:60}.

ẓann

Probability. That which has not reached the level of certainty (*yaqīn*). Speculative, uncertain, speculation, supposition, likely, probable. The opposite of *yaqīn* (certainty). See also *yaqīn qaṭʿī*.

Zaydī

Known as the Shīʿī Seveners; a Shīʿī branch that today pre-dominates in Yemen. See also Ismāʿīlī, and Jaʿfarī.

Works Cited

بسم الله الرحمن الرحيم

Arabic Works

Abū Ḥayyān al-Andalusī, Muḥammad b. Yūsuf. *Tafsīr al-Baḥr al-Muḥīṭ*. Eds. ʿĀdil ʿAbd al-Mawjūd and ʿAlī Muḥammad Muʿawwaḍ. Beirut: Dār al-Kutub al-ʿIlmiyyah, 1993.

Abū Zahrah, Muḥammad. *Uṣūl al-Fiqh*. Cairo: Dār al-Fikr al-ʿArabī, n.d.

al-Albānī, Muḥammad Nāṣir al-Dīn. *Hijab al-Mar'ah al-Muslimah*. Cairo: Al-Maktabah al-Salafiyyah, 1374.

___. *Silsilat al-Aḥādīth al-Ḍaʿīfah wa al-Mawḍūʿah*. Riyadh: Maktabat al-Maʿārif, 1988.

___. *Silsilat al-Aḥādīth al-Ṣaḥīḥa*. Beirut: al-Maktab al-Islāmī, 1972.

al-ʿĀlim, Yūsuf Ḥāmid. *al-Maqāṣid al-ʿĀmmah li al-Sharīʿah al-Islāmiyyah*. Herndon, Va.: International Institute of Islamic Thought, 1991.

al-Alūsī, Abū al-Faḍl Shihāb al-Dīn Maḥmūd. *Rūḥ al-Maʿānī fī Tafsīr al-Qur'ān al-ʿAẓīm wa al-Sabʿ al-Mathānī*. Beirut: Dār Iḥyā' al-Turāth al-ʿArabī, 1985.

al-Āmidī, Sayf al-Dīn Abū al-Ḥasan ʿAlī b. Abī ʿAlī b. Muḥammad. *al-Iḥkām fī Uṣūl al-Aḥkām*. Cairo: Muḥammad ʿAlī Sābī, 1968.

___. *al-Iḥkām fī Uṣūl al-Aḥkām*. Ed. Sayyid Jamīlī. Beirut: Dār al-Kitāb al-ʿArabī, 1984.

al-As'adī, Muḥammad 'Ubayd Allāh. *al-Mūjaz fī Uṣūl al-Fiqh*. N.p.: Dār al-Salām, 1990.

al-Asnawī, Jamāl al-Dīn Abī Muḥammad 'Abd al-Raḥīm b. al-Ḥasan. *Nihāyat al-Sūl fī Sharḥ Minhāj al-Wuṣūl ilā 'Ilm al-Uṣūl*. Ed. Sha'bān Ismā'īl. Beirut: Dār Ibn Ḥazm, 1999.

al-'Ayīnī, Badr al-Dīn Aḥmad. *'Umdat al-Qārī Sharḥ Ṣaḥīḥ al-Bukhārī*. Beirut: Dār al-Fikr, n.d.

Ayyūb, Ḥasan. *al-Sulūk al-Ijtimā'ī fī al-Islām*. Cairo: Dār al-Buḥūth al-'Ilmiyyah, 1979.

al-Badakhshī, Muḥammad b. al-Ḥasan. *Sharḥ al-Badakhshī Manāhij al-'Uqūl ma'a Sharḥ al-Asnawī Nihāyat al-Sūl*. Beirut: Dār al-Kutub al-'Ilmiyyah, 1984.

Badrān, Badrān Abū al-'Aynayn. *Uṣūl al-Fiqh*. Cairo: Dār al-Ma'ārif, 1965.

al-Baghawī, Ḥusayn b. Mas'ūd. *Sharḥ al-Sunnah*. Beirut: Dār al-Fikr, 1994.

al-Bahūtī, Manṣūr b. Yūnus. *Kashshāf al-Qinā' 'an Matn al-Iqnā'*. Ed. Abū 'Abd Allāh Ismā'īl. Beirut: Dār al-Kutub al-'Ilmiyyah, 1997.

Balīq, 'Izz al-Dīn. *Minhāj al-Ṣāliḥīn*. Beirut: Dār al-Fatḥ, 1978.

Bāqir al-Ṣadr, Muḥammad. *Durūs fī 'Ilm al-Uṣūl*. Beirut: Dār al-Kitāb al-Libnānī, 1978.

al-Baṣrī, Abū al-Ḥusayn Muḥammad b. 'Alī b. al-Ṭayyib. *al-Mu'tamad fī Uṣūl al-Fiqh*. Ed. Khalīl al-Mays. Beirut: Dār al-Kutub al-'Ilmiyyah, 1983.

___. *Kitāb al-Mu'tamad fī Uṣūl al-Fiqh*. Ed. Muḥammad Ḥamīd Allāh, Muḥammad Bakr, and Ḥasan Ḥanafī. Damascus: Institut Français, 1964.

al-Bayhaqī, Abū Bakr Aḥmad b. al-Ḥusayn b. 'Alī. *Kitāb al-Sunan al-Kubrā*. Beirut: Dār al-Ma'rifah, n.d.

al-Bukhārī, 'Alā' al-Dīn. *Kashf al-Asrār*. Beirut: Dār al-Kitāb al-'Arabī, n.d.

al-Bukhārī, Muḥammad. *al-Adab al-Mufrad.* Beirut: Mu'assasat al-Kitāb, 1986.

al-Burūsī, Ismā'īl Ḥaqqī. *Tanwīr al-Adhhān min Tafsīr Rūḥ al-Bayān.* Ed. Muḥammad 'Alī al-Ṣābūnī. Damascus: Dār al-Qalam, 1989.

al-Dāraquṭnī, 'Alī b. 'Umar. *Sunan al-Dāraquṭnī.* Ed. Majdī b. Sayyid al-Shūrī. Beirut: Dār al-Kutub al-'Ilmiyyah, 1996.

al-Dawālībī, Muḥammad Ma'rūf. *Madkhal ilā 'Ilm Uṣūl al-Fiqh.* 5th ed. N.p.: Dār al-'Ilm li al-Malāyīn, 1965.

al-Dawīsh, Aḥmad b. 'Abd al-Razzāq, ed. *Fatāwā al-Lajnah al-Dā'imah li al-Buḥūth al-'Ilmiyyah wa al-Iftā'.* Riyadh: Dār 'Ālam al-Kutub, 1991.

al-Dībānī, 'Abd al-Majīd 'Abd al-Ḥamīd. *al-Minhāj al-Wāḍiḥ fī 'Ilm Uṣūl al-Fiqh wa Ṭuruq Istinbāṭ al-Aḥkām.* Binghāzī: Dār al-Kutub al-Waṭaniyyah, 1995.

al-Dimashqī, Abū 'Abd Allāh 'Abd al-Raḥmān. *Raḥmat al-Umma fī Ikhtilāf al-A'imma.* Kuwait: Maktabat al-Bukhārī, n.d.

al-Dimashqī, Abū Ḥafṣ 'Umar b. 'Alī Ibn 'Ādil. *al-Lubāb fī 'Ulūm al-Kitāb.* Eds. 'Ādil Aḥmad 'Abd al-Mawjūd and 'Alī Muḥammad Mu'awwaḍ. Beirut: Dār al-Kutub al-'Ilmiyyah, 1998.

Fakhr al-Dīn al-Rāzī, Muḥammad b. 'Umar b. al-Ḥusayn. *'Ilal al-Ḥadīth.* Beirut: Dār al-Ma'rifa, 1985.

___. *al-Maḥṣūl fī 'Ilm Uṣūl al-Fiqh.* Beirut: Dār al-Kutub al-'Ilmiyya, n.d.

___. *al-Maḥṣūl fī 'Ilm Uṣūl al-Fiqh.* Ed. Ṭāhā Jābir Fayyāḍ al-'Alwānī. 3rd ed. Beirut: Mu'assasat al-Risāla, 1997.

___. *al-Maḥṣūl fī 'Ilm Uṣūl al-Fiqh.* Beirut: Dār al-Kutub al-'Ilmiyya, 1988.

___. *al-Tafsīr al-Kabīr* (*a.k.a. Mafātīḥ al-Ghayb*). Beirut: Dār al-Kutub al-'Ilmiyya, 1990.

al-Ghazālī, Abū Ḥāmid Muḥammad b. Muḥammad. *Iḥyā' 'Ulūm al-Dīn.* Cairo: Dār al-Ma'rifah, n.d.

___. *al-Mankhūl min Ta'līqāt al-Uṣūl.* Damascus: Dār al-Fikr, 1980.

___. *al-Mustaṣfā min ʿIlm al-Uṣūl*. Ed. Ibrāhīm Muḥammad Ramaḍān. Beirut: Dār al-Arqam, n.d.

___. *al-Mustaṣfā min ʿIlm al-Uṣūl*. Baghdad: Maktabat al-Mathannā, n.d.

al-Ghazālī, Muḥammad. *Dustūr al-Wiḥdah al-Thaqafiyyah Bayn al-Muslimīn*. Cairo: Dār al-Ansar, 1981.

___. *Humūm Dāʿiyah*. Cairo: Dār al-Bashīr, 1984.

___. *Kayf Nafham al-Islām*. Cairo: Dār al-Kutub al-Islāmiyyah, 1983.

___. *Khuluq al-Muslim*. Cairo: Dār al-Kutub al-Islāmiyyah, 1983.

___. *al-Sunnah al-Nabawiyyah Bayn Ahl al-Fiqh wa Ahl al-Ḥadīth*. Cairo: Dār al-Shurūq, 1989.

al-Ghiṭāʾ, Muḥammad al-Ḥusayn Āl Kāshif. *Naqḍ Fatāwā al-Wahhābiyyah*. Beirut: Markaz al-Ghadīr, 1999.

al-Ḥakīm al-Nīsābūrī, Abū ʿAbd Allāh. *al-Mustadrak ʿalā al-Ṣaḥīḥayn*. Beirut: Dār al-Maʿrifah, n.d.

al-Harawī, Abū ʿUbayd al-Qāsim b. Salām. *Gharīb al-Ḥadīth*. Beirut: Dār al-Kutub al-ʿIlmiyyah, 1986.

al-Ḥarrānī, Aḥmad b. Ḥamdān. *Ṣifat al-Fatwā wa al-Muftī wa al-Mustaftī*. Ed. Muḥammad Nāṣir al-Albānī. Damascus: al-Maktab al-Islāmī, 1380.

Harrās, Muḥammad Khalīl. *al-Ḥarakah al-Wahhābiyyah: Radd ʿalā Maqāl li al-Duktūr Muḥammad al-Bahī fī Naqd al-Wahhābiyyah*. Beirut: Dār al-Kitāb al-ʿArabī, n.d.

al-Ḥaṭṭāb, Abū ʿAbd Allāh. *Mawāhib al-Jalīl li Sharḥ Mukhtaṣar Khalīl*. Beirut: Dār al-Kutub al-ʿIlmiyyah, 1995.

al-Hindī, ʿAlāʾ al-Dīn ʿAlī al-Muttaqī b. Ḥusām al-Dīn al-Burhān Fawzī. *Kanz al-ʿUmmāl fī Sunan al-Aqwāl wa al-Afʿāl*. Beirut: Muʾassasat al-Risāla, 1985.

Ibn ʿAbd al-Barr, Abū ʿUmar Yūsuf b. ʿAbd Allāh b. Muḥammad al-Nimrī. *al-Tamhīd li-mā fī al-Muwaṭṭaʾ min al-Maʿānī wa al-Asānīd*. Eds. Muṣtafā al-ʿAlawī and Muḥammad al-Bakrī Morroco: Maktabat Faḍālah, 1982.

Ibn ʿAbd al-Wahhāb, Muḥammad. *Kitāb al-Tawḥīd alladhī huwa Ḥaqq Allāh ʿalā al-ʿAbīd.* Cairo: Dār al-Maʿārif, 1974.

Ibn ʿAbd al-Wahhāb, Sulaymān. *al-Ṣawāʿiq al-Ilāhiyyah fī al-Radd ʿalā al-Wahhābiyyah.* Ed. Bassām ʿAmqiyyah. Damascus: Maktabat Ḥarrāʾ, 1997.

Ibn Abī Shaybah, Abū Bakr ʿAbd Allāh b. Muḥammad. *al-Kitāb al-Muṣannaf fī al-Aḥādīth wa al-Āthār.* Ed. Muḥammad ʿAbd al-Salām Shāhīn. Beirut: Dār al-Kutub al-ʿIlmiyyah, 1995.

Ibn ʿĀbidīn, Muḥammad Amīn. *Ḥāshiyat Radd al-Muḥtār.* Cairo: Muṣṭafā al-Bābī, 1966.

Ibn al-ʿArabī, Abū Bakr Muḥammad b. ʿAbd Allāh. *Aḥkām al-Qurʾān.* Ed. ʿAlī Muḥammad al-Bijāwī. Beirut: Dār al-Maʿrifah, n.d.

Ibn al-Athīr, Abū al-Saʿādāt al-Mubārak b. Muḥammad al-Jazrī. *al-Nihāyah fī Gharīb al-Ḥadīth wa al-Athar.* Ed. Abū ʿAbd al-Raḥmān b. ʿUwīḍah. Beirut: Dār al-Kutub al-ʿIlmiyyah, 1997.

Ibn ʿAṭiyyah al-Andalusī, Abū Muḥammad ʿAbd al-Ḥaqq b. Ghālib. *al-Muḥarrar al-Wajīz fī Tafsīr al-Kitāb al-ʿAzīz.* Ed. ʿAbd al-Salām ʿAbd al-Shāfī. Beirut: Dār al-Kutub al-ʿIlmiyyah, 1993.

Ibn Badrān, Badrān Abū al-ʿAynayn. *Nuzhat al-Khāṭir al-ʿĀṭir* Beirut: Dār al-Kutub al-ʿIlmiyyah, 1922.

Ibn Bāz, ʿAbd al-ʿAzīz b. ʿAbd Allāh b. ʿAbd al-Raḥmān. *Majmūʿ Fatāwā.* Ed. ʿAbd Allāh b. Muḥammad b. Aḥmad al-Ṭayyār. Riyadh: Dār al-Waṭan, 1416 A.H.

___. *Majmūʿ Fatāwā wa Maqālāt Mutanawwiʿah.* Ed. Muḥammad b. Saʿd al-Shawīʿ. Riyadh: Maktabat al-Maʿārif lī al-Nashrwa al-Tawzīʿ, 1992.

Ibn Fawzān, Ṣāliḥ b. Fawzān b. ʿAbd Allāh. *al-Muntaqā min Fatāwā Faḍīlat al-Shaykh Sāliḥ b. Fawzān b. ʿAbd Allāh al-Fawzān.* Ed. ʿĀdil b. ʿAlī b. Aḥmad al-Farīdān. 2nd ed. Madīnah: Maktabat al-Ghurbān al-Athariyyah, 1997.

Ibn Ḥajar al-ʿAsqalānī, Aḥmad b. ʿAlī. *al-Durar al-Kāminah fī Aʿyān al-Miʾah al-Thāminah.* Ed. ʿAbd al-Wārith Muḥammad ʿAlī. Beirut: Dār al-Kutub al-ʿIlmiyyah, 1997.

___. *Fatḥ al-Bārī fī Sharḥ al-Bukhārī*. Beirut: Dār al-Fikr, 1993.

___. *Fatḥ al-Bārī Sharḥ Ṣaḥīḥ al-Bukhārī*. Eds. Muḥammad Fu'ād 'Abd al-Bāqī and Muḥibb al-Dīn al-Khaṭīb. Beirut: Dār al-Ma'rifah, n.d.

___. *Taqrīb al-Tahdhīb*. Ed. 'Abd al-Wahhāb 'Abd al-Laṭīf. Cairo: n.p., 1975.

Ibn Ḥajar al-Haytamī. *al-Fatāwā al-Kubrā al-Fiqhiyyah*. Beirut: Dār al-Kutub al-'Ilmiyyah, 1983.

Ibn Ḥanbal, Aḥmad. *Musnad al-Imām Aḥmad b. Ḥanbal*. Ed. 'Alī Ḥasan al-Ṭawīl, Samīr Ṭāhā al-Majdhūb, and Samīr Ḥusayn Ghāwī. Beirut: al-Maktab al-Islāmī, 1993.

Ibn Ḥazm, Abū Muḥammad 'Alī b. Aḥmad b. Sa'īd. *al-Muḥallā bi al-Āthār*. Ed. 'Abd al-Ghaffār al-Bandārī. Beirut: al-Kutub al-'Ilmiyyah, n.d.

Ibn Ḥibbān, Muḥammad. *al-Majrūḥīn min al-Muhaddithīn wa al-Ḍu'afā' wa al-Matrūkīn*. Ḥalab: Dār Wa'y, 1397 A.H.

Ibn Jār Allāh, Muḥammad b. Aḥmad al-Ṣa'adī al-Yamānī. *al-Nawāfiḥ al-'Aṭirah fī al-Aḥādīth al-Mushtahirah*. Ed. Muḥammad 'Abd al-Qŭdir 'Aṭā. Beirut: Mu'assasat al-Kutub al-Thaqāfiyyah, 1992.

Ibn al-Jawzī, Abū al-Faraj 'Abd Raḥmān. *Kitāb Aḥkām al-Nisā'*. Beirut: Mu'assasat al-Kutub al-Thaqāfiyyah, 1992.

___. *Kitāb al-Mawḍū'āt*. Beirut: Dār al-Kutub al-'Ilmiyyah, 1995.

___. *Zād al-Masīr fī 'Ilm al-Tafsīr*. Ed. Aḥmad Shams al-Dīn. Beirut: Dār al-Kutub al-'Ilmiyyah, 1994.

Ibn Kathīr, 'Imād al-Dīn Abī al-Fidā' Ismā'īl. *al-Bā'ith al-Hathīth Sharḥ Ikhtiṣār 'Ulūm al-Ḥadīth*. Beirut: Dār al-Kutub al-'Ilmiyyah, 1983.

___. *Mukhtaṣar Tafsīr Ibn Kathīr*. Ed. Muḥammad 'Alī al-Ṣabūnī. Beirut: Dār al-Qur'ān al-Karīm, 1981.

Ibn Khaldūn, Abū Zayd 'Abd al-Raḥmān b. Muḥammad. *al-Muqaddimah*. Beirut: Dār Iḥyā' al-Turāth, n.d.

Ibn Manẓūr, Abū al-Faḍl Jamāl al-Dīn Muḥammad b. Makram. *Lisān al-'Arab*. Beirut: Dār Ṣādir, n.d.

Ibn Mufliḥ, Abū Isḥāq Burhān al-Dīn. *al-Mubdiʿ fī Sharḥ al-Muqniʿ*. Ed. ʿAlī ʿAbd Allāh Āl Thānī. Beirut: al-Maktab al-Islāmī, 1974.

Ibn al-Nujaym, Zayn al-Dīn b. Ibrāhīm b. Muḥammad al-Miṣrī al-Ḥanafī. *Sharḥ al-Baḥr al-Rāʾiq Sharḥ Kanz al-Daqāʾiq*. Beirut: Dār al-Kutub al-ʿIlmiyyah, 1997.

Ibn Qayyim al-Jawziyyah, Shams al-Dīn Abī ʿAbd Allāh Muḥammad b. Abī Bakr. *ʿAwn al-Maʿbūd Sharḥ Sunan Abī Dāwūd*. Ed. ʿAbd al-Raḥmān Muḥammad ʿUthmān. 2nd ed. Medina: al-Maktabah al-Salafiyyah, 1968/1969.

___. *Iʿlām al-Muwaqqiʿīn ʿan Rabb al-ʿĀlamīn*. Ed. ʿAbd al-Raḥmān al-Wakīl. Cairo: Maktabat Ibn Taymiyyah, n.d.

___. *Rawḍat al-Muḥibbīn wa Nuzhat al-Mushtāqīn*. Ed. al-Sayyid al-Jamīlī. 6th ed. Beirut: Dār al-Kitāb al-ʿArabī, 1999.

Ibn Qudāmah, Abū Muḥammad ʿAbd Allāh. *al-Mughnī*. Beirut: Dār Iḥyāʾ al-Turāth al-ʿArabī, n.d.

Ibn Rushd (I), Abū al-Walīd Muḥammad b. Aḥmad. *al-Muqaddimāt al-Mumahhidāt*. Ed. Muḥammad Ḥajjī. Beirut: Dār al-Gharb al-Islāmī, 1988.

Ibn Rushd (II), Abū al-Walīd Muḥammad b. Aḥmad b. Muḥammad b. Aḥmad. *Bidāyat al-Mujtahid wa Nihāyat al-Muqtaṣid*. Beirut: Dār al-Kutub al-ʿIlmiyyah, 1997.

___. *Faṣl al-Maqāl fī mā bayna al-Sharīʿah wa al-Ḥikmah min al-Ittiṣāl*. Ed. Muḥammad ʿImārah. 2nd ed. Cairo: Dār al-Maʿārif, 1983.

Ibn al-Ṣalāḥ al-Shahrazūrī, Abū ʿAmr ʿUthmān b. ʿAbd al-Raḥmān. *Adab al-Muftī wa al-Mustaftī*. Ed. Muwaffaq b. ʿAbd Allāh b. ʿAbd al-Qādir. N.p.: Maktabat al-ʿUlūm wa al-Ḥikam, 1986.

___.*ʿUlūm al-Ḥadīth*. Damascus: Dār al-Fikr, 1986.

Ibn Taymiyyah, Taqī al-Dīn. *Darʾ Taʿāruḍ al-ʿAql wa al-Naql ʾaw Mawāfaqat Ṣaḥīḥ al-Manqūl li Ṣarīḥ al-Maʿqūl*. Ed. Muḥammad Rashād Sālim. Riyadh: Dār al-Kunūz al-Adabiyyah, n.d.

___. *al-Qaḍāʾ wa al-Qadar*. Ed. Aḥmad ʿAbd al-Raḥīm al-Sāyiḥ and al-Sayyid al-Jamīlī. Beirut: Dār al-Kitāb al-ʿArabī, 1991.

___. *Majmūʿat al-Rasāʾil wa al-Masāʾil*. Ed. Muḥammad Rashīd Riḍā. Mecca: Dār al-Bāz, 1976.

___. *al-Tafsīr al-Kabīr*. Ed. ʿAbd al-Raḥmān ʿUmīrah. Beirut: Dār al-Kutub al-ʿIlmiyyah, n.d.

ʿItr, Nūr al-Dīn. *Manhaj al-Naqd fī ʿUlūm al-Ḥadīth*. Damascus: Dār al-Fikr, 1981.

al-Jāḥiz, ʿAmr b. Baḥr b. Maḥbūb. "Kitāb al-Qiyān" in *Rasāʾil al-Jāḥiẓ: al-Rasāʾil al-Kalāmiyyah*. Ed. ʿAlī Abū Milḥim. Beirut: Dār al-Hilāl, 1987.

___. "Kitāb al-Nisāʾ" in *Rasāʾil al-Jāḥiẓ: al-Rasāʾil al-Kalāmiyyah*. Ed. ʿAlī Abū Milḥim. Beirut: Dār al-Hilāl, 1987.

al-Jaṣṣāṣ, Abū Bakr Aḥmad b. ʿAlī al-Razī. *Aḥkām al-Qurʾān*. Beirut: Dār al-Kutub al-ʿIlmiyyah, 1994.

___. *al-Ijmāʿ*. Ed. Zuhayr Shafīq Kabbī. Beirut: Dār al-Muntakhab al-ʿArabī, 1993.

al-Jirāḥī, Ismāʿīl b. Muḥammad al-ʿAjlūnī. *Kashf al-Khafāʾ wa Muzīl al-Ilbās ʿan mā ishahar min al-Aḥādīth ʿalā Alsinat al-Nās*. 2nd ed. Beirut: Dār Iḥyāʾ al-Turāth al-ʿArabī, 1968.

___. *Kashf al-Khafāʾ wa Muzīl al-Ilbās*. Beirut: Muʾassasat al-Risāla, 1983.

al-Jurjānī, Abū Aḥmad ʿAbd Allāh b. ʿUdayy. *al-Kāmil fī Ḍuʿafāʾ al-Rijāl*. Eds. ʿĀdil Aḥmad ʿAbd al-Mawjūd and ʿAlī Muḥammad Muʿawwaḍ. Beirut: Dār al-Kutub al-ʿIlmiyyah, 1997.

al-Juwaynī, *Imām al-Ḥaramayn* Abū al-Maʿālī. *al-Burhān fī Uṣūl al-Fiqh*. Cairo: Dār al-Anṣār, 1400 A.H.

___. *Kitāb al-Ijtihād min Kitāb al-Talkhīṣ*. Damascus: Dār al-Qalam, 1987.

al-Kalūzānī, Abū al-Khaṭṭāb Maḥfūẓ b. Aḥmad b. al-Ḥasan. *al-Tamhīd fī Uṣūl al-Fiqh*. Ed. Muḥammad b. ʿAlī b. Ibrāhīm. Mecca: Markaz al-Baḥth al-ʿIlmī wa Iḥyāʾ al-Turāth al-Islāmī, 1985.

al-Kāsānī, Abū Bakr b. Masʿūd. *Badāʾiʿ al-Ṣanāʾiʿ fī Tartīb al-Sharāʾiʿ*. Eds. ʿAlī Muḥammad Muʿawwaḍ and ʿĀdil ʿAbd al-Mawjūd. Beirut: Dār al-Kutub al-ʿIlmiyyah, 1997.

al-Khan, Muṣṭafā et. al. *Nuzhat al-Muttaqīn Sharḥ Riyāḍ al-Ṣāliḥīn.* Beirut: Mu'assasat al-Risāla, 1987.

al-Khaṭīb al-Baghdādī, Abū Bakr Aḥmad b. 'Alī b. Thābit. *Kitāb al-Faqīh wa al-Mutafaqqih.* N.p.: Maṭba'at al-Imtiyāz, 1977.

al-Kīlānī, 'Abd al-Qādir Ibn al-Sayyid Muḥammad. *al-Nafḥah al-Zakiyyah fī al-Radd 'alā al-Firqah al-Wahhābiyyah.* Damascus: Maṭba'at al-Fayḥā', 1340 A.H.

Kishk, Muḥammad Jalāl. *Akhṭar min al-Naksah.* Kuwait: Dār al-Bayān, 1967.

___. *al-Ghazw al-Fikrī.* 4th ed. Cairo: al-Mukhtār al-Islāmī, 1975.

___. *al-Naksah wa al-Ghazw al-Fikrī.* Beirut: Dār al-Kitāb al-'Arabī, 1969.

al-Kiyyā al-Harrāsī, 'Imād al-Dīn b. Muḥammad. *Aḥkām al-Qur'ān.* Eds. Mūsā Muḥammad 'Alī and 'Izzat 'Alī 'Īd 'Aṭiyyah. Cairo: Dār al-Kutub al-Ḥadītha, 1974.

al-Lāmishī, Abū al-Thanā' Maḥmūd b. Zayd. *Kitāb fī Uṣūl al-Fiqh.* Ed. 'Abd al-Majīd Turkī. Beirut: Dār al-Gharb al-Islāmī, 1995.

Maḥmaṣānī, Ṣubḥī. *Falsafat al-Tashrī' fī al-Islām.* 3rd ed. Beirut: Dār al-'Ilm li al-Malāyīn, 1961.

al-Makkī, Ibn Aḥmad. *Manāqib Abī Ḥanīfah.* Beirut: Dār al-Kitāb al-'Arabī, 1981.

Mālik b. Anas. *al-Muwaṭṭa'.* Ed. Bashshār 'Awād Ma'rūf. 2nd ed. Beirut: Dār al-Gharb al-Islāmī, 1997.

al-Maqdisī, Shams al-Dīn Muḥammad b. Mufliḥ. *Uṣūl al-Fiqh.* Ed. Fahd b. Muḥammad al-Sadhān. Riyadh: Maktabat al-'Ubaykān, 1999.

al-Māwardī, Abū al-Ḥasan 'Alī b. Muḥammad b. Ḥabīb. *al-Ḥāwī al-Kabīr fī Fiqh Madhhab al-Imām al-Shāfi'ī.* Eds. 'Alī Muḥammad Mu'awwaḍ and 'Ādil Aḥmad 'Abd al-Mawjūd. Beirut: Dār al-Kutub al-'Ilmiyyah, 1994.

___. *al-Nukat wa al-'Uyūn.* Ed. al-Sayyid b. 'Abd al-Maqṣūd b. 'Abd al-Raḥīm. Beirut: Dār al-Kutub al-'Ilmiyyah, 1992.

al-Mawdūdī, Abū al-Aʿlā. *al-Ḥijāb*. Cairo: Dār al-Anṣār, 1977.

al-Mubārakfūrī, Muḥammad. *Tuḥfat al-Aḥwadhī fī Sharḥ Jāmiʿ al-Tirmidhī*. Beirut: Dār al-Kutub al-ʿIlmiyyah, n.d.

al-Muqaddim, Muḥammad Aḥmad Ismāʿīl. *ʿAwdat al-Ḥijāb*. Riyadh: Dār Ṭaybah, 1996.

Mutahhari, Murtaza. *Masʾala-i Hijāb*. Tehran: Anjuman-i Islām-yi Pizhishkan, 1969.

al-Nasafī, Abū Barakāt ʿAbd Allāh b. Aḥmad b. Maḥmūd Ḥāfiẓ al-Dīn. *al-Baḥr al-Rāʾiq Sharḥ Kanz al-Daqāʾiq*. Ed. Zakariyyā ʿUmayrāt. Beirut: Dār al-Kutub al-ʿIlmiyyah, 1997.

___. *Tafsīr al-Nasafī*. Cairo: Dār Iḥyāʾ al-Kutub al-ʿArabiyyah, n.d.

al-Nawawī, Muḥyī al-Dīn b. Sharaf Abu Zakariyyā. *Riyāḍ al-Ṣāliḥīn*. Beirut: Dār al-Khayr, 1993.

___. *al-Majmūʿ Sharḥ al-Muhadhdhab*. Cairo: Dār al-Fikr, n.d.

___. *al-Minhāj Sharḥ Ṣaḥīḥ Muslim al-Ḥajjāj*. Ed. Khalīl Maʾmūn Shīḥā. Beirut: Dār al-Maʿrifah, 1996.

___. *Sharḥ Ṣaḥīḥ Muslim al-Musammā al-Minhāj Sharḥ Ṣaḥīḥ Muslim b. Ḥajjāj*. Beirut: Dār al-Maʿrifah, 1996.

___. *Sharḥ Ṣaḥīḥ Muslim*. Beirut: Dār al-Qalam, n.d.

al-Qaraḍāwī, Yūsuf. *al-Imām al-Ghazālī bayn mādiḥīh wa nāqidīh*. Egypt: Dār al-Wafāʾ, 1988.

___. *al-Ṣaḥwah al-Islāmiyyah bayn al-Juḥūd wa al-Taṭarruf*. Qatar: Kitāb al-Ummah, 1402 A.H.

al-Qarāfī, Shihāb al-Dīn Abū al-ʿAbbās. *al-Dhakhīrah*. Ed. Saʿīd Aʿrāb. Beirut: Dār al-Gharb al-Islāmī, 1994.

___. *al-Iḥkām fī Tamyīz al-Fatāwā ʿan al-Aḥkām wa Taṣarrufāt al-Qāḍī wa al-Imām*. Ed. Abū Bakr ʿAbd al-Rāziq. Cairo: al-Maktab al-Thaqāfī lī al-Nashr wa al-Tawzīʿ, 1989.

al-Qurṭubī, Abū ʿAbd Allāh Muḥammad b. Aḥmad al-Anṣārī. *al-Jāmiʿ li Aḥkām al-Qurʾān*. Beirut: Dār al-Kutub al-ʿIlmiyyah, 1993.

Quṭb, Muḥammad. *Shubuhāt Ḥawl al-Islām*. Cairo: Dār al-Shurūq, 1974.

al-Ramlī, Shams al-Dīn Muḥammad. *Nihāyat al-Muḥtāj ilā Sharḥ al-Minhāj*. Beirut: Dār Iḥyā' al-Turāth, 1992.

al-Rāzī, Fakhr al-Dīn Muḥammad b. ʿUmar b. al-Ḥusayn. *ʿIlal al-Ḥadīth*. Beirut: Dār al-Maʿrifah, 1985.

___. *al-Maḥṣūl fī ʿIlm Uṣūl al-Fiqh*. Beirut: Dār al-Kutub al-ʿIlmiyyah, n.d.

___. *al-Maḥṣūl fī ʿIlm Uṣūl al-Fiqh*. Ed. Ṭāhā Jābir Fayyāḍ al-ʿAlwānī. 3rd ed. Beirut: Mu'assasat al-Risālah, 1997.

___. *al-Maḥṣūl fī ʿIlm Uṣūl al-Fiqh*. Beirut: Dār al-Kutub al-ʿIlmiyyah, 1988.

___. *al-Tafsīr al-Kabīr (a.k.a. Mafātīḥ al-Ghayb)*. Beirut: Dār al-Kutub al-ʿIlmiyyah, 1990.

al-Rustāqī, Khamīs b. Saʿīd al-Shaqaṣī. *Manhaj al-Ṭālibīn wa Balāgh al-Rāghibīn*. Oman: Wizārat al-Turāth al-Qawmī wa Thaqāfī, n.d.

al-Sakhāwī, Shams al-Dīn Muḥammad b. ʿAbd al-Raḥmān. *al-Ḍaw' al-Lāmiʿ li-Ahl al-Qarn al-Tāsiʿ*. Beirut: Maktabat al-Ḥayāh, n.d.

___. *al-Maqāṣid al-Ḥasanah fī Bayān Kathīr min al-Aḥādīth al-Mushtahirah ʿalā al-Alsinah*. Ed. Muḥammad ʿUthmān al-Khasht. 2nd ed. Beirut: Dār al-Kitāb al-ʿArabī, 1994.

Ṣāliḥ, Subḥī. *ʿUlūm al-Ḥadīth*. Beirut: Dār al-ʿIlm, 1991.

al-Ṣanʿānī, Abū Bakr ʿAbd al-Razzāq. *al-Muṣannaf*. Ed. Ḥabīb al-Raḥmān al-Aʿẓamī. Beirut: al-Maktab al-Islāmī, 1983.

al-Sarakhsī, Abū Bakr Muḥammad b. Aḥmad b. Abī Sahl. *al-Muḥarrar fī Uṣūl al-Fiqh*. Beirut: Dār al-Kutub al-ʿArabiyyah, 1996.

___. *Uṣūl al-Sarakhsī*. Beirut: Dār al-Kutub al-ʿIlmiyyah, 1993.

al-Ṣāwī, Aḥmad. *Ḥāshiyat al-ʿAllāmah al-Ṣāwī ʿalā Tafsīr al-Jalālayn*. Beirut: Dār Iḥyā' al-Turāth al-ʿArabī, n.d.

al-Shāfiʿī, Abū ʿAbd Allāh Muḥammad b. Idrīs. *al-Umm*. Beirut: Dār al-Fikr, n.d.

Shāh Walī Allāh al-Fārūqī al-Dahlawī, Aḥmad b. ʿAbd al-Raḥīm. *al-Inṣāf fī Bayān Sabab al-Ikhtilāf fī al-Aḥkām al-Fiqhiyyah*. Cairo: al-Maṭbaʿah al-Salafiyyah, 1385 A.H.

al-Shahrastānī, Muḥammad b. ʿAbd al-Karīm Abī Bakr Aḥmad. *al-Milal wa al-Niḥal*. Eds. Amīr ʿAlī Mihannā and ʿAlī Ḥasan Fāʿūr. 5th ed. Beirut: Dār al-Maʿrifah, 1996.

Sharīf, Hāshim. *al-Marʾah al-Muslimah Bayn Ḥaqīqat al-Sharīʿah wa Zayf al-Abāṭīl*. Alexandria: Dār al-Maʿrifah al-Jāmiʿiyyah, 1987.

al-Shāṭibī, Ibrāhīm b. Mūsā. *al-Muwāfaqāt fī Uṣūl al-Sharīʿah*. Ed. ʿAbd Allāh Darrāz. Cairo: Dār al-Fikr al-ʿArabī, n.d.

al-Shawkānī, Muḥammad b. ʿAlī b. Muḥammad. *Nayl al-Awṭār*. Cairo: Dār al-Ḥadīth, n.d.

___. *al-Qawl al-Mufīd fī Adillat al-Ijtihād wa al-Taqlīd*. Cairo: Maktabat al-Qurʾān, 1988.

___. *Ṭalab al-ʿIlm wa Ṭabaqāt al-Mutaʿallimīn: Adab al-Ṭalab wa Muntahā al-ʿArab*. N.p.: Dār al-Arqam, 1981.

al-Shaybānī, ʿAbd al-Raḥmān b. ʿAlī b. Muḥammad b. ʿUmar. *Kitāb Tamyīz al-Ṭayyib min al-Khabīth fī mā yadūr ʿalā Alsinat al-Nās min al-Ḥadīth*. Beirut: Dār al-Kitāb al-ʿArabī, n.d.

al-Shinqīṭī, Muḥammad al-Amīn b. Muḥammad al-Mukhtār al-Jakanī. *Aḍwāʾ al-Bayān fī Īḍāḥ al-Qurʾān bi al-Qurʾān*. Beirut: ʿĀlam al-Kutub, n.d.

al-Shīrāzī, Abū Isḥāq Ibrāhīm. *Sharḥ al-Lumʿa*. Ed. ʿAbd al-Majīd Turkī. Beirut: Dār al-Gharb al-Islāmī, 1988.

al-Suyūṭī, Jalāl al-Dīn ʿAbd al-Raḥmān b. Abī Bakr. *al-Durr al-Manthūr fī al-Tafsīr bi al-Maʾthūr*. Cairo: Maṭbaʿat al-Anwār al-Muḥammadiyyah, n.d.

___. *Ikhtilāf al-Madhāhib*. Ed. ʿAbd al-Qayyūm Muḥammad Shafīʿ al-Basṭāwī. Cairo: Dār al-Iʿtiṣām, 1404 A.H.

___. *al-Jāmiʿ al-Ṣaghīr min Ḥadīth al-Bashīr al-Nadhīr*. Ed. Muḥammad Muḥyī al-Dīn ʿAbd al-Ḥamīd. Cairo: Dār Khadamāt al-Qurʾān, n.d.

___. *Sharḥ al-Suyūṭī ʿalā Sunan al-Nasāʾī*. Beirut: Dār al-Qalam, n.d.

al-Ṭabarānī, Abū al-Qāsim Sulaymān b. Aḥmad. *al-Muʿjam al-Kabīr*. Ed. Ḥamdī ʿAbd al-Majīd al-Salafī. Beirut: Dār Iḥyāʾ al-Turāth al-ʿArabī, 1985.

al-Ṭabarī, Abū Jaʿfar Muḥammad b. Jarīr. *Jāmiʿ al-Bayān fī Tafsīr al-Qur'ān*. Beirut: Dār al-Maʿrifah, 1989.

al-Tirmidhī, Abū ʿAbd Allāh Muḥammad al-Ḥakīm. *Nawādir al-Uṣūl fī Maʿrifat Aḥādīth al-Rasūl*. Beirut: Dār Ṣādir, n.d.

al-Ṭūfī, Najm al-Dīn. *al-Bulbul fī Uṣūl al-Fiqh*. Cairo: Maktabat al-Shāfiʿī, 1989.

al-Ṭūsī, Abū Jaʿfar Muḥammad b. al-Ḥasan b. ʿAlī. *al-Mabsūṭ fī Fiqh al-Imāmiyyah*. Tehran: al-Maṭbaʿah al-Ḥaydariyyah, 1387 AH.

al-ʿUkbarī, Abū ʿAlī al-Ḥasan b. Shihāb al-Ḥasan. *Risālah fī Uṣūl al-Fiqh*. Ed. Muwaffaq b. ʿAbd Allāh b. ʿAbd al-Qādir. Mecca: al-Maktabah al-Makkiyyah, 1992.

al-Urmawī, Sirāj al-Dīn Maḥmūd b. Abī Bakr. *al-Taḥṣīl min al-Maḥṣūl*. Ed. ʿAbd al-Ḥamīd ʿAlī Abū Zaynad. Beirut: Mu'assasat al-Risālah, 1988.

al-ʿUthaymīn, Muḥammad al-Ṣāliḥ. *Fatāwā al-Shaykh Muḥammad al-Ṣāliḥ al-ʿUthaymīn*. Ed. Ashraf b. ʿAbd al-Maqṣūd ʿAbd al-Raḥīm. Riyadh: Dār ʿĀlam al-Kutub, 1991.

al-Yamanī, Abū Muḥammad. *ʿAqā'id al-Thalāthah wa al-Sabʿīn Firqah*. Ed. Muḥammad b. ʿAbd Allāh Zarabān al-Ghāmidī. Medina: Maktabat al-ʿUlūm wa al-Ḥikam, 1414 AH.

al-Zamakhsharī, Abū al-Qāsim Jārr Allāh Maḥmūd b. ʿUmar. *al-Kashshāf ʿann Ḥaqā'iq al-Tanzīl wa ʿUyūn al-Aqāwīl fī Wujūh al-Ta'wīl*. Beirut: Dār al-Fikr, n.d.

al-Zarkashī, Shams al-Dīn Muḥammad b. ʿAbd Allāh. *al-Baḥr al-Muḥīṭ*. Cairo: Dār al-Ṣafwah, 1988.

Zayd, Muṣṭafā. *al-Maṣlaḥah fī al-Tashrīʿ al-Islāmī wa Najm al-Dīn al-Ṭūfī*. 2nd ed. Cairo: Dār al-Fikr al-ʿArabī, 1964.

Zīdān, ʿAbd al-Karīm. *al-Mufaṣṣal fī Aḥkām al-Mar'ah wa al-Bayt al-Muslim*. Beirut: Mu'assasat al-Risālah, 1994.

al-Zuḥaylī, Wahbah. *al-Wasīṭ fī Uṣūl al-Fiqh al-Islāmī*. 2nd ed. Beirut: Dār al-Fikr, 1969.

English Works

Abou El Fadl, Khaled. "Ahkam al-Bughat: A Study of Irregular Warfare and the Law of Rebellion in Islam." In *Cross, Crescent and Sword: The Justification and Limitation of War in Western and Islamic Traditions*. Eds. James Turner Johnson and John Kelsay. Westport, Conn.: Greenwood Press, 1990.

___. "The Common and Islamic Law of Duress." *Arab Law Quarterly* 2 (1991): 121-159.

___. *Conference of the Books: The Search for Beauty in Islam*. Lanham, Md.: University Press of America, 2001.

___. "Islamic Law and Muslim Minorities: The Juristic Discourses on Muslim Minorities from the 2nd/8th to the 11th/17th Centuries." *Journal of Islamic Law and Society* 1, no. 2 (1994): 141-187.

___. "Legal Debates on Muslim Minorities: Between Rejection and Accommodation." *Journal of Religious Ethics* 22, no. 1 (1994): 127-162.

___. *Rebellion and Violence in Islamic Law*. Cambridge: Cambridge University Press, 2001.

___. *Speaking in God's Name: Islamic Law, Authority and Women*. Oxford: Oneworld Press, 2001.

Abrahamov, Binyamin. "Ibn Taymiyya on the Agreement of Reason with Tradition." *Muslim World* 82 (1992): 256-272.

Ahmad, Qeyamuddin. *The Wahabi Movement in India*. Calcutta: Firma K.L. Mukhopadhyay, 1966.

Ahmed, Akbar S. *Discovering Islam: Making Sense of Muslim History and Society*. London: Routledge, 1988.

___. *Postmodernism and Islam: Predicament and Promise*. London: Routledge, 1992.

___. *Toward Islamic Anthropology: Definition, Dogma, and Directions*. Ann Arbor, Mich.: New Era Publications, 1986.

Ahmed, Leila. *Women and Gender in Islam*. New Haven, Conn.: Yale University Press, 1992.

Ajami, Fouad. *The Arab Predicament: Arab Political Thought and Practice Since 1967*. Rev. ed. Cambridge: Cambridge University Press, 1992.

Akhtar, Shabbir. *A Faith for All Seasons: Islam and the Challenge of the Modern World*. Chicago, Ill.: Ivan R. Dee, 1990.

An-Na'im, Abdullahi Ahmed. *Toward an Islamic Reformation: Civil Liberties, Human Rights, and International Law*. Syracuse, N.Y.: Syracuse University Press, 1990.

Arkoun, Mohammed. *Rethinking Islam*. Trans. R. Lee. Boulder, Colo.: Westview Press, 1994.

Ayoub, Mahmoud M. *The Qur'ān and its Interpreters*. Albany, N.Y.: State University of New York, 1984.

Bagby, Ihsan Abdul-Wajid. "Utility in Classical Islamic Law: The Concept of Maṣlaḥah in Uṣūl al-Fiqh." Ph.D. diss., University of Michigan, 1986.

Balkhi, Fasihuddin. *Wahabi Movement*. New Delhi: Classical Publishing Company, 1983.

Blankinship, Khalid Yahya. *The End of the Jihād State: The Reign of Hishām Ibn 'Abd al-Malik and the Collapse of the Umayyads*. Albany, N.Y.: State University of New York Press, 1994.

Cantori, Louis J. "Religion and Politics in Egypt." In *Religion and Politics in the Middle East*. Ed. Michael Curtis. Boulder, Colo.: Westview Press, 1981.

Cook, Michael. "On the Origins of Wahhabism." *Journal of the Royal Asiatic Society*. Series 3, 2.2 (1992): 191-202.

Cleveland, William L. *A History of the Modern Middle East*. Boulder, Colo.: Westview Press, 1994.

Crone, Patricia and Martin Hinds. *God's Caliph: Religious Authority in the First Centuries of Islam*. Cambridge: Cambridge University Press, 1986.

Dallal, Ahmad. "The Origins and Objectives of Islamic Revivalist Thought, 1750-1850." *Journal of the American Oriental Society* 113.3 (1993): 341-359.

Dutton, Yasin. *The Origins of Islamic Law: The Qur'an, the Muwaṭṭa', and Madinan 'Amal*. Richmond, U.K.: Curzon Press, 1999.

El Guindi, Fadwa. *Veil: Modesty, Privacy and Resistance*. Oxford: Berg, 1999.

Fadel, Muhammad. "Ibn Ḥajar's Hady al-Sārī: A Medieval Interpretation of the Structure of Al-Bukhārī's al-Jāmiʿ al-Ṣaḥīḥ: Introduction and Translation." *Journal of Near Eastern Studies* 54, no. 3 (1995): 161-197.

Fakhry, Majid. *A History of Islamic Philosophy*. 2nd ed. New York: Columbia University Press, 1983.

Goldrup, Lawrence Paul. "Saudi Arabia: 1902-1932: The Development of a Wahhābī Society." Ph.D. diss., University of California Los Angeles, 1971.

Gracia, Jorge J.E. *Texts: Ontological Status, Identity, Author, Audience*. Albany, N.Y.: State University Press of New York, 1996.

Haddad, Yvonne Yazbeck. "The Dynamics of Islamic Identity in North America." In *Muslims on the Americanization Path?* Ed. Yvonne Yazbeck Haddad and John L. Esposito. Oxford: Oxford University Press, 2000.

___, ed. *The Muslims of America*. Oxford: Oxford University Press, 1991.

Hasan, Ahmad. *The Doctrine of Ijmāʿ in Islam*. Islamabad: Islamic Research Institute, 1978.

Hodgson, Marshall G.S. *The Venture of Islam: Conscience and History in a World Civilization*. 1974. Reprint, Chicago, Ill.: University of Chicago Press, 1977.

Hourani, George F. "Divine Justice and Human Reason in Muʿtazilite Ethical Theology." In *Ethics in Islam*. Ed. Richard G. Hovannisian. Malibu, Calif.: Undena Publications, 1985.

Iṣik, Hüseyin Hilmi. *Advice for the Wahhābī*. 2nd ed. Istanbul: Özal Matbaasi, 1978.

___. *The Religion Reformers in Islam*. 3rd ed. Istanbul: Waqf Ikhlas Publications, 1978.

Izutsu, Toshihiko. *Ethico-Religious Concepts in the Qur'ān*. Montreal: McGill University Press, 1966.

___. *God and Man in the Koran*. 1964. Reprint, North Stratford, N.H.: Ayer Company Publishers, 1995.

Jackson, Sherman A. "The Alchemy of Domination? Some Ash'arite Responses to Mu'tazilite Ethics." *International Journal of Middle Eastern Studies*, 31 (1999): 185-201.

Kaba, LansinÈ. *The Wahhabiyya: Islamic Reform and Politics in French West Africa*. Evanston: Northwestern University Press, 1974.

Kamali, Mohammad Hashim. *Principles of Islamic Jurisprudence*. Cambridge: Islamic Texts Society, 1991.

Kerr, Malcolm H. *Islamic Reform: The Political and Legal Theories of Muḥammad 'Abuh and Rashīd Riḍā*. Berkeley and Los Angeles: University of California Press, 1966.

Khadduri, Majid. *The Islamic Conception of Justice*. Baltimore, Maryland: Johns Hopkins University Press, 1984.

Lane, E.W. *Arabic-English Lexicon*. Cambridge, England: Islamic Texts Society, 1984.

Leaman, Oliver. *An Introduction to Medieval Islamic Philosophy.* London: Cambridge University Press, 1985.

Macleod, Arlene Elowe. *Accommodating Protest: Working Women, The New Veiling, and Change in Cairo*. New York: Columbia University Press, 1991.

Marsot, Afaf Lutfi al-Sayyid. "The Ulama of Cairo in the Eighteenth and Nineteenth Century." In *Scholars, Saints, and Sufis*. Ed. Nikki Keddi. Berkeley: University of California Press, 1972.

___. *A Short History of Modern Egypt*. 1985. Reprint, Cambridge: Cambridge University Press, 1994.

___. *Egypt in the Reign of Muhammad Ali*. Cambridge: Cambridge University Press, 1984.

___. *Women and Men in Late Eighteenth-Century Egypt*. Austin, Tex.: University of Texas Press, 1995.

Mernissi, Fatima. *The Veil and the Male Elite*. New York: Addison-Wesley Publishing Company, 1991.

Minces, Juliette. *Veiled Women in Islam*. Trans. S.M. Berrett. Watertown, Massachusetts: Blue Crane Books, 1994.

Mir-Hosseini, Ziba. *Islam and Gender: The Religious Debate in Contemporary Iran*. Princeton: Princeton University Press, 1999.

Modarressi, Hossein. *Crisis and Consolidation in the Formative Period of Shiʿite Islam*. Princeton: Darwin Press, 1993.

Moore, Kathleen M. *Al-Mughtaribūn: American Law and the Transformation of Muslim Life in the United States*. Albany, N,Y.: State University of New York Press, 1995.

___. "The Hijab and Religious Liberty: Anti-Discrimination Law and Muslim Women in the United States." In *Muslims on the Americanization Path?* Eds. Yvonne Haddad and John Esposito.Oxford: Oxford University Press, 2000.

Moosa, Ebrahim. *Ghazali of Tus: His Life, Works and Teachings*. Oxford: Oneworld Publications, 2000.

Mortimer, Edward. *Faith and Power: The Politics of Islam*. New York: Vintage Books, 1982.

Opwis, Felicitas Meta Maria. "Maṣlaḥa: An Intellectual History of A Core Concept in Islamic Legal History." Ph.D. diss., Yale University, 2001.

Pedersen, Johannes. *The Arabic Book*. Trans. Geoffrey French. Princeton: University of Princeton Press, 1984.

Pipes, Daniel. "In Muslim America: A Presence and a Challenge." *National Review* (February 21, 2000): 40-1.

al-Qaraḍāwī, Yūsuf. *Islamic Awakening Between Rejection and Extremism*. Ed. A.S. al-Shaikh-Ali and Mohamed B.E. Wasfy. Herndon, Va: International Institute of Islamic Thought, 1991.

Rahman, Fazlur. *Islam*. New York: Holt, Rinehart and Winston, 1966.

___. *Islamic Methodology in History*. Islamabad: Islamic Research Institute, 1965.

___. *Major Themes of the Qur'ān.* Minneapolis, Minn.: Bibliotheca Islamica, 1994.

___. *Revival and Reform in Islam: A Study of Islamic Fundamentalism.* Ed. Ebrahim Moosa. Oxford: Oneworld Publications, 2000.

Reinhart, A. Kevin. *Before Revelation: The Boundaries of Muslim Moral Thought.* Albany, N.Y.: State University of New York Press, 1995.

Roded, Ruth. *Women in Islamic Biographical Collections: From Ibn Sa'd's to Who's Who.* Boulder, Colo.: Lynne Rienner Publishers, 1994.

Rodinson, Maxime. *Islam and Capitalism.* Trans. Brian Peace. Austin, Tex.: University of Texas, 1978.

Roy, Olivier. *The Failure of Political Islam.* Trans. Carol Volk. Cambridge, Mass.: Harvard University Press, 1994.

Sachedina, Abdulaziz Abdulhussein. *The Just Ruler in Shi'ite Islam: The Comprehensive Authority of the Jurist in Imamite Jurisprudence.* Oxford: Oxford University Press, 1988

___. *The Islamic Roots of Democratic Pluralism.* Oxford: Oxford University Press, 2001.

Said, Edward. *Orientalism.* New York: Vintage Books, 1979.

Sakr, Ahmad H. *Understanding Halal Foods: Fallacies and Facts.* Lombard, Ill.: Foundation For Islamic Knowledge, 1996.

Shaarawi, Huda. *Harem Years: The Memoirs of an Egyptian Feminist.* Trans. Margot Badran. New York: The Feminist Press, 1987.

Shahin, Emad Eldin. *Political Ascent: Contemporary Islamic Movements in North Africa.* Boulder, Colo.: Westview Press, 1997.

Sharī'atī, 'Ali. *On the Sociology of Islam.* Trans. Hamid Algar. Berkeley: Mizan Press, 1979.

Siddiqi, Muhammad Zubayr. *Hadith Literature.* Cambridge: Islamic Texts Society, 1993.

Spectorsky, Susan A., trans. *Chapters on Marriage and Divorce: Responses of Ibn Ḥanbal and Ibn Rāhwayh.* Austin, Tex.: University of Texas Press, 1993.

Suleiman, Michael W., ed. *Arabs in America: Building a New Future.* Philadelphia: Temple University Press, 1999.

Tucker, Judith E. *In the House of the Law: Gender and Islamic Law in Ottoman Syria and Palestine.* Berkeley and Los Angeles: University of California Press, 1998.

Turner, Bryan S. *Weber and Islam.* London: Routledge and Kegan Paul, 1974.

Uddin, Zaheer. *A Handbook of Halaal and Haraam Products.* New York: Center for American Muslim Research and Information, 1994.

Wadud-Muhsin, Amina. *Qur'an and Woman: Rereading the Sacred Text from a Woman's Perspective.* Oxford: Oxford University Press, 1999.

Watt, W. Montgomery. *The Formative Period of Islamic Thought.* Oxford: Oneworld Publications, 1998.

Weiss, Bernard. *The Search for God's Law.* Salt Lake City, Utah: University of Utah Press, 1992.

Index

بسم الله الرحمن الرحيم

K

L

M